KU-255-514

TRAVELLERS
SURVIVAL KIT

Mozambique

TRAVELLERS
SURVIVAL KIT

Mozambique

Adam Lechmere

Published by Vacation Work, 9 Park End Street, Oxford
www.vacationwork.co.uk

TRAVELLERS SURVIVAL KIT MOZAMBIQUE

by Adam Lechmere

Editor: Ian Collier

First published 1999

Copyright © Vacation Work 1999

ISBN 1-85458-223-2 (softback)

No part of this publication may be stored, reproduced or transmitted
in any form or by any means without the prior
written permission of the publisher

Cover design and chapter headings by
Miller, Craig and Cocking Design Partnership

Typeset by Worldview Publishing Services (01865-201562)

Maps by Andrea Pullen

Chapter Headings by Beccy Blake

Cover Photograph
Dhows at Maxixe
by Adam Lechmere

Printed by William Clowes Ltd., Beccles, Suffolk, England

Contents

PRACTICAL INFORMATION

REGIONS OF MOZAMBIQUE

MAPS

Preface

I like to spend some time in Mozambique
The sunny sky is aqua blue

Bob Dylan, *Mozambique*

Between 1976 and 1992, Mozambique was effectively cut off from the world. It was an enigma, this beautiful country that inspired Bob Dylan but was caught up in a desperate civil war which made it simply too dangerous for most travellers to contemplate. Backpackers would get as far as the Chimanimani Mountains on the Zimbabwe border and gaze out towards the Indian Ocean, far away over forbidden territory, with *Mozambique*'s lyrics echoing on their headphones.

Writing a book about Mozambique is a bittersweet experience. It's a pleasure to describe such a wonderful country, you feel as many people as possible should experience its delights, but you don't want to encourage mass tourism. Too many visitors and things will change. Foreigners may not be welcomed so readily; people won't invite you into their houses on a moment's aquaintance and sit you down for a meal, as they do now. It is common to be waiting – hours – for a bus and to be quizzed by teenagers, children and adults, all wanting to get a look at you, and your gear, and your books. If the country is flooded with tourists they'll perhaps be more interested in your spending power.

Mozambique is exquisitely beautiful. Its 2,500 kilometre coastline, fringed with swaying palms and sweeping stretches of white sand, is the stuff of many dreams. There are no ice-cream sellers or t-shirt hawkers on the beaches – there's usually no one at all, apart from a fisherman maybe, glimpsed picking his way along distant rocks. Many of the towns and villages are built on foundations laid by Muslim merchant seamen a thousand years ago, some – like Ibo – are half-populated ghost-towns, their crumbling buildings only a hundred years old. And there are other ruins, like the enormous Chongoene Hotel at Xai-Xai, once a haunt of the Mozambican elite. Its elegant terraces are now cracked and overgrown, the dining room is strewn with rubble, and filthy picture windows barely reflect the immense green sea beyond.

Chongoene is derelict, but there are plans to do it up. It's the same up and down the coast – everyone has plans. A South African couple in Vilanculos, for example – it could be anywhere – are waiting for government rubber stamps to complete a deal, another man has a diving concession with plans to open a campsite, another is lounging on a beach somewhere, thinking about setting up a couple of reed huts and a bar, and charging people a dollar a night.

Many town hotels might not be first-rate, but you can always find a beach cabin or a campsite. If you fancy sleeping on the sand under the palms, you can do that as well. The land is fertile. You can pick oranges off the trees, or buy them from people who picked them ten minutes before you. A man will sell you a fish as you emerge from your tent at five in the morning.

This beautiful land has had a terrible time for most of the last 500 years. Mozambicans have been enslaved, colonised, forced to work on building sites, down mines and in the fields. In 1975 the Portuguese grudgingly bestowed independence on a country crippled by 10 years of independence war. The new rulers presided over a population so starved of education that there was 90 per cent illiteracy. Rhodesia and South Africa fomented civil war, which went on with unparalleled savagery for 17 years. When it finished, Mozambique was shattered. At the beginning of the 1990s it was the poorest country in the world.

You wouldn't know it now. Mozambique bears many signs of a country emerging from years of conflict – the exploded lorries rusting in the fields, mine-clearing squads, aid-workers in every town. It is still near the bottom of every index of poverty, and improvements come slowly. But you see very few signs of the trauma that must remain after so devastating a war. Tourists are treated with courtesy; the country seems full of optimism.

Development continues apace. Roads are being rebuilt and hotels renovated from Maputo to Pemba. The political situation (with elections due in late 1999) is stable. Tourism is picking up and will increase as airports like Pemba start taking international flights; in ten years you'll no longer have 20 kilometres of beach to yourself, and getting to places like Pangane and Ibo will not require two gruelling days on the back of a *chapa* and a three-hour walk through the surf. When Mozambique is firmly on the tourist map it will still be entrancing, but if you want a sense of adventure and discovery, now is the time to go.

Adam Lechmere
London
March 1999

Acknowledgements

Thanks to Hannah Griffiths for invaluable help with the section on the Beira Corridor, to Samantha Cloud for a series of very useful e-mails about Beira and its surrounds, Frank Habsburg in Tete, Mike Croll for his encyclopaedic knowledge of landmines, Ruth Hansford, Joshua Marcuson, Cora at Austral, and the people of Mozambique who showed such kindness and hospitality to a sweating foreigner with bad Portuguese and an absurd method of eating oranges. Lastly to Rosalind for contributions to the Quelimane section – and skilful negotiation of the fine line between patience and exasperation.

To Rosalind and Susannah

While every effort has been made to ensure that the information contained in this book is as up-to-date as possible, some details are bound to change within the lifetime of this edition, and readers are strongly advised to check facts and credentials themselves.
The *Travellers Survival Kit: Mozambique* will be revised regularly. We are keen to hear comments, criticisms and suggestions from both natives and travellers. Please write to the author at Vacation Work, 9 Park End St, Oxford OX1 1HJ. Those whose contributions are used will be sent a complimentary copy of any Vacation Work title.

MOZAMBIQUE AND ITS PEOPLE

GEOGRAPHY

Mozambique fits like a piece of jigsaw into the complicated political geography of southern Africa. It is shaped more or less like the letter Y, with the left fork truncated, and Malawi plunging deep into the central cleft. It shares borders with Tanzania, Swaziland, South Africa, Zimbabwe, Zambia and Malawi. For the last three, Mozambique represents the only route to the Indian Ocean.

Occupying the eastern edge of the great southern African escarpment, Mozambique's mountainous interior falls to a broad plateau descending to coastal hills and plain. The astonishingly beautiful 2,750km coastline is fringed with lagoons, coral reefs and strings of islands. Several major rivers rise in the interior – the Zambezi, the Limpopo, the Rovuma, the Lúrio, the Save and the Lebombo – flowing eastwards and into the Indian Ocean. The Zambezi, which saw some of Livingstone's most famous exploits, is Africa's fourth largest river; the Limpopo in the south of the country is the tenth largest. Mozambique has 200km of Lake Niassa (Lake Malawi) within its borders, and has one of the biggest man-made lakes in Africa, that retained by the massive Cahora Bassa dam in Tete province.

Although the predominant geography of Mozambique is coastal lowland and savannah plain, the interior is mountainous. The country's highest peak is the 2,436m Mount Binga, in the Chimanimani range on the Zimbabwean border. Other mountains which top the 1,800m mark are Gorongosa (1,862m), Domue in Tete province (2,095m) and Mount Namuli near Gurúe (2,419m). As the foothills of these mountains descend to plateau there are some splendid granite outcrops. None of these has facilities for tourism, but many represent some of the most challenging climbing in the world.

Vegetation consists of savannah, open bushveldt and grassland. Most of the highlands are covered in dense miombo forest (known in the west as brachystegia), while the prevailing vegetation in the lowlands is scrubby bushland. Mozambique is very fertile, supporting vast coconut plantations around Inhambane and Quelimane, citrus groves in Manica, cashew nuts (Mozambique was once the world's largest producer of cashews), sugar cane, maize and tropical hardwoods. There is very little rainforest in Mozambique. You will find it on Mount Gorongosa's upper slopes, in the Chimanimani mountains, and on Murrumbala, Chiperone and Namuli in Zambesia province.

CLIMATE

Mozambique's climate is sub-tropical to tropical. In the winter months of May to October temperatures on the coast do not get higher than 20-25°C. During the summer months of November to April – the rainy season – temperatures are higher (27-31°C on the coast, and as high as 40°C inland) and conditions can be extremely humid, especially on the north coast and inland. Rainfall varies from an annual level of 500mm in the interior of Gaza province, to almost 2,000mm in the highlands of Niassa province. The annual rainfall in the British Isles, in comparison, is 850mm. The wettest areas of the country are the highlands east of Malawi; the south is much drier and hotter. Mozambique is vulnerable to powerful weather systems – in 1996, Cyclone Bonita cut a swathe of destruction through Zambesia province.

HISTORY

Mozambique before 1500

The East African coast and interior – modern-day Mozambique, Zimbabwe and Malawi – has been inhabited for thousands of years. The Batwa peoples came in from the west of Africa about 3,000 years ago, and Bantu speakers began to migrate into east Africa about 1,000 years later. From then until the 19th century the region was dominated by a succession of powerful warrior-tribes – the Great Zimbabwe, the Monomotapa, the Moravi, the Tonga, the Makua, the Nguni. It was a feudal society: chieftains levied taxes, collected tributes, raised armies and controlled trade while the people grew sorghum and millet, fished and bred cattle. Since the 4th century AD the Iron Age peoples of the high veldt of what is now Zimbabwe built stone platforms on which huts and other buildings were erected. Some of these societies were highly sophisticated. They measured their wealth in cattle, but also mined and washed for gold which they sold to Arab traders from the north, and the Muslim settlements along the coast.

Most sophisticated of all was the extraordinary kingdom of Great Zimbabwe, which lasted a thousand years, from the 5th to the middle of the 15th century. It was distinguished from the stone-platform builders of the high veldt by its elaborate tradition of stone wall building, which during the period of ascendancy became artistically and technically masterful.

The influence of Great Zimbabwe spread over vast areas of central and eastern Africa, but the kingdom's capital was abandoned around the end of the 15th century, for reasons which are not entirely clear but may have been the

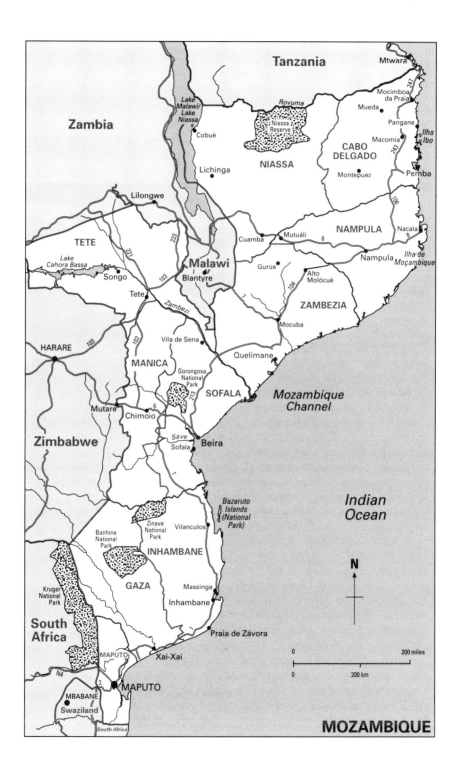

The Slave Trade

Slaves had been a part of the east African economy long before the arrival of the Portuguese. Captured in war and in slaving raids between tribes, they were bought and sold up and down the coast. They were the mainstay of the prazos, and were divided into many different ranks and categories. Some entered service voluntarily – to become the slave of a prazeiro *was often seen as an opportunity for betterment. Slaves were far more than manual workers: they ran households, went on diplomatic missions, commanded armed forces and undertook trading expeditions. But in the mid-18th century the Industrial Revolution in Europe changed the nature of slavery, causing a massive increase in demand and making the trade into an international and highly lucrative business.*

The French sugar producers of the Indian Ocean islands, the Caribbean colonies and the Americas all suddenly found a need for huge armies of labourers, and they looked to Africa to supply them. Portugal at first stuck to its policy of not allowing any trade with foreign powers, but the huge profits to be made from slaves resulted in an illicit trade growing up all along the coast. Depending on the governor of the area in question, slavery went on either formally or informally from the Bazaruto Islands to Ibo, with Ilha de Moçambique a centre of activity.

Before the 1760s about 1,000 slaves a year had been exported from Ilha de Moçambique and Ibo Island. During that decade numbers went up to about 1,500 annually from these islands alone, and as demand intensified, so trade increased. By the 1820s, 20,000 slaves a year were leaving Mozambique's ports. The Makua of present-day Cabo Delgado were particularly enthusiastic at meeting the demand, but caravans came in from all over the country, from Sofala, Inhambane, Zambésia and from the north, and ships left from all points on the coast. After 1807, when Britain abandoned the slave trade altogether and the French and Dutch suspended operations, Portugal found new outlets in Brazil, North America and Cuba.

When Britain managed to persuade Brazil (in 1830) and Portugal (in 1842) to abolish the trade, it went underground. Angoche, Quelimane and other coastal towns, which were enjoying unaccustomed prosperity because of slavery, were loath to give it up. Islands like Ibo were perfect for illicit operations, as the approach waters were too shallow for British gunboats patrolling the coast, and Arab dhows laden with slaves could slip in and out unmolested. Between 1836 and 1841, from Quelimane, Ilha de Moçambique and other ports, more than 65,000 slaves were exported.

Slavery continued for most of the rest of the century. As markets closed, others opened up. The demand from Brazil ended in 1851, but Cuba and the United States continued to import thousands of slaves. When those markets dried up, Mozambique's resourceful slavers found new outlets, in Madagascar, and its satellite sugar-growing islands of Nosy Bé and

> *Mayotte. Visitors to Quelimane and other slave towns at first noticed nothing: the trade officially did not exist. Gradually the signs would become apparent – the large numbers of whalers and capacious barges off the coast, huge sums of money changing hands. For many of the* prazo-owning *Afro-Portuguese, slaving was a form of gambling, with massive rewards if a voyage was successful. Uncooperative governors were bribed or intimidated into silence, or murdered. It was not until the end of the century that slavery petered out, although the Makua – almost totally outside Portuguese control – continued to ship slaves to Madagascar until well into the 20th century. For Mozambicans, slavery did not really end until the 1960s, when the hated* chibalo *system of forced labour came to an end. Up to then they were – quite legally – press-ganged to work on railways, roads and plantations, and carry out any other work required by the Portuguese. When* chibalo *was finally abolished, the change from forced to voluntary labour cannot have been that radical: thousands were already working on the Lourenço Marques port and railway, or had contracted themselves to South African labour recruiters.*

result of civil war sparked off by a secession struggle. By the middle of the 16th century the great stone citadels had become mysterious ruins. The decline of Great Zimbabwe coincides neatly with the rise of one of the most powerful African empires, the Monomotapa dynasty.

When Vasco Da Gama first rounded the Cape of Good Hope in 1498 and put in at Ilha De Moçambique, the Monomotapa Empire was the most powerful state of central and southern Africa. Ruled by Karanga chiefs, it extended from the Kalahari Desert to the Indian Ocean, controlled millions of subjects and dominated the market in gold, copper, ivory, ambergris and other goods, which they traded with Arab-Swahili merchant sheiks of the coast. In turn, these merchants commanded the attention of the Portuguese adventurers who came looking for the source of the gold they had seen in North Africa.

The east African coast has been a centre of international trade for thousands of years. The ancient Egyptians knew it in 2,500BC, and they were followed by the Phoenicians and Romans, and, from about the 7th century AD, Arab traders began to settle. Madagascar was their first trading post, but from the 9th century the greatest trading centre was the city of Sofala, ruled by a sheikh who controlled a complex web of foreign and internal commerce. Visiting traders sought his permission to buy and sell ivory and cloth, and in return he would supply warehousing facilities, access to trade routes and the services of ships' pilots, boat builders and repairmen. Through polygamous marriages he was linked to chieftaincies of the Sofala hinterland. Sofala was the trading capital of the area, but it was not the only centre of commerce. Just down the coast was the island of Chiloane, then Mambone at the mouth of the Save river, and further south still the Bazaruto islands. Trade was rich: as well as ivory, gold and copper, there was turtleshell, ambergris and pearls, cotton cloths, woven mats and baskets. Sofala was also well-known for its iron: farming implements, spears and axes, and hooks and chains for fishing. Boat-building too was an important industry.

The arrival of the Portuguese

Vasco da Gama was by no means the first Portuguese navigator to arrive in Mozambique. Throughout the latter half of the 15th century, his countrymen had been exploring southern and eastern Africa. By 1444 they had sailed as far south as Senegal, and over the next 50 years they reached the Gambia river, Sierra Leone and São Tomé.

King João of Portugal had long been interested in capturing the gold trade and in forging new trading alliances, if necessary by conquest. The towns of Kilwa and Sofala, which he believed to be richer in gold than they actually were, were prime targets for another important reason: ships sailing between India and Europe could use them as way stations to reprovision and repair, offload the sick and employ fresh crews.

By 1505 the Portuguese had decided to take control of Kilwa and Sofala, which, with their fast, well-armed ships, they did with very little trouble. It soon became evident that a base between the two cities was needed, and in 1507 Ilha de Moçambique was taken over, and a factory and customs house built.

The Portuguese never intended to drive out the sheikhs, preferring to make them middlemen for trade with the interior. But conflicts erupted from the start, with serious disturbances breaking out in Sofala, and relations in Kilwa deteriorating so badly that traders stopped calling there, local merchants left the city, and in 1513 the Portuguese pulled out altogether. For the next 20 years the Portuguese established themselves along the coast with violence, intimidation and extortion. Any ships sailing without Portuguese protection would be plundered, and tribute was exacted from the coastal towns. Between 1505 and 1530 cities in Cabo Delgado and the Querimbas were attacked and plundered, and raiding parties penetrated as far north as Mombasa in what is now Kenya.

Over the ensuing decades the Portuguese consolidated their hold over the coastal towns – the mighty fort of São Sebastião was started on Ilha de Moçambique in 1546, and by the 1560s all the major centres along the coast had resident Portuguese. An Afro-Portuguese community began to assert itself, as soldiers deserted from the garrisons and got in with local chiefs by marrying their daughters and lending assistance with military operations. In fact it was the Afro-Portuguese who were responsible for most of the colonisation of the interior of Mozambique: many built power bases of their own, formed private armies and established themselves not only on the coast, but along the southern bank of the Zambesi as far inland as Tete.

The coming of the Portuguese had a far-reaching effect on the local economy. With fortified centres like Ilha de Moçambique becoming more and more populous (numbers at the fort could be swelled by as many as 1,000 if a fleet was wintering there) food supply was of paramount importance. Prodigious quantities of staples such as sorghum, rice, corn, meat, salt, oil and chickpeas were needed to feed the garrisons up and down the coast. Economic activity expanded in other areas. The ivory and gold trades employed hundreds of Africans; slaves were brought to the coast to act as interpreters or orderlies in the hospitals and warehouses. The building and maintaining of forts employed thousands of skilled men and labourers, from carpenters to stone masons, blacksmiths to cooking-oil makers.

The 1590s onwards

For most of the 16th century Portuguese power in Mozambique faced few threats from the sea. The Turks regularly attacked their ships, but never seemed to be more than an annoyance. In the 1590s the English and the Dutch began to take an interest in the trading possibilities, using excellent Portuguese maps and charts and with faster, stronger and better-armed ships. The Portuguese protected their possessions jealously, refusing any foreign ships revictualling rights, producing deliberately misleading maritime charts and conducting a propaganda campaign by accusing the English of cannibalism. During the early part of the 17th century, the English seized Portuguese merchantmen and stole their cargoes, but it was the Dutch who decided simply to invade Portugal's strongholds and add them to their empire.

It was lucky for the Portuguese that they had spent the last 50 years building their impregnable fortresses, because their other defences were in many ways shambolic. The garrison at São Sebastião was in a pathetically weak condition when the Dutch attacked, but the fort's massive walls and strategic position thwarted them. Despite several attempts over the next three decades, no foreign power was able to take the fort nor make much of a dent in the Portuguese east African empire. Commentators have suggested that Ilha de Moçambique has had an incalculable effect on the history of the region: if the Dutch had managed to take the island they would have ousted the Portuguese, and may not have had to found the Cape Colony further south, the settlement that gave birth to the Afrikaaner nation.

Portuguese domination of the East African interior

Portuguese influence over the interior came about gradually, and not as a result of any policy of conquest on the part of the Crown. Although several military expeditions were sent up the Zambesi, and northwards to try and conquer the powerful Monomotapa kingdom, they were for the most part unsuccessful. There was always an official interest in penetrating inland and along the coast, and forays were made to Angoche and up and down the coast from Sofala. But most of the real work of colonisation was done by Afro-Portuguese half-castes (*mazungos*), superannuated soldiers, deserters, former slaves and refugees from war or famine, who made their way inland, married,

The Prazos

The history of Mozambique is inextricably bound up with the history of the Prazos da Coroa, *land rights granted by the Portuguese crown. Seen from a colonial point of view* prazos *were official land grants handed out by the colonial power, but from the African angle they operated exactly as chieftaincies. The Crown gave land to Jesuits and Dominicans, to superannuated soldiers, to Portuguese merchants, and to the widows and orphans of those who had died in its service. Although Portugal tried to control* prazeiros, *and claimed ownership of any gold or silver found, in reality most of them were quite beyond the power of the Crown, keeping private armies and exerting influence over local chiefs. The authorities contented themselves with the fact that maintaining Portuguese rule was generally in the* prazeiros' *interests.* Prazos *were leased for three generations, and the leaseholder undertook to develop the land, keep order, maintain roads and government buildings and provide military assistance when the government needed it. By the 18th century the captaincies of Sofala, Sena, Tete and Quelimane were* prazo-held. *They were a feudal aristocracy that dominated the affairs of the region, influencing crown-appointed captains by being the only source of labour and soldiers.*

One of the most interesting aspects of the system was that prazos *were handed down from mother to daughter. They were granted to Portuguese women on the condition they married a Portuguese (this would encourage men to seek wealthy marriages and settle in East Africa). Although the men usually ran the* prazo, *if an ambitious woman held the legal title she could exploit it. There were many egregious characters amongst the* donas *who held* prazos, *among them Dona Ines Gracias Cardoso who increased her land by several judicious marriages, and the 'haughty and proud' Dona Luiza Michaela da Cruz, who kept a large force of armed slaves and allegedly poisoned her third husband. She was indicted in 1874 for 80 murders, accused of having her victims bound and thrown to the crocodiles.*

It should be remembered that many of the tribes of Mozambique were also matrilineal, and the prazos *would not therefore have been seen as an aberration. They dominated the government of Mozambique for at least three centuries until their abolition in the 1930s, and must account in large part for the fact that Mozambican women today are amongst the most independent in Central and eastern Africa.*

and became – in some cases – powerful chieftains in their own right. Issues of land rights and ownership were later formalised into the *prazo* system, which is described in more detail below.

Life in the coastal stations was hard. Food was scarce, pay sporadic, the forts were hot and uncomfortable, and there were precious few women. It was unsurprising that soldiers should be tempted to try their fortune inland, trading their weapons and military expertise, marrying chiefs' daughters and fighting local wars. By the end of the 16th century there were *mazungo* enclaves from the Querimba to the Bazaruto Islands, and along the south bank of the Zambesi as far west as Tete. The *mazungo* class was extraordinarily adept. In many ways they were like the convicts of Botany Bay who made their fortunes and became part of the Australian establishment. *Mazungos* were often rejects and wanderers: a Portuguese deserter or convict could become an influential member of *mazungo* society, while a freed slave or refugee could make his way in an Afro-Portuguese private army or household.

Mazungos therefore were locally very powerful, and although they kept Portuguese names, were nominally Catholics, they were as much African as Portuguese. Many of them were quite African in appearance, they led an African way of life, married and formed family and chiefly ties. The head of a *mazungo* family in Sena or Tete would have a Portuguese town house, but in rural areas he would live as a chief. The Portuguese regarded them as Catholics, but they would as soon consult a *nganga* (witchdoctor) as a priest.

While the Afro-Portuguese were forming their fiefdoms, the Portuguese Crown still had expansionist dreams. In 1545 the Spanish *conquistadores* discovered rich seams of silver at Potosí in Bolivia, and the Portuguese clung to the belief that they would find their Potosí in Angola or at Chicoa on the Zambesi, north-west of Tete. During the 16th century various expeditions into the interior were mounted. In 1560 a Jesuit priest called Gonçalo da Silveira went to the court of the Monomotapa to see if he could convert what was then the most powerful empire in east Africa to Christianity. He was welcomed with gifts and then murdered after a short stay. In the 1570s Francisco Barreto, sometime galley captain and former governor, put together a force of 1,000 veterans of Mediterranean warfare and set off to capture the mines of the Monomotapa. This band of cut-throats made their way up the Zambesi, pillaging and sacking Muslim towns and putting entire populations to the sword, before meeting their nemesis in the form of marauding Maravi warriors from the west. Other expeditions fared as badly, but the Portuguese were successful in one respect. They may not have found the fabled mines or defeated the Monomotapa, but they wiped out most of the Muslim populations of the Zambesi delta, and established a lasting Portuguese presence in Sena and Tete.

The 19th Century

From 1794 until the 1830s Mozambique was devastated by a series of terrible droughts, completely altering the social, economic and political nature of the country. Communities were decimated by starvation, and by the exodus of the able-bodied migrating to better-watered areas. So severe was the hunger between 1794 and 1802 that a contemporary writer described people falling dead on the beaches at Inhambane as they searched for shellfish. Early in the 19th century things improved, but the rains failed again in 1817. The Zambesi valley was badly affected: the *prazos* were overrun by armed bands searching for food, their slaves dispersed, and roads and buildings fell into disrepair. The great gold fairs of Manica and Zumbo stopped completely. Swarms of locust turned the skies black and descended on what crops had managed to survive, stripping them to the ground.

African and Afro-Portuguese societies fared far worse than the Portuguese, who occupied the coastal stations and could be supplied by sea. The droughts decimated Afro-Portuguese communities, many of whom emigrated to Brazil and India. The *prazos* of the Zambesi delta were taken over by powerful and aggressive barons, who spent the next few decades hunting elephants for ivory, slave-raiding and pursuing bloody vendettas against each other.

The effect on African society was more far-reaching still. The great Karanga and Maravi kingdoms disintegrated, and the Monomotapa chieftaincy became moribund. Drought struck the Nguni people – cattle farmers, artisans and traders of the area south of Delagoa Bay (present-day Maputo) – who raided their neighbours for cattle, and eventually started the greatest warrior migration southern Africa has ever seen, giving birth to the Zulu nation. Throughout the early 19th century, different Nguni warbands – Ndwandwe, Swazi and Zulu – moved into Mozambique. They attacked Inhambane, Madanda and Quissanga, and in 1830 raided Sofala, where the ancient fort gave refuge for the last time to the terrified Portuguese community.

The 1840s also saw a massive increase in illicit slaving (see *The Slave Trade*), and radical alterations in the trading culture that had barely changed for centuries. While the gold trade dried up, world markets demanded more and more ivory, and old-fashioned hunting methods gave way to organised parties of men with firearms. This was a far cry from the ivory caravans of the Bisa and Yao tribes that had been winding their way down to the coastal trading stations for centuries.

As the 19th century progressed, Britain began having an influence on Mozambique. Although the Scramble for Africa did not really get going until 1876 (when King Leopold of the Belgians first decided to take some of the wealth of the unexplored continent, and set off a rush by the leaders of European powers to build empires in Africa) Britain was already busy putting stakes in the ground. It had largely ignored eastern Africa until it acquired control of South Africa in 1806 and Mauritius in 1810, when the government began to take an interest in the coast, and in particular the splendid natural harbour of Delagoa Bay. Throughout the early years of the century Britain tried to persuade Portugal to abolish slavery, and when a treaty giving rights of mutual search was finally signed in 1842, her warships regularly patrolled the coast. Other interests surfaced: after their settlement of the Transvaal in the 1830s the Boers reached Delagoa Bay in an attempt to open a road to the sea. The British government was also alarmed at French interest in Madagascar, and in 1820 raised the Union Flag in the southern part of Delagoa Bay, prompting a series of disputes that were not to be settled until 1875, when French-brokered treaties were signed giving Portugal the right to Delagoa Bay and surrounding land.

As the Scramble for Africa intensified in the 1870s, with Britain, France and Germany all vying for possessions on the very borders of Mozambique, Portugal decided it had to assert its claim to the land it had occupied for over 300 years. In answer to the hugely popular exploits of David Livingstone, exploratory expeditions were organised by the Lisbon Geographical Society in order to open up trade routes between Mozambique and Angola – and to show that Portugal did indeed own eastern and central Africa. In the two decades leading up to the final parcelling-out of land in 1891, a series of stand-offs and tense diplomatic incidents almost descended into war when the British government delivered an ultimatum to Portugal, after giving the adventurer Cecil Rhodes rights to parts of the Zambesi valley. Although it certainly had historic claims to the land, Portugal backed out.

The moment that the ultimatum was delivered in January 1890 was the moment – as one commentator puts it – that the music stopped. A treaty was signed by Britain and Portugal, and after much arbitration (with Portugal still hoping for a corridor of land linking Angola to Mozambique) borders were agreed. The country that Portugal was left with reflected its history of involvement: seaports from Ibo to Lourenço Marques were included, along with the trading hinterland on which they depended. Delagoa Bay remained Portuguese, but was almost surrounded by South Africa. Portugal kept the Zambesi delta, as far west as Zumbo, as well as Sena and Tete (which however was surrounded by British territory in the shape of Malawi). The northern border with Tanzania (then German East Africa) was simpler, being the administrative border formed between the regions of Mozambique Island and Mombasa. Germany was to be the arbitrator in the event of a dispute over any of the borders.

Thus at the end of the 19th century Portugal found itself nominally colonial owner of a land over which it had never really had any control. From then on, it set about trying to pacify its new possession.

Mozambique as a Portuguese colony 1890-1975

Portuguese pacification of the interior was long and bloody, involving a series of debilitating battles during the first decades of the new century. The Gaza monarchy – ruling great tracts of land south of the Zambesi – was the most powerful of the African chieftaincies, ruled first by the Nguni warlord Soshongane, who died in 1856, and later by Gungunhana, on whom the Portuguese declared war in 1895. Although defeated, Gungunhana remained a potent emblem of resistance in Mozambique – a grandfather of Samora Machel was a commander in one of his armies. Portugal conquered the Zambesi valley in 1902, and bought the Makua and Yao under their control ten years later.

The colonisers' method was to first subdue a territory by military means and then to grant concessions to companies to administer the area. Only Nampula, Gaza, Inhambane and Maputo provinces were directly administered by the colonial state. The Niassa Company and the Mozambique Company were both set up with French and British investments in the last decade of the 19th century. There were other charters, such as the British Sena Sugar Estates, the last of which existed until 1941. The area south of the Save river was reserved as a labour pool for the South African Witwatersrand Native Labour Association (WNLA).

The charter companies raised most of their income through taxes and *chibalo* – forced labour. Mozambicans were recruited to work on roads, railways, plantations and mines, and those in the catchment area of the WNLA went to work in the gold and diamond mines of South Africa; part of their wages were paid in gold directly to the Portuguese government. Some 150,000 workers went to South Africa every year – by 1900 up to half the male population would be absent at any one time. During the colonial years hundreds of thousands of Mozambicans escaped *chibalo* by crossing the borders to Rhodesia and Malawi and trying their luck with comparatively less repressive regimes.

In 1926 the fascist dictator Antonio Salazar came to power in Portugal. Seeking to make Portugal and her empire a self-sufficient whole he abolished the charter companies and introduced forced cultivation of cotton and rice. He also formalised forced labour, and introduced a form of apartheid based on indigenous and non-indigenous classes. The former – Africans – had no legal rights, had to carry identity cards, and had to fulfil forced labour requirements. The latter included Afro-Portuguese, Indians, Chinese and naturally the Portuguese and other Europeans. A tiny minority of indigenous people could become non-indigenous or *assimilado*. To be assimilated a Mozambican had to be able to read and write, and to have rejected African customs. Only around one per cent of the population managed to change their status in this way.

One of the major obstacles to becoming *assimilado* was the near impossibility of learning. Schooling was left mainly to religious orders. The

Catholic church (which happily used forced labour to build the cathedral in Maputo) was regarded as a 'civilising influence' but Protestants, who encouraged literacy in Mozambican languages, were barely tolerated. Some Mozambicans succeeded in getting an education: Eduardo Mondlane was taught by a Protestant mission.

The Salazar years may have been repressive, but they saw Mozambique enjoying something of an economic boom. Forced agricultural schemes led to a huge rise in cotton and rice production; during the Second World War Portugal's neutrality meant that Mozambique could concentrate on increasing food production. During the post-war period manufacturing industry diversified, especially in Lourenço Marques and Beira. The capital had been moved to Lourenço Marques in 1902, and it benefitted from a share of South Africa's railway traffic, as Beira did from its rail link with Rhodesia. Most of Mozambique's railways were built with British expertise and capital – by 1963 the country had six separate railway systems.

The struggle for Independence

After the Second World War, while many African nations were clamouring for independence, Portugal clung to her colony. Neutral during the war, it did not have to contend with a vociferous resistance movement bolstered by soldiers who had fought for freedom, only to return home to find they were second-class citizens. Immigration to Mozambique increased in the post-war period, even while the movement for independence began to gather steam.

At first resistence was sporadic and localised. Few Africans were educated, and it was difficult to organise a coherent opposition. Any dissidence was quickly suppressed by the government authorities, the military, and the hated PIDE secret police. Then in 1960, troops opened fire on a peaceful demonstration in the town of Mueda in Cabo Delgado. Some 600 demonstrators died in the slaughter, Mueda became the symbol of Portuguese oppression, and served to concentrate the energies of anti-colonial groups both in Mozambique and abroad. In 1962 several anti-colonial organisations were invited by Julius Nyerere, president of Tanzania, to set up headquarters in the capital Dar es Salaam. They joined forces to form Frelimo – the Frente de Libertação de Moçambique (Mozambique Liberation Front) – under the leadership of Eduardo Mondlane, who had been born in Gaza and later had become a university lecturer in the United States. Frelimo began an armed campaign of resistance to Portuguese rule in September 1964, by attacking a garrison at the town of Chai, in Cabo Delgado.

Working from its base in Tanzania, and with strong Makonde support, Frelimo was initially successful in the north. They drove out the Portuguese and organised villages into 'liberated zones', setting up schools, shops and health clinics in the areas they controlled. But Frelimo was quickly riven by internal divisions, and Mondlane was killed by a letter bomb in 1969, allegedly sent by Frelimo defectors.

Samora Machel, one of Frelimo's guerilla commanders and also from Gaza province, succeeded to the leadership. As Portugal held more and more tenaciously to power, Frelimo became isolated from Europe and received increasing support from the Soviet Union and China. As the movement began to expand southwards into Tete, the Portuguese government launched operation Gordian Knot in 1970, a massive counter-offensive in which napalm and scorched-earth tactics were used. In 1972 commandos massacred hundreds of villagers in an attack on Wiriamu in Tete province. But political events in Portugal – there was an army coup in 1974 – severely weakened the regime's willingness to fight for its colony, and 60,000 troops were withdrawn. Exactly ten years after the first shots were fired in Chai, the Lusaka Accord was signed, ending colonial rule and handing over government to a very surprised Frelimo. In June 1975, Samora Machel became president of the People's Republic of Mozambique.

From Independence to the Present Day

Machel found himself in charge of a country in a state of total disarray. Over 90 per cent of the population was illiterate, there was very little infrastructure that had not been destroyed in the ten-year war, and the departing Portuguese had sabotaged much of what was left. The scuppered ships in Beira harbour still bear witness to their bitterness at losing their colony. Frelimo acted quickly to unify the country, imposing one-party rule and incarcerating opposition leaders in 're-education camps' – allegations of torture and mistreatment of prisoners in some camps have never been properly answered. Religious groups were suppressed and a secret police force (SNASP) set up. At the same time hospitals, schools and missions were nationalised and vastly improved: the number of primary school pupils doubled in seven years, and health clinics multiplied throughout the country. In 1977 Frelimo declared itself a Marxist-Leninist party, dedicated to the education of the masses and the destruction of capitalism.

While all this was going on, Machel was antagonising the Ian Smith regime in neighbouring Rhodesia, and the South African government, by supporting liberation movements in their countries. Smith set up Renamo (Resistência Nacional Moçambicana – Mozambican National Resistance) in 1976 with the aim of destabilising Mozambique. When Rhodesia won its independence and became Zimbabwe in 1980, South Africa took over support of Renamo, in order to counteract Mozambique's support for anti-apartheid activists, and to block Zimbabwe's access to the sea via Mozambique.

This was the period of greatest activity for Renamo. With South Africa's support, membership increased to over 8,000, and by 1982 it posed a serious threat to the government. Despite savage methods and well-documented human rights abuses Renamo was also able to draw support from a good deal of internal hostility to the government.

Even after the 1984 Nkomati Accords, in which Mozambique and South Africa pledged to cease hostilities, Renamo continued its operations. It was now covertly supported by South Africa, provisioning itself from the local population. It recruited by kidnapping young men and boys, and instilled terror by mutilating civilians, including children. Renamo's aim was to destroy schools, roads, hospitals and anything else that represented government support and security. There were terrible massacres as Renamo launched offensives along the Zambesi valley from their base in Gorongosa. In 1986 Samora Machel died when the plane he was travelling in crashed near Mbunzi on the South African border. The circumstances of his death have never been explained, although it seems certain there was foul play. By 1988, with external support drying up for both sides, the war was at stalemate.

Machel's successor Joaquim Chissano tried hard to negotiate a settlement. He initiated a major review of Frelimo's policies, including a retreat from Marxism. It was not until 1990 that Frelimo and Renamo agreed to a partial cease-fire, allowing negotiations to continue throughout 1991 and 1992, although fighting persisted in the north, and the country's problems were made worse by drought and chronic food shortages. After many rounds of dialogue, Chissano and Renamo leader Afonso Dhlakama finally signed the General Peace Agreement in Rome on 4 October 1992, with the support of the United States, Britain, France, Portugal and the United Nations. A UN peace-keeping force, ONUMOZ, oversaw the two-year transition period – the last contingents left Mozambique in 1995. By the end of 1995 the 1.7 million refugees who had fled Mozambique returned, in the largest repatriation ever seen in sub-Saharan Africa. In addition, some 4 million people who had been internally displaced returned to their homes.

The first multi-party elections were held – fairly peacefully – in 1994, with an 85 per cent turn-out. Fourteen parties contested seats, and there were 12 presidential candidates. Chissano was returned to power, but without an overall majority. To most observers' surprise, Renamo gained 38 per cent of the vote, including majorities in five provinces. Dhlakama complained of irregularities but accepted the result.

Since that date reforms have continued. The National Assembly got off to a shaky start when Renamo walked out in protest over a secret vote to elect the Speaker, but it is generally reckoned to be maturing fast. The situation is an odd one: of the two main parties, one is reformed Marxist-Leninist, used to wielding absolute power, while the other is a reformed guerilla movement. There is conflict, but both parties manage to co-exist, with liberal helpings of criticism from an unfettered national press and an increasingly assertive civil society.

More reforms were introduced in 1998 with the drafting of a new constitution. The main changes include provisions for enhancing the role of the opposition leader and opposition parties, the setting up of an advisory body for the president, the strengthening of parliament and the prime minister, and the replacement of the national flag (with its depiction of a machine gun) and the national anthem, both of which tend to glorify war and the ruling party.

The next elections are scheduled for October 1999. Renamo is still a relatively weak opposition, not helped by its lack of concrete policies, other than being anti-Frelimo. It remains to be seen whether Mozambique will shift towards a system of dominant one-party politics, or if it will become a truly stable multi-party democracy.

POLITICS

The Republic of Mozambique is a modern, multi-party democracy with universal suffrage. The executive branch of the government consists of the president and the Council of Ministers, the legislative branch is the National Assembly, and the judiciary consists of a Supreme Court, provincial, district and municipal courts. There are two main political parties: the ruling Frente de Libertação de Moçambique (the Mozambique Liberation Front – Frelimo), and the opposition party, the Resistência Nacional Moçambicana (Mozambican National Resistance – Renamo). A third party, the Uniao Democratica (UD) is much weaker than its main rivals. The president of the Republic is Joaquim Chissano; the leader of the opposition Afonso Dhlakama.

THE ECONOMY

Until 1975 Mozambique's economy was based almost entirely on the export of agricultural products – shrimp, cashews, copra, sugar, tea, cotton and citrus fruits – to Portugal. There was also a limited manufacturing sector around the shipping and transportation that went with such exports. At independence, some quarter of a million Portuguese pulled out, taking a huge amount of technical expertise with them, and leaving behind a largely illiterate, unskilled population. Frelimo immediately set out to replace capitalism with Marxism, nationalising factories and forming collective farms. Armed resistence from Renamo quickly put paid to most trade and industry by destroying factories, roads and cutting off the rural population from the cities. By the mid-1980s the economy was in ruins.

Today Mozambique is one of the poorest countries in the world, with a struggling economy crippled by an external debt that stands at over $5.2 billion (of which $144 million is owed to the UK, and $1.6 billion to the former Soviet Union). Joining the World Bank and the International Monetary Fund (IMF) in 1984 did little good for the average Mozambican: Frelimo borrowed heavily to buy arms during the war and put little of it into the infrastructure. The economy is now entirely dependent on foreign loans and aid. Although many of the nation's roads, factories, hotels and public buildings are being rebuilt with aid, Mozambique still labours under the burden of a debt which requires $460,000 per day to service. In order to qualify for debt relief, the government must cut public spending, leading to further dependence on aid donors. Even with debt relief, from 2000-2003 the country will still be required to pay some $90 million per year in debt service payments.

At present an estimated 80 per cent of the population supports itself on subsistence agriculture and fishing. The staple is maize, rice is grown on the flood plains of major rivers, but all wheat is imported. Five times as much food and other products are imported than exported.

But the economy is picking up. Mozambique is an astonishingly fertile country; its prawns – before the Soviet factory ships overfished the waters – were famous throughout the world, and crops from maize and cashews to fruit and cotton grow fast in the rich soil of the coastal plain. There is still an excellent rail network linking Mozambique's coast with all its landlocked neighbours. An informal economy is thriving along all the nation's borders. Industry is being privatised and is sucessful in urban areas like Maputo, Beira and Nampula. Arterial roads are being rebuilt apace – heavy trucks laden with goods are now a common sight on the main highway, the EN1. The Cahora Bassa dam is now sending electricity to South Africa and will soon supply most of Mozambique. Lastly – and perhaps most importantly for the economy – tourism is on the increase. Soon national parks will be restocked with game, and hotels (which are already springing up all over the country) will service well-heeled tourists and not just the army of aid workers and the odd adventurous backpacker.

AID AGENCIES IN MOZAMBIQUE

Mozambique receives over $1 billion annually in aid from a variety of international governments and non-governmental organisations (NGOs). Aid organisations concentrate not only on sustainable development, helping to make agriculture and industry more efficient, and improving education and health throughout the country, but also in lobbying governments to reduce Mozambique's international debt.

It should be remembered that although Mozambique currently receives a vast proportion of its Gross National Product in foreign aid, the government is fighting to reduce this dependency. Similarly, most aid agencies concentrate on sustainable development – that is, using aid to create a situation in which communities can fend for themselves rather than be forever dependent on handouts.

As well as the proliferation of foreign NGOs in Mozambique, there are also many highly effective local NGOs. These include MULEIDE, which is concerned with women, the law and development, and the two main NGOs which work with landmine victims, the Mozambican Association of Disabled People (ADEMO) and the Mozambican Association of Disabled Soldiers (ADEMIMO). See also the section on Landmines in *Crime and Safety (page 97)*.

Aid agencies operating in Mozambique come from the UK, Ireland, Scandinavia, the United States and Canada. The British and Irish governments pledge considerable amounts of money to Mozambique. Britain aims to increase an annual investment of £20 million to an estimated £38 million by 2001; Ireland has a £22 million development plan, giving to provinces where Ireland is the only international donor.

The British NGO Oxfam has worked in Mozambique since 1984. During the civil war, Oxfam concentrated on emergency relief and rural community development projects. It now helps communities to grow a wider range of crops and get better access to markets, supports disabled people, and lobbies creditor governments to reduce Mozambique's external debts. Another British NGO, Christian Aid, has been working in the country since the mid-1970s. It works with local organisations such as the Christian Council of Mozambique and the Rural Association for Mutual Support (ORAM). The primary focus for Christian Aid's involvement is long-term rural development. The Irish NGO Trocaire works in Maputo province, Zambesia, Nampula and Sofala, concentrating on human rights issues, agriculture and other development areas.

Scandinavian aid agencies are very active in Mozambique. The Danish government has increased its aid from $25 million to $42 million since 1997, money that goes towards agriculture, health, education and justice. Swedish donations total some $65 million, financing projects in education, public administration, agriculture, energy, roads and bridges. Norway supplies $50 million annually – Mozambique is at the top of the list of African countries it regards as a priority for assistance – through the Norwegian Agency for International Development (NORAD). Other European agencies include the Swiss organisation Helvetas, which works mainly in the north of Mozambique, and various Finnish organisations. KEPA is a group of Finnish NGOs that has worked in Mozambique since 1992, focusing on social welfare, especially working with local disabled people's associations. KEPA also runs cultural programmes like community theatre projects, and works with government ministries on such areas as deafness and mental and physical disabilities.

One of the largest international NGOs operating in Africa is the Humana People to People organisation, an international grouping of aid organisations.

The Mozambican arm of Humana is ADPP (Ajuda de Desenvolvimiento de Povo para Povo) – now registered as a private Mozambican association – runs schools and other education projects, child aid and family projects with the object of improving living conditions, teacher training and the running of schools. It is funded mostly by the sale of second-hand clothes in Europe.

USAID (United States Agency for International Development) is the leading US government agency responsible for administration of economic and humanitarian assistance. It has operated in Mozambique since 1984. Its stated plan for the 1996-2001 period is to work to increase rural household income, help the government to work with local civil society nationally and locally, and improve maternal, child health and family planning services.

The United Nations is also very active in Mozambique. ONUMOZ (the United Nations Operation in Mozambique) was established in 1992 to monitor the transition to peace, and its last remaining officers left in 1995. Since then UNICEF (United Nations Children's Fund), UNHCR (United Nations High Commission for Refugees) and the UN World Food Programme (WFP) have all been involved in various capacities. In 1999 the WFP pledged $2.4 million to help victims of flooding in the central and southern provinces.

Mine clearance is another major aid area. The best-known organisation in the country is the Halo Trust (whose patron, Princess Diana, garnered massive publicity), which works mainly in the north of the country. Another large mine-clearance operation is COCAMO (Cooperation Canada-Mozambique), which in early 1999 pledged $1.7 million for demining operations in Maputo, Inhambane and Nampula provinces.

POPULATION

According to the 1997 census, the population of Mozambique is 15.7 million. This figure is considerably lower than the 18 million plus inhabitants that was projected from the 1980 census, mainly because the post-civil war baby boom that was expected never materialised, the fertility rate has not grown in line with predictions, and the infant mortality rate has not fallen as expected.

Forty-six per cent of the population is under 15 and more than 70 per cent is under 30. Average life expectancy is 46 years (45 for men and 48 for women). The infant mortality rate is 135 per 1,000 live births (as compared to 6 per 1,000 live births in the UK), and the maternal mortality rate is 1,500 per 100,000 live births (the figure is 9 per 100,000 in the UK).

LIFE IN MOZAMBIQUE

While in the larger towns life is nearly as cosmopolitan as in any city in the west, the majority of the population (over 60 per cent) lives in rural areas and makes a living from the land. Because so much of the industrial and business infrastructure of the country was destroyed during the civil war, relatively few people are formally employed, and those that do have regular jobs tend to live in the cities. The first priority for people in rural areas is to feed their families. Those that have a plot of land and tools will grow maize, cassava and sweet potatoes, or rice in low-lying marshy areas. On the coast there is plenty of fish, which will be supplemented with green vegetables and sauces made from coconut and chillies. On special occasions a chicken might be killed. In most parts of Mozambique fruit – oranges, papaya, mangoes and pineapples – is plentiful and cheap, but inland in dryer areas it is harder to come by.

Traditionally it is the women who do most of the work in the fields and look after the family, while men take charge of house-building, hunting, burning charcoal and protecting the crops from animals. It is men who usually own bicycles, so often it's the husband who takes produce to market – which can sometimes be several days' ride. Many people have no concept of a regular income. Money will be available around harvest time, but when that is spent, existence can be hand-to-mouth. A family member may catch fish to sell at market, or grow a few vegetables to sell, and men burn wood to make charcoal to sell, or cut down trees to sell to timber companies.

Family life in Mozambique has been disrupted for decades. Before the war it was common for men to be working hundreds of miles away for months at a time. The war itself caused upheavals that are still being felt, and the resulting economic chaos hasn't helped. It's not uncommon for families to be headed by women; either the husband has been killed in the war or has left home to find work. In situations where a woman is left on her own she may in turn leave her family in the care of her eldest daughter while she goes to work.

The UK charity (NGO) Christian Aid gives this example of a typical rural family in Nampula province. The father is a policeman in the far north of the province and is away for months at a time. The mother works 15 miles away, leaving early on Monday morning and returning Friday evening or Saturday morning. Her home is run by her eldest daughter, who is 15, and who cooks for her two sisters, gets them to school and then goes to school herself. She says that despite the hard work she likes it when her mother's away, as her sisters have to do what she says.

THE PEOPLE

Most Mozambicans come from seven or eight dominant ethnic groups: the Tsonga in the south; the Gitonga around Inhambane; the Shopi around Quissico and north of the Limpopo river; the Macua and the Makonde in the north; the Sena and Ndau in the Zambesi valley. Mozambicans have been mixing with different cultures for centuries and have absorbed many different characteristics and customs. Arabs had been trading and living along the coast for hundreds of years before the arrival of the Portuguese, and when the new colonizers arrived they quickly settled and intermarried, creating a rich cultural mix. Mozambicans today – especially in the cities – reflect that melding of races and ideas. More than anything the Portuguese influence is visible, in the architecture and the food, the music, the cafés, nightclubs and bars.

Meeting the people

If you speak the most rudimentary Portuguese you'll find Mozambicans easy to get on with. If you can only grunt the words for 'yes', 'no' and 'Is this the bus for Pemba?', try the international language of football and cigarettes, which you'll find is a great ice-breaker. The generosity and friendliness of Mozambicans puts many Westerners to shame. Travelling in a country that has emerged – the poorest in the world – from 17 years of savage war, you will be constantly delighted by people's lack of suspicion and willingness to engage you in conversation. Children have the most heart-breaking smiles; give an old lady your hard-won seat on a crowded truck, and six people will squash up to make you a space.

The war is bound to have left some form of collective trauma. You may also meet surliness and suspicion, but seldom aggression. Remember also that much of Mozambique was completely cut off from the West for many years, and in many areas a gangly youth with a red face and a pack on their back is likely to excite a good deal of curiosity, which normally manifests itself as hospitality. If you're waiting for a lift at some dusty junction town, and someone tries out his English ('Hey, my friend!'), invites you into his house and gives you a plate of mandioca or a chicken leg, accept it graciously. You'll do wonders for the next backpacker that tramps through.

Outside Maputo and Beira young women often don't take kindly to being addressed, and confine themselves to pointing and giggling at you if you're a man, and staring with a mixture of fascination and disdain if you're a woman.

Women in Mozambique

Most Mozambican ethnic groups are matrilineal, and the *prazos* (see *History*, above), the semi-feudal system by which much of the country was administered for several hundred years of Portuguese dominance, was based on inheritance through the female line. For the first half of the 20th century hundreds of thousands of men went to work in South Africa, leaving the women to run their families and livings. Add to that the fact that Frelimo has some progressive pro-women policies, and it is easy to see why Mozambican women have a strong tradition of independence and influence. Mozambique is one of the few southern African countries where you will see women – even in rural areas – smoking in public, and in the larger towns it's not unusual to see groups of women out together at a café, something that would be extremely unusual in Zambia and unheard-of in Malawi. Thirteen per cent of the total of members of parliament are women, a figure that compares interestingly with the UK's eight per cent.

But in the most isolated rural areas, customs continue which do little to support women's lives. Girls get married as young as 14 or 15, and widows have little status, often facing eviction by their in-laws. Customary law still permits the husband's relatives to seize the house and property after his death, although modern Mozambican law does not recognise this. Supporting a family while the husband is absent and perhaps not sending any support can be a heavy burden. Family health suffers as women struggle to produce enough food: malnutrition is one of the most common health problems for children and adults. As the economy improves things will get better, but at the moment, for the majority of Mozambican women living outside the cities, life is hard.

PHOTOGRAPHY

If you want to photograph a public building, a bridge or any such sensitive installation, get permission first. On no account try to photograph governor's residences and government buildings outside Maputo – you are not even allowed to walk past these places on the same side of the road, and taking a picture could get you into serious trouble, or at least make you liable to a crippling fine or bribe. In most places, your camera will generate great interest and you'll be mobbed by youths wanting their photograph taken. Many people assume all cameras are Polaroids and will want to see the picture immediately. Be very tactful with older people, as they are often suspicious of cameras and resent having their pictures taken. With anyone else, just ask, and they'll happily pose for you.

RELIGION AND TRADITIONAL BELIEFS

There is no official religion in Mozambique. Some 30 per cent of those who profess religious beliefs are Christian; another 20 per cent are Muslim. Fifty per cent of the population follow traditional African religions. The Frelimo government's Marxist-Leninist stance led them to outlaw tribal traditions and animist religions as superstitious: many practices such as polygamy, traditional healing and initiation rites were banned. But many communities continue such traditions, and even more so since the ban was lifted in 1990. In the more isolated rural areas of the north young people must still pass through rites of passage. Some traditions, like scarification of the flesh of women, are dying out, but others are still followed. Makua girls reaching puberty are forbidden to put salt on their food during rituals, and must never use salt during menstruation. Elder women take young girls into the bush where they learn about adult life, marital relations and respect for parents. At the end of a week they ritually bathe, are anointed with oil and don a veil before being taken to the house of the chief, who gives them each a gift before lifting the veil. Similarly, adolescent Makonde boys are taken into the bush to learn a man's duties – house-building, bush-clearing, and the necessity of providing clothes for one's wife. They also learn the Mapiko dance, for which they wear masks carved out of soft *njala* wood. You can see Mapiko dances, with their pantomime costumes and villainous characters, in many villages and towns in the north. They have a real carnival atmosphere with loud drums and cymbals, and an enthusiastic crush of people. Nowadays, like the older generation all over the world, Makonde elders complain that things aren't what they used to be and that Mapiko has lost its mystery.

In Cabo Delgado you will also see young girls and women with white-painted faces and arms. This is purely cosmetic: the paste is ground from the bark of the nciro tree, and is supposed to protect the skin from the drying effects of sun and wind.

LANGUAGE

Portuguese is the official language of the country, the language of government, business and the law, teaching in high schools and universities. In fact it is actually only spoken by some 25 per cent of the population – those who have been to school – and you will certainly come across many people who speak only their local language. But for practical purposes if you speak Portuguese you will be able to get by anywhere in Mozambique. Even in cities English is not widely spoken, although things are changing, mainly due to the fact that it is the language of all Mozambique's neighbours.

Apart from Portuguese, there are 33 languages in Mozambique, all of which belong to the Bantu family. Many of these are spoken by a few thousand people, but the main groups and their dialects – Makua-Lomwe in the north, Tsonga in the south, Shona in central Mozambique and Sena in the northwest – are spoken at home by over 50 per cent of the population. KiSwahili is fairly widely spoken in the northern coastal areas, and some Zulu is spoken in the south.

Other main languages are Maconde (spoken in Cabo Delgado), Gitonga (the Inhambane area up to Morrumbane), Ndau (south of Beira), Ronga (Maputo province), Yao (around Lake Niassa), and Changana (Gaza province).

LEARNING PORTUGUESE

You should learn the basics of Portuguese before you go to Mozambique. A smattering of the language will make a huge difference to the ease with which you travel around the country. There's a wide range of phrase books, videos and tapes on the market; the BBC produces very good ones (particularly their *Talk...* course for absolute beginners), but other publishers such as Hugo and Berlitz are just as comprehensive. Take a good phrase book and pocket dictionary with you – they weigh little and are extremely useful in the myriad situations in which you may find yourself utterly lacking the ability to communicate. Below is a brief introduction to pronunciation and some useful phrases, and a glossary of some words and acronyms that may be found in the text. More specialised glossaries can be found at the beginning of the sections on Money, Communications, Eating and Drinking, Entertainment, Shopping, Health and Hygiene, and Crime and Safety.

Pronunciation

Vowels

a	as in 'father'	*gato*
e	as in 'get' or the 'a' in 'gate'	*hotel* or *dizer*
i	as in 'meet'	*filha*
o	as in 'pot' or as in 'note'	*mosca* or *boca*
u	as in 'foot'	*nunca*

Consonants

c (followed by 'e' or 'i')	's' as in 'single'	*cidade*
c	'c' as in 'candle'	*cabra*
ç	soft 'z' as in 'zebra'	*Moçambique*
ch	'sh' as in 'shake'	*chá*
g (followed by 'e' or 'i')	'jz' as in 'measure'	*gente*
g	'g' as in 'good'	*gasolina*
j	'jz' as in 'measure'	*jornal*
lh	'll' as in 'million'	*mulher*
m (at the end of a word)	is hardly pronounced	*sim*
nh	'y' as in 'yellow'	*banho*
r	rolled as in Scots 'Edinburgh'	*caro*
rr	strong roll	*corrida*
s (in the middle or end of a word)	'sh' as in 'finish'	*escola*
qu	'qu' as in 'queen'	*quando*
qu	'k' as in 'kilo'	*quilo*
x	'sh' as in 'shake'	*Maxixe*
z (at the end of a word)	'jz' as in 'measure'	*paz*
z (in the middle of word)	'z' as in 'zoo'	*fazer*

Useful Words and Phrases

hello	*olá*	(ohlah)
goodbye	*adeus*	(adyoosh)
good morning	*bom dia*	(bohm deeyah)
good afternoon	*boa tarde*	(boah tahrd)
good night	*boa noite*	(boah noyt)
how are you?	*como está?*	(kohmoo istah?)
very well, thanks	*muito bem, obrigado/a*	(mweeto bem, ohbrigahdoo/a)
yes sim	*(seehm)*	
no não	*(nohw)*	
please	*por favor*	(pohr favohr)
thank you (very much)	*(muito) obrigado/a*	(mweeto ohbrigahdoo/a)
don't mention it	*de nada*	(day nahdaa)
excuse me (I'm sorry)	*desculpe*	(dis-koolp)
excuse me (may I?)	*com licença*	kohm lee-sensa)
how much is it?	*quanto é*	(kwantoo e)
good	*bom/boa*	(bohm/boha)
bad	*mau/má*	(maoo/mah)
I don't understand	*não entendo*	(nohw ayntehndoo)
do you speak English?	*Fala inglês?*	(fahla eenglaysh?)
I speak very little Portuguese	*falo muito pouco português*	(fahloo mweeto pohkoo poortoogaysh)
Is there anyone here who speaks English?	*há alguém que fale inglês?*	(ah alghem ki fahli eenglaysh?)
could you show me in the book?	*podia-me mostrar no livro?*	(pohdeea-mi mohstrar noo leevro?)
my name is...	*chamo-me*	(shamoo mi)
what's your name?	*como se chama?*	(kohmoo si shama?)
could you repeat that?	*podia repetir?*	(poodea rripeteer?)
a little more slowly	*mais devagar*	(miysh dayvagahr)
It doesn't matter	*não importa*	(nohw eemportah)
That's fine, that's great	*muito bem*	(mweeto behm)
Where is...?	*onde é?*	(ohndee e?)
toilet	*casa de banho*	(kahsa di bahnyoo)
What time?	*A que horas?*	(ah kay orash?)
Could you help me?	*podia-me ajudar?*	(pohdeea-mi azhoodar?)
What is it called in Portuguese?	*Como se chama em português?*	(kohmoo si shama ehm poortoogaysh?)

Days

Note that the weekdays are often abbreviated to segunda, terça, etc

Sunday	*o domingo*
Monday	*a segunda-feira*
Tuesday	*a terça-feira*
Wednesday	*a quarta-feira*
Thursday	*a quinta-feira*
Friday	*a sexta-feira*
Saturday	*o sábado*

Months

January	*Janeiro*
February	*Fevereiro*
March	*Março*
April	*Abril*
May	*Maio*
June	*Junho*
July	*Julho*
August	*Agosto*
September	*Setembro*
October	*Outubro*
November	*Novembro*
December	*Dezembro*

Seasons

spring	*a primavera*
summer	*a verão*
autumn	*o outono*
winter	*o inverno*

General time phrases

day	*o dia*
week	*a semana*
fortnight	*quinze dias*
month	*o mês*
year	*o ano*
today	*hoje*
tomorrow	*amanhã*
yesterday	*ontem*
last night	*ontem à noite*
last week	*na semana passada*
next week	*na semana que vem*
next Monday	*na próxima segunda-feira*

in the morning	*de manha*
in the afternoon/evening	*de tarde*
at night	*à noite*

Nationality and status

I am English	*sou inglês/esa*
Scottish	*escocês/esa*
Welsh	*galês/esa*
Irish	*irlandês/esa*
Australian	*austaliano/a*
a New Zealander	*neo zelandês/esa*
United States	*os Estados Unidos*
American	*americano/a or estadunidense* (m and f)
married	*casado/a*
single	*solteiro/a*
engaged	*comprometido/a*
man	*o homem*
woman	*o mulher*
husband	*o marido*
wife	*a mulher*
boyfriend/girlfriend	*o namorado/a*
boy	*o rapaz*
girl	*a rapariga*
child/children	*a criança/as crianças*
son/daughter	*o filho/a*
sons and daughters	*os filhos*

Numbers

zero	*zero*
one	*um/a*
two	*dois/duas*
three	*três*
four	*quatro*
five	*cinco*
six	*seis*
seven	*sete*
eight	*oito*
nine	*nove*
ten	*dez*
eleven	*onze*
twelve	*doze*
thirteen	*treze*
fourteen	*catorze*

fifteen	*quinze*
sixteen	*dezasseis*
seventeen	*dezassete*
eighteen	*dezoito*
nineteen	*dezanove*
twenty	*vinte*
twenty-one	*vinte e um/a*
twenty-two	*vinte e dois/duas*
twenty-three	*vinte e três*
twenty-four	*vinte e quatro*
twenty-five	*vinte e cinco*
thirty	*trinta*
thirty-one	*trinta e um/a*
forty	*quarenta*
fifty	*cinquenta*
sixty	*sessenta*
seventy	*setenta*
eighty	*oitenta*
ninety	*noventav*
one hundred	*cem*
a hundred and one	*cento e um/a*
two hundred	*duzentos/as*
three hundred	*trezentos/asv*
four hundred	*quatrocentos/as*
five hundred	*quinhentos/as*
one thousand	*mil*
ten thousand	*dez mil*
one million	*um milhão*
two million	*dois milhãos*

Glossary of words and acronyms used in the text

câmbio	bureau de change
capulana	brightly-coloured all-purpose wrap worn by women
chapa	a pick-up truck or lorry with seats operating as a short- or long-distance taxi
Frelimo	Frente de Libertação de Moçambique (Mozambique Liberation Front)
machamba	small plot of land for cultivation
machimbombo	bus
marimba	type of xylophone
Mapiko	a dance performed by the Makonde people
mazungo	(archaic) person of mixed race

miombo	tree, also called brachystegia, native to Mozambique
NGO	Non-Governmental Organisation, aid agency or charity
prazo	large semi-feudal estate
prego	bread roll with beef filling
Renamo	Resistência Nacional Moçambicana (Mozambican National Resistance)
TDM	Telecomunicações de Mocambique – the national telephone company

FURTHER READING

General

If you want a background to the history of European involvement in Africa a good start would be *The Scramble For Africa* by Thomas Pakenham (Abacus, London, 1992), a highly readable account the Great Powers' race for colonial possessions at the end of the 19th Century. Another general history is *Africa* edited by Phyllis M. Martin and Patrick O'Meara (Indiana University Press, 3rd edition, 1995). If you are interested in Livingstone you could start with Tim Jeal's *Livingstone* (Pimlico, London, 1973), or go straight to the tormented explorer's great work, the *Narrative Of An Expedition To The Zambesi And Its Tributaries 1858-1864*. On this expedition Livingstone travelled through the centre of Mozambique. He writes about the slave trade at Quelimane, the vast amounts of game in the bush, the dense population on the shores of Lake Niassa, the rapids at Cahora Bassa. He may have been driven, even demented, but his descriptions are fresh and evocative – it is a fascinating read.

Of the hundreds of books on Africa today there are one or two that give a particularly good perspective on the continent: *Africa Now – People, Policies, Institutions* edited by Stephen Ellis (Heinemann 1996) is a collection of essays compiled for a conference in 1995, and *Into The House Of The Ancestors – Inside The New Africa* (John Wiley and Sons 1998) by Karl Maier, the former Africa correspondent for the Independent newspaper in the UK, is based on interviews with traditional healers, chiefs, businessmen, generals, scientists, poets, politicians and a whole spectrum of African society. It looks at the spirit of Africa at a turning point in the continent's history, and how Africans connect tradition to development. Lastly, Nigerian writer and Nobel Laureate Wole Soyinka's *The Open Sore Of A Continent* (Oxford University Press, 1996) covers more than Nigeria, looking at questions of nationhood, identity and the general state of African culture and politics at the end of the 20th century

Mozambique

The definitive history is the erudite and exhaustive *A History of Mozambique* by Malyn Newitt (Hurst and Company, London, 1995; Wits University Press,

South Africa, 1995). *Confronting Leviathan: Mozambique Since Independence* by Margaret Hall and Tom Young (Hurst and Company, London, 1997) is a detailed history of the country since 1975. Another excellent book is *Machel of Mozambique* by Iain Christie (Zimbabwe Publishing House, Harare, 1988), a highly-respected biography of Samora Machel.

The Mozambican Peace Process In Perspective (Conciliation Resources, London, 1998), published by a London-based NGO, gives a detailed, balanced background to the events leading up to 1992 and the aftermath of the war, together with primary materials. As a potted history, *Mozambique: Rising From The Ashes* by Rachel Waterhouse (Oxfam, UK and Ireland, 1996) is useful, if a little over-sympathetic towards Frelimo.

Two very readable books are Nick Middleton's entertaining travelogue *Kalashnikovs and Zombie Cucumbers: Travels In Mozambique* (Phoenix, London, 1994), the account of a journey around the country during and just after 1992, and *Viva Mozambique* by Sally Crooks (Starling Books), the author's experience of five years living in the country as it went from war to peace.

Other historical and socio-economic texts on Mozambique tend to be too academic for the layman's needs. Worth looking at, however, are Joseph Hanlon's *Peace Without Profit* (1996) and *Mozambique: Who Calls The Shots?* (1991), both published by Heinemann, which discuss the West's involvement in the restructuring of Mozambique, and the complex relationship between aid donors and the crisis-hit government. If you are interested in ONUMOZ, the United Nations' mission to manage the transition to democracy, *Mozambique: UN Peacekeeping in Action 1992-1996* by Richard Synge (United States Institute of Peace Press) is a readable account.

Lastly, *The History of Landmines* by Mike Croll (Leo Cooper/Pen and Sword, 1998) is a comprehensive study, with detailed sections on the landmine situation in Mozambique.

Mozambican literature

One of the best sources in English of Mozambican writers is the Heinemann African Writers Series, who publish both Mia Couto and Luis Honwana, two of Mozambique's best-known writers. You should also make every effort to get hold of *Short Stories From Mozambique*, edited by Richard Bartlett (COSAW Publishing, Johannesburg, 1995).

As the South African writer Albie Sachs says in his introduction to this anthology, during the colonial years 'culture was not seen as a weapon of struggle. It was part of struggle.' Frelimo was full of poets and writers. Luis Honwana, Frelimo member and Samora Machel's Minister of Culture between 1982 and 1991, documented the effects of war in stories like *We*

Killed Mangy-Dog (available in the anthology above). Other modern writers include Ungulani Ba Ka Khosa, Suleiman Cassamo, Mia Couto (Frelimo fighter and later director of the Mozambican Information Agency) and the poet Helder Muteia, a key member of the Association of Mozambican Writers.

Mozambican fiction naturally gives an entirely different perspective to that of travelogues and guide books. Lília Momplé's *No-one Killed Suhura* (in *Short Stories from Mozambique*), depicts the powerlessness of a local girl and her grandmother against the eventually murderous advances of a Portuguese official, on Ilha de Moçambique. In Mia Couto's *Voices Made Night* (Heinemann), ordinary Mozambicans' lives are – sometimes comically – disrupted by war and poverty. A young cowherd is horrified when his uncle's prize ox is blown up by a mine; an old man tells his wife he must dig her grave now because he won't have the strength to do it when she dies. Other books to look out for are Couto's *Every Man Is A Race* and Lina Magaia's *Dumba Nengue Run For Your Life*. One of the most powerful accounts of the terrible disruption of war is *A Shattering of Silence* by Farida Karodia, which describes a young girl's journey through Mozambique after the killing of her family.

Of the hundreds of Mozambican poets, one of the most famous is Jose Craveirinha, who wrote about the conditions of the poorest of his countrymen in the late 1940s, and was arrested as a dissident by the Portuguese. His most famous work, *Poem Of The Future Citizen* is not published in the UK but you should be able to find it in Maputo libraries.

If you want to study Mozambican literature in greater detail, one of the best critical works is *The Post Colonial Literature of Lusophone Africa* by Patrick Chabal et al. (Hurst, 1996).

Bookshops
London has the best selection of travel bookshops. *Stanfords* (12-14 Long Acre, London WC2E 9LP; tel 0207 836 1321; fax 0207 836 0189; e-mail: sales@stanfords.co.uk) is probably the best stocked with guides, related literature and maps. *Daunt Books* (83 Marylebone High Street, London W1M 4DE; tel 0207 224 2295) specialises in travel literature and rare and out-of-print books – and also has a beautiful 19th century interior. The bookshop in the *Africa Centre* (38 King Street, London WC2E 8JT; tel 0207-240 6649; fax 0207-497 0309; e-mail: africabooks@dial.pipex.com) has the best selection of books on Mozambique.

Specialist travel bookshops out of London are more scarce. In Manchester, *Dillons* (2-4 Saint Ann's Square, Manchester M2 7HH; tel 0161-832 0424; fax 0161-831 7786; e-mail: manchstr@dillons.co.uk) has a very good travel section. *The Map Shop* (15 High Street, Upton-upon-Severn, Worcestershire WR8 0HJ; tel 01684 593 146; e-mail: themapshop@btinternet.com; website:

www.themapshop.co.uk) has a national reputation and stocks all types of guides as well as maps.

Almost all of the books above, and many more besides, are available from www.amazon.co.uk, and from amazon.com in the USA.

PRACTICAL INFORMATION

Mozambique is not one of the most popular southern African destinations, so you won't find too many flight bargains. You could find a slightly less expensive flight to Harare, Dar es Salaam or another neighbouring capital, but you'll spend the difference anyway making your way into Mozambique. The best options for flying are detailed below. If you are including Mozambique in a wider tour of the continent there are many overland routes you can take. The most frequented are through Malawi, Zimbabwe and South Africa, but there are several other border crossings, some of them – like the Newala/Mocimboa do Rovuma route from Tanzania – hardly used by travellers and requiring a good deal of initiative and stamina. One of the most exciting things about travelling in Mozambique is the feeling of newness and exploration. You may not be David Livingstone, but you can choose routes that Westerners haven't travelled for years. You could well be stranded for days on a track which sees a vehicle once a week, but that lends a nice sense of adventure to your trip.

BY AIR

From the UK and Europe the most popular route to Mozambique is via Johannesburg from London. South African Airways have the most competitive flights, with return fares ranging between £550-1,200 for direct flights from London, including a one hour connecting flight to Maputo. British Airways have direct flights to Johannesburg and Cape Town with connecting flights to Maputo via Linhas Aéreas de Moçambique (LAM), Mozambique's national carrier and South African Airways, these cost around £1,100. Richard Branson's Virgin Atlantic have direct flights to Johannesburg with connecting flights to Maputo on South African Airlines, their round-trip prices range from £800-1,000. Air France also flies from London to Johannesburg, with an overnight stopover in Paris, flights cost between £1,600 and £2,120. The Portuguese carrier TAP has direct flights from

Lisbon, which you can connect to with BA from London for around £2,250, as well as a co-shared service with LAM.

LAM has flights from Johannesburg to Maputo six times a week (not Saturdays), and several times a week from the other neighbouring capitals. LAM also flies direct from Johannesburg to Beira and Vilanculos. The charter company Metavia Airlines serves Maputo from Johannesburg and also from Nelspruit, Richard's Bay and Durban.

You can also fly into Lilongwe in Malawi, Dar es Salaam in Tanzania, or the Zimbabwean capital Harare, but these routes will work out no cheaper than going via Johannesburg.

From the USA

The most convenient and cheapest US city from which to fly to Africa is New York, followed by Atlanta, Chicago and Cincinnati. As a guide, prices range between $2,400-2,700 for coach class returns from New York and $2,800-3,100 from Los Angeles. Flights from the West Coast usually stage through New York or occasionally Miami, so it may be possible to get cheaper connections across the US. The main routes used are via Johannesburg and then onto Maputo. South African Airways fly direct to Johannesburg from New York —a 12-hour flight with a refuelling stop in the Cape Verde Islands. In low season you should expect to pay around $1,200 to Johannesburg, and a further $250 for the flight to Maputo. In high season you should add around $350 to that price. From Chicago (via Europe) to Johannesburg and on to Maputo, the minimum cost would be around $1,650.

Virgin Atlantic, BA and Air France all have flights from the New York airports to Mozambique which stage through London, Paris and Johannesburg; with west coast flights connecting via New York. American Airlines have direct flights to Johannesburg connecting on to Maputo with South African or LAM, their flights from Los Angeles stage through New York or Miami.

As many carriers stage through London, even from the West Coast, another option for travellers from the USA is to get a flight across the Atlantic to London and then see what you can pick up in there, although most travel agents advise this will work out no cheaper than flying direct.

From Australia

As with Europe and America most flights stage via Johannesburg, although Qantas have flights to Harare giving you the options of continuing overland or with a connecting flight. Qantas have flights to Johannesburg which connect to Maputo with either LAM or South African. These can be direct from Sydney to Johannesburg or connecting via Perth with South African. An economy return will cost A$2,499, and be valid from 5 days to six months.

Useful Addresses:

Air France: 1st Floor, 10 Warwick Street, London, W1R 5RA; tel 0207-474

5555; Website www.airfrance.fr/
120 West 56th Street, New York, NY 10019, USA; tel 1-800-237 2747.
American Airlines: 4200 Amon Carter Boulevard, MD 2644, Dallas Fort
Worth Airport, Texas 75261, USA; tel (freephone) 1-800-321 2121;
Website wwwr3.aa.com/
45-46 Picadilly, London, W1V 9AJ; tel 0208-572 5555.
British Airways: Waterside, PO Box 365, Harmondsworth, UB7 0GB; tel
0208-759 5511; Website www.british-airways.com
British Airways can be contacted anywhere in the USA on (freephone) 1-
800-AIRWAYS.
Linhas Aéreas de Moçambique: Ave Karl Marx 220, Maputo, Mozambique;
tel 01-426001/4.
Qantas: Chifley Square, 70 Hunter Street, Sydney, Australia; tel 131313
(information and reservations); Website www.qantas.com.au
Level 4, 841 Apollo Street, El Segundo, Los Angeles, CA 90425, USA; tel
800-227-4500 (reservations).
South African Airways: St George's House, 61 Conduit Street, London, W1R
0NE; tel 0207-312 5002; Website www.saa.co.za
Suite 1600, 16th Floor, 515 East Las Olas Boulevard, Fort Lauderdale,
Florida 33301, USA; tel 1-800-722 9675 (reservations); Website www.saa-
usa.com
9th Floor, 5 Elizabeth Street, Sydney, NSW 2000, Australia; tel 612-9223
4448.
TAP: 38-44 Gillingham Street, London; tel 0207-828 0262. Website
http://restaurantes.netopia.pt/tap/
3rd Floor, 608 Fifth Avenue, New York, USA; tel 212-969-5775.
Virgin Atlantic: Virgin Megastore, 14-16 Oxford Street, London W1; tel (UK
reservations) 01293-747747; Website www.fly.virgin.com
100 E. 42nd Street, New York, NY 10017, USA; tel 800-862 8621.

TOUR OPERATORS AND TRAVEL AGENTS

There is a list of useful flight finder websites at the end of the *Help and
Information* section.

UK

Trailfinders stitch together flights all over the world and are particularly good
at finding the cheapest round-the-world tickets. STA travel and Campus
Travel have very good websites with flight-finding services. A couple of
London agents specialise in Africa: all addresses are given below.

Trailfinders: 42-50 Earl's Court Road, London W8 6FT (tel 0207-938 3366);
194 Kensington High Street, London W8 6BD (tel 0207-938 3939); and

branches in Birmingham (tel 0121-236 1234); Bristol (tel 0117-929 9000); Glasgow (tel 0141-353 2224); Manchester (tel 0161-839 6969); Newcastle (tel 0191-261 2345).

STA: 85 Shaftesbury Avenue, London W11; tel 0207-361 6161, and branches in Manchester (tel 0161-834 0668); Leeds, Bristol, Oxford, Glasgow etc – see website at www.sta-travel.co.uk for details and flight finder.

African Travel Specialists: Glen House, Stag Place, London SW1; tel 0207 630 5434.

Africa Travel Centre: Medway Court, Leigh Street, London WC1; tel 0207-387 1211.

Campus Travel: www.usitcampus.co.uk. Flight finding service: no Mozambique fares but you might pick up a cheap one to South Africa or Tanzania.

Acacia Expeditions; tel 0207 706 4700; e-mail: acacia@afrika.demon.co.uk. Organise trips from Johannesburg taking in Maputo, Xai-Xai, Inhambane, Kruger National Park.

USA

A look through the Yellow Pages will bring up any number of travel agents dealing with South Africa, although very few deal directly with Mozambique. The UK operator Abercrombie and Kent, who are just starting to run packages to southern Mozambique have an office in Illinois. One of the best New York agents with specialist knowledge of Mozambique is Africa Travel.

Abercrombie and Kent, 1520 Kensington Road, Oak Brook, Illinois 60523; tel 630-954 2944; fax 630-954 3324; e-mail: info@abercrombiekent.com

Africa Travel, 1170 Broadway, Suite 311, New York, NY 10001; tel 212-481 3850; e-mail: cdscks89@aol.com

Lion Roars Safaris, 505 Beachland Boulevard, Suite 1-219, Vero Beach, FL 32963. Tel 561-234 9201; fax 561-234 9202; e-mail: sales@lionroars.com.

Triple A Corporate Travel, tel 913-649 1504 (Based in Kansas, will stitch together USA-Mozambique flights, also organises discounts for aid agency staff.)

South Africa and Swaziland

There are many agencies in South Africa specialising in tours to Mozambique, offering all-in packages including fishing, safaris, diving, catamaran trips and the like. Some of the main operators are listed below.

Mozambique Connection: Tel 011-626 2650/1144; fax 011-626 1149, and in Inhambane and Tofu; tel. 023-29021; e-mail: mozcon@pixie.co.za. Tours to destinations from Inhaca Island to Pemba.

Moçambique Tours (Durban): Tel 031-303 2190; fax 031-303 2396; e-mail: mit@iafrica.com; website: www.durban.org.za/mph/mit. Tours to Inhaca Island, Bazaruto Islands, Vilanculos.

Moçambique Adventure Safaris: Tel 082-494 1735; website: www. adventure.co.za/mozambique.htm. Diving, game fishing, spear fishing.

Mozambique National Tourist Co: Johannesburg; tel 011-339 7275/81; fax 011-339 7295. Maputo; tel 01-421794/8; e-mail: entur@virconn.com; website: www.entur.imoz.com. Tours to Ponta Malongane, Ponta do Ouro, Xai-Xai, Vilanculos, Bazaruto Islands.

OVERLAND ROUTES

From South Africa

Private Car
The Komatipoort-Ressano Garcia border crossing is 470km east of Johannesburg on good roads. The journey from Johannesburg to the border by car takes about five hours, with a further one and a half hours from Ressano Garcia to Maputo, also on a good road. If you need to break your journey to avoid driving the last stretch to Maputo after dark, there is a campsite and a hotel in Komatipoort. If you are coming up from Durban you can cross at the Ponta do Ouro border at the southern tip of Mozambique. The road between Ponta do Ouro and Maputo is in a very bad state of repair and should only be attempted in a 4WD.

Public Transport
Several bus companies run between Johannesburg, Durban and Maputo. *Panthera Azul* (tel 011-331 7409; fax 011-337 7409) leave at 7.30am Monday to Saturday, and an hour later on Sunday, and an overnight bus leaves at 9pm. *Tropical Air Tours* (011-337 9169/8946) have daily buses between Johannesburg and Maputo via Nelspruit, as do *Translux*. Panthera Azul (031-309 7798 in Durban) run twice a week between Maputo and Durban (See p.118 for contact numbers in Maputo). The journey from Johannesburg to Maputo takes about 10 hours.

Hitching
It's not advisable to hitch in or out of Johannesburg; once at Ressano Garcia it should not be difficult to pick up a lift for the 100km to Maputo.

Train
The luxurious Trans-Lubombo Express goes from Durban to Maputo twice a week on Tuesdays and Fridays, leaving at 7.30pm and arriving at 6.15pm the following day. There are also trains from Johannesburg. Further details

and contact numbers are given in the *Arrival and Departure* section of *Maputo*.

From Zimbabwe

The section *Beira* in the chapter on *Sofala and Manica* covers the overland route from the Zimbabwean town of Mutare to Beira in detail. This is one of the most popular routes into Mozambique, the roads are in good condition and the trip can easily be done in a saloon car. There is plenty of public transport and hitching is perfectly viable.

From Malawi

There are a number of different border crossings from Malawi to Mozambique. If you are heading for Quelimane you should cross at Milange; if you want to go to Tete first, then Zóbuè is the obvious border to head for. If you are heading for Nampula the best route is between Mangochi and Cuamba. For the far north of the country and Lake Niassa, you can go via Likoma Island, from where ferries cross to Cóbuè and other towns. Foreigners entering Mozambique by land from Malawi have to pay $5 immigration tax. Getting a visa should not be problem – there are immigration offices in the larger towns you pass through.

Private car
The journey from Blantyre to Tete takes about four hours on good roads. Other road routes are covered in *Public transport* below and should present no problems for a 4WD.

Public transport
Regular buses connect Blantyre with Harare via Zóbuè and Tete, leaving Blantyre at 6am and arriving in Tete at midday. You may find you have to pay the full fare to Harare if you get on at Blantyre, so an alternative is to get out at Mwanza (where there is a hotel) on the Malawian side and catch another bus through to Tete. There are also buses from Lilongwe to Tete via Dedza in the north, but note that this route is over very bad roads, the buses are scarce, and there are few other vehicles so hitching will be a very slow option.

If you want to cross the Zambesi and go on to Beira (see *Beira* p.166), you could get one of the two or three buses a day from Blantyre to Nsanje at the southern tip of Malawi. Some buses go straight through; others stop at Nsanje, from where you can pick up another lift to the border. At the border you can pick up a lift going to Vila Nova de la Frontera and Nhamalábue, and cross the Zambesi by bridge at Vila de Sena or the car ferry at Caia, for which you might have to wait several hours.

For Nampula, there are frequent minibuses from Mangochi to Namwera and the border. There are places to stay at Namwera. It's quite possible to walk the last 2km from here to the border if there seems to be no bus. It's then a further 6km to Mandimba from where there are frequent *chapas* to Cuamba.

Your final option – the crossing at Milange, on the road between Blantyre and Mocuba – is not particularly satisfactory because of the dearth of transport along the final leg of the journey. There are frequent buses from Blantyre, taking three to four hours to get as far as the Malawian border at Muloza. From there it's 1km to the border post at Milange, and a little further to the town itself, where there is a pensão and bank. There are few vehicles using the road between Milange and Mocuba so be prepared to wait days for a lift. Once you get to Mocuba (where there are places to stay) you'll have no trouble getting a lift to Quelimane or Nampula. Use this route only if you must get straight to Quelimane; if you're going to Nampula, take the train from Cuamba.

Train
This is the best and most enjoyable way of getting to Nampula. There is a twice-weekly train from Balaka to the border at Nayuchi (this is a rail crossing only) via Liwonde, from where you can walk to the small town of Interlagos on the Mozambican side and catch a freight train to Cuamba. For trains from Cuamba to Nampula see *Nampula* p.204. Note there are daily trains connecting Blantyre with Balaka, arriving mid-morning, which should give you enough time to make the border and the Cuamba connection. If you arrive too late there is a pensão at Interlagos.

Boat
Also a very pleasant option. The Malawian boat *Ilala* goes up and down Lake Malawi once a week in either direction, stopping at Likoma Island twice a week. In Malawi you can catch the boat at Monkey Bay, Chipoka, Nkhotakota, Likoma, Nkhata Bay and Chilumba, as well as many other smaller ports. Check locally for times. Once on Likoma (see *Niassa* p.224 for more details) you can get a local boat across to Cóbuè, or to Metangula, 100km south.

From Tanzania

The Tanzanian route is one of the longest and most difficult for overland travellers. At present (though there are plans for a bridge) the only way across the Rovuma river is by canoe. In the wet season (November to April) the current is too fast for that, and the approach roads become almost impassable, effectively closing the border. There is another canoe crossing north of

Mocimboa do Rovuma; if you decide to take that route you should expect to cover around 40km on foot or bicycle. You can also catch a dhow from Msimbati, 12km south of Mtwara, to Mocímboa da Praia. When the monsoon winds are blowing from the south (between April and September) the voyage can take four or five days or longer, and should not be attempted.

In the right weather the border is perfectly passable. Once you have got to Mocimboa da Praia you will have no problem getting a lift down to Pemba. Don't go this way if you are in any sort of hurry – even in the dry season the 350km journey can take up to 18 hours, over some of the worst roads in Mozambique.

Public Transport
From Mtwara get a lift south to the border at Mwambo. Then you will probably have to walk the 5km to the river – local boys act as porters if you want to conserve your energy and offload your pack. Once you've crossed the river by dugout canoe, there is another 2km walk to the Mozambican border post at Namiranga, where there is an immigration office. Transport through to Palma (50km south) and Mocimboa is scarce, but you should be able to get a lift.

If you are fit and adventurous, and time is not a problem, you could take the route between Masasi and Mueda, crossing the river at Mocimboa do Rovuma, a village about 150km inland along the border. This is the heart of Makonde territory, remote and beautiful country, where you are highly unlikely to meet a motor vehicle: travellers tell tales of days spent hiking along roads impassable to anything but a bicycle. From Masasi or Mtwara take one of the regular buses to Newala, where there are places to stay. From Newala you will probably have to walk the 40km to the border post, although you may well be able to pay someone to act as a bicycle taxi. Once across the river it is about 20km to Mocimboa do Rovuma (again, transport is scarce) and a further 50km south to Mueda. You should be able to get a lift for the last stretch, although you should be prepared to wait a couple of days at least for any sort of vehicle to pass.

Boat
From Msimbati (served by bus from Mtwara) you can arrange a lift on a fishing dhow to Palma or Mocimboa da Praia. At the best estimate this should take 10-12 hours, although make sure the monsoon is not blowing from the south (see above). Dhow journeys can seem very romantic, as indeed they are when they last only a couple of hours, but remember they are working fishing boats, there is no shelter of any sort, nor any toilet facilities. You should also take adequate food and water for a trip that could last more than a day. Before you leave try and ascertain whether the dhow captain is going all the way to Palma or Mocimboa, or if his journey ends several kilometres short.

From Zambia

There are two routes into Mozambique from Zambia, via Chanida and Cassacatiza on the northern border, and via the Zumbo border post at the far western end of the Cahora Bassa lake. Both routes are very rarely used by travellers, because most people heading for Tete come in from Malawi. The 280km road between Cassacatiza and Tete is in fair condition and can be covered in 4WD, but there is very little public transport. However, it is a beautiful and hilly part of the country, and on your way to Tete you might consider taking a 100km detour via Vuende to Furancungo (see *Tete* for details). There are few vehicles in these parts and you may have to wait hours – or days – for a lift.

Crossing the Zambesi at Zumbo (one of the largest and most important Portuguese settlements in eastern Africa in the early 18th century) and then hitching your way through to Songo and Tete could be fascinating. There is some doubt as to whether foreigners are allowed across the border at all, although as it's a route much frequented by locals its worth a try.

Passports

All visitors to Mozambique need a full ten-year passport. Keep a photocopy of your passport separately, and a record of its number and date and place of issue in a third safe place. This will make it easier to get a replacement should it be lost or stolen.

Visas

All visitors require a visa, which you can get at any Mozambican embassy, consulate or high commission abroad (see list below) or through the National Tourist Company in Johannesburg. Visas are either single-entry or multiple-entry: if you're intending to cross over into Malawi or any other neighbouring country and return to Mozambique you'll need a double-entry visa. Visas are valid for a stay of up to 30 days. If you want to extend your visa after that you can do it at any immigration office (in all the provincial capitals and in certain other towns detailed in the text), as long as you don't stay more than three months.

In the UK, single-entry visas cost £35, multiple entry £70. You can order them by post from the Mozambique High Commission in London_they normally take five days to deliver but you can get an express service on the same day for £60, or within 24 hours for £55. In the USA visas can be obtained from the Embassy in Washington and usually take two weeks to process, however for a higher fee they can be obtained in two days; a single entry visa costs $20 ($40 for two-day service) and a multiple entry visa costs $40 ($60).

You should not arrive at a border without a visa, despite stories you will hear about people buying visas on the spot. You will almost certainly be refused entry, and even if you did manage to bribe an official into letting you in – itself a dangerous thing to attempt – you would have to explain at the next police checkpoint how you managed to get into the country without a valid visa.

List of Mozambican Embassies and consulates abroad

United Kingdom   21 Fitzroy Square, London W1P 5HJ; tel 0207-383 3800; fax 0207-383 3801.

United States   Embassy of the Republic of Mozambique, Suite 570, 1990 M Street NW, Washington DC 20036, USA; tel 202-293-7146, fax 202-835-0245.

South Africa   PO Box 40750, 199 Beckett St, Arcadia, 0083 Pretoria; tel 012-343 7840.

252 Jeppe Street, 7th Floor, Cape York Building, Johannesburg; tel 011-336 1819; fax 011-336 9921.

45 Castle Street, Cape Town; tel 021-262-944/5; fax 021-262 946.

320 West Street, Durban; tel 031-304 0222; fax 031-304 0774.

43 Brown Street, Nelspruit; tel 013-752 7396; fax 013-753 2088.

In Johannesburg, visas can also be arranged with the Empresa Nacional de Turismo; tel 011-339-7275; fax 011-339 7295.

France   82 Rue Laugier, 75017 Paris; tel 01-4764 9132; fax 01-4267 3828.

Germany   Adenauerallee 46, 53113 Bonn; tel 0228224024; fax 0228-213920.

Italy   Via Nazionale 5, 2 Piano, Int 4, 00184 Roma; tel 06-3751 4852.

Malawi   PO Box 30579, Lilongwe 3; tel 0265-78410.

Portugal   7 Avenue Berna, Lisboa 1000; tel 01-797 1994.

Russia   Ul Gilyarovskovo 20, Moscow; tel 095-284 4007; fax 095-200 4235.

Swaziland	Highlands View, Princes Drive Road, PO Box 1212, Mbabane; tel 0268-43700; fax 0268-43692.
Tanzania	PO Box 15274, 25 Garden Ave, Dar es Salaam; tel 051-67843.
Zambia	Lufubu Road, Plot No 5627, PO Box 34877, Kalundu, Lusuka; tel 01-29 1251; fax 01-29 0411.
Zimbabwe	152 Herbert Chitpo Ave, PO Box 4608, Harare; tel 04-79 0837; fax 04-73 2898.

bank	*o banco*
bill	*a conta*
bureau de change	*o câmbio*
black market	*o mercado preto*
change (small coins)	*os trocos*
change (verb)	*cambiar*
credit card	*o cartão de crédito*
dollar	*o dólar*
money	*o dinheiro*
receipt	*o recibo*
pound sterling	*a libra esterlina*
travellers cheque	*o travellers cheque*

MONEY IN MOZAMBIQUE

The Mozambican unit of currency is the **Metical**, almost always used in its plural form of **Meticais**, or its short form Mt. At the time of writing there are around Mt 20,000 to the £1 Sterling (Mt11,500 to US$1). Mozambicans will frequently knock off three zeros when quoting a price: if something costs Mt15,000, they may simply say, '*Quinze*'. One thousand is often referred to as *quantos* (pronounced 'consh'), so Mt100,000 becomes *cem quantos*. Notes are available in denominations of Mt5,000 up to Mt100,000. The smallest coin is Mt500, the largest Mt1,000. There are still Mt500 and Mt 1,000 notes in circulation; ragged as cobwebs and usually held together with tape, they are still legal currency.

Acceptable Currencies

With very few exceptions (ie some big city hotels) the metical is acceptable currency for all transactions. The US dollar is accepted hard currency all over Mozambique. South African rands in the south, Zimbabwean dollars north of the Zambesi, and kwacha on the Malawian borders, are also accepted. The pound sterling is not recognised as currency but can be changed in the larger banks in the big cities.

Change

Except in Maputo and especially north of the Zambesi, getting change can be a problem. Make sure you always have small denomination notes and a handful of coins about you, as it can be irritating constantly to be given IOU's. It is a good idea to check whether change is available before you buy something.

CHANGING MONEY

Changing money should not be a problem in Mozambique. Do not rely on being able to change travellers cheques: though they are the safest way to carry money, you may find yourself far away from a bank that will change them for you. You should take enough US dollars or South African rands in cash to ensure that if you cannot change travellers cheques you will not be stuck without cash. Even if you find it impossible to change them into meticais, dollars and rands are accepted throughout the country as hard currency. Most branches of the larger banks exchange foreign currency for meticais; there are also *câmbios* (bureaux de change) in the main cities. Branches of Banco Standard Totta de Moçambique, Banco Comercial e de Investimientos (BCI) and Banco Comercial de Moçambique can be found in most towns. There are now branches of Banco International de Moçambique (BIM) in Maputo, Beira, Nampula and Nacala. BCI and BIM are generally the only banks that exchange travellers cheques, **and will only do so if you can produce a receipt**. Most banks are open from 8 to 11am and from 2 to 3.30pm.

The Polana Hotel in Maputo changes travellers cheques, for a high commission. Only the largest banks and the biggest hotels in Maputo accept credit or debit cards; in the rest of the country they are practically useless as a source of cash or means of payment.

Money Transfers

It used to be impossible to get money transferred from your bank at home to Mozambique, but now – as long as you are in a big enough town – your only problem should be the several days it takes for the transfer to go through. UK high street banks (and major banks in most of Europe, the US and Australasia) will happily transfer money to a Mozambican bank, but they cannot guarantee the cash will be released to you when it arrives. If you are stuck without cash (if all your money is stolen for example) you should first contact your embassy and ask what they advise. You can also go directly to one of the major banks listed above, ask which European bank they deal with, and take the transaction from there. This will only work in the provincial capitals – banks in other towns are unlikely to have any sort of system set up to deal with international transfers. Remember that you should look on this as a last resort, and make sure you take enough money with you to ensure you don't run out.

The Black Market

A black market for cash operates in most of Mozambique. You will get the best rate for US dollars, but South African rands, Zimbabwe dollars and Malawi kwacha are also accepted. There should be no danger involved in using this method to buy your meticais, as long as you don't do it openly on the street, where you are likely to be conned. Where relevant, established money changers are mentioned in the text. If you cannot get to a bank and have no other means of obtaining meticais, ask in hotels and restaurants if there is anywhere you can change foreign currency. Don't accept lower than the going rate.

BUDGETING

Mozambique is not cheap compared to its neighbours. Tourists are frequently shocked by their basic day-to-day expenditure – food, public transport and accommodation all cost a good deal more than they do in Malawi or Tanzania. Mozambique's economy has been destroyed by 17 years of civil war, and a tourist infrastructure is something that takes years to develop. Until very recently Mozambique saw no tourists, except for the handful of hardy South Africans and Zimbabweans that continued to come in for the fishing, and for those that flew straight into the Bazaruto Islands. Furthermore, Mozambicans themselves did not travel around their country. As a result there are very few decent mid-range hotels, and what passes for upmarket outside of Maputo is often mean, dirty – and overpriced. Similarly, restaurants are often pretentious and pricey. Public transport is also more expensive than you will be used to if you have come from another southern or east African country.

You should be prepared to spend between $30 and $40 a day if you are staying in hotels, less if you are camping. As *Accommodation* p.72, makes clear, the latter is frequently the best option. If you are staying in hotels you should budget for at $15-20 per day for a double room, or $5 per day if you are camping. The cheapest meal in a mid-range restaurant will cost from $2-5 (as an example, half a chicken with salad in Gúrúe would be $3-4). If you are camping and buying all your own food in markets, you can budget for considerably less. Peripherals like beer are expensive: the average cost of a can or bottle of Mozambican Castle is $1.30, rising to $1.50 in the far north of the country. Public transport should work out at around $5 per day.

Carrying Money

Keep most of your cash and your passport in a fabric money belt under your shirt, and distribute emergency supplies – say $100 – around your backpack or suitcase. Safeguarding your money and valuables is covered in more detail under *Crime and Safety* p.93.

air mail	*por avião*
code	*o indicativo*
envelope	*o envelope*
fax	*o fax*
e-mail	*o e-mail*
collect call (reverse charge)	*a chamada a pagar pelo destinatário*
magazine	*a revista*
newspaper	*o jornal*
out of order	*avariado*
parcel	*o embrulho*
post (noun)	*o correio*
post box	*o marco de correio*
postcard	*o postal*
post office	*o correio*
rate	*a tarifa*
stamp	*o selo*
telephone	*o telefone*
telephone call	*a chamada*
I want to make a telephone call to England	*quero ligar para a Inglaterra*
telephone directory	*a lista telefónica*
telephone receiver	*o auscultador*

TELEPHONE

Outside the cities there are very few private telephones in Mozambique, so public telephones are readily available and reasonably efficient. All larger towns have a TDM (Telecomunicações de Moçambique) call centre from where you can make international and national calls. These are mentioned in the text where relevant. Local calls can be made from phone boxes or from staffed public call booths in cafés and restaurants. Bear in mind that making international calls from your hotel will cost you around $30 for three minutes, three or four times as much as from a public call centre. A cellular phone network covers Maputo, Matola and Xai-Xai.

Fax

The big Maputo hotels have fax facilities, as do some hotels and call centres outside the capital, but it is an expensive and unreliable way of communicating, and in any case is fast being superseded by e-mail.

E-MAIL

The Internet is not a medium that is by any means widespread in Mozambique; at the time of writing there is only one cybercafe in Maputo (*Connection Time*, Ave 24 de Julho 377 (near the Geology Museum); tel 01-499147; e-mail webmaster@contime.com; Website: www.contime.com). But it's an area that is developing so fast that by the early part of the new century you will certainly be able to communicate by e-mail in many more places than you can now. You can send and receive e-mails at the Polana and the Cardoso Hotels in Maputo, for the price of a local call. Several other hotels and hostels around the country – especially the ones that are more geared to backpackers, like Fim do Mundo in Angoche – will take in and send e-mails for you.

MAIL

Mozambican post is slow but reliable. International letters cost just over $1, postcards $1.30. Post Offices normally keep office hours morning and afternoon. Poste Restante is not generally to be relied upon. It is far better for a letter to be sent 'to be awaited' (*esperar*) at a large hotel (preferably one you're staying in, although this is not essential). It should be addressed as follows:

Esperar: Livingstone, Sr D (Sra for Senhora, Sr for Senhor)
Hotel Polana
Ave Julius Nyerere 1380
Maputo
Moçambique

MEDIA

Newspapers

Newspapers and magazines have burgeoned since the end of the war, with numerous new and independent publications coming on the market. The two main daily newspapers, *Noticias* (and its Sunday sister, *Domingo*), published in Maputo, and *Diario do Moçambique*, published in Beira, are considered to be sympathetic to the establishment and the Frelimo government in particular. More independent is the weekly newspaper *Savana* launched in 1993. Much more interesting, because they are produced by young, independent journalists and are fiercely critical of Frelimo, are the newsletters *Metical* and *Mediafax*. Published by the same group as *Savana,* both are distributed by fax. Weekly magazines include the interesting *Tempo*. There is little published in English, except for the dry *Mozambique Inview*, and *Time Out Moçambique*, a bi-annual tourist guide. The national news agency, AIM, has an excellent website, in English, at www.poptel.org.uk/mozambique-news/

In 1997 a European Union initiative earmarked funds until September 1999 for six regional newspapers to be started in Matola, Lichinga, Inhambane, Chimoio, Gaza and Pemba. They include *O Amanhã, Baía, Megajornal* and *Voz de Pemba*, and are published two to four times a month. All production costs are met from abroad, and young journalists are trained up on the job. They are interesting and well-written and aim at sustainability; it will be interesting to see which ones survive and prosper when funding stops.

Newspapers can be bought from kiosks and street-sellers. You will find international publications like the *Guardian Weekly*, the *Economist* , South African and other African journals in the lobby of the Polana and Cardoso hotels in Maputo, and in bookshops like Sensacãos in Maputo.

Television and Radio

TV Moçambique (TVM) and the independent RTK are the two main television stations in Mozambique. RTK has an English-language bias, while TVM concentrates on news and imported films. There are also a number of satellite channels available, such as the BBC's Discovery channel and South African stations. According to 1998 statistics there are only three televisions and 38 radios per 1,000 people in Mozambique (compared to over 600 TVs and 1,433 radios per 1,000 in the UK).

Radio Moçambique has an English-language service, Radio Maputo. The BBC World Service can be picked up anywhere in Mozambique on short wave on the following frequencies: 1197, 90200, 6005, 3255, 6190, 9600, 11940, 21660, 15400, 11835. For the most up-to-date information write to World Service Publicity (PO Box 76, Bush House, London WC2B 4PH; tel 0207 257 2211) or check the website at www.bbc.co.uk/worldservice.

The Internet

At the time of writing the only places you'll be able to access the Internet in Mozambique are the Polana and Cardoso hotels in Maputo, and the cybercafe Connection Time (see *E-mail* above). If you have your own laptop and modem you'll be lucky to find a compatible telephone socket outside of Maputo. At the end of the *Help and Information* section there is a list of websites it is worth having a look at before you go – where relevant they are repeated in the text.

accident	*o acidente*
aeroplane	*o avião*
airport	*o aeroporto*
arrival	*a chegada*
bicycle	*a bicicleta*
breakdown	*o avariado*
bus	*o autocarro, o machimbombo*
bus station	*a estação de autocarros*
bus stop	*a paragem de autocarros*
car	*o carro*
car hire	*aluguer de automóveis*
customs	*alfândega*
daily	*diário*
departure	*a partida*
diesel	*o gasóleo*
(is it) far(?)	*(fica)longe(?)*
flight	*o voo*
garage	*o garagem*
insurance	*o seguro*
lorry, truck	*o camião*
mechanic	*o mecânico*
near (to)	*perto (de)*
passenger	*o passageiro*
petrol	*a gasolina*
platform	*a linha, a plataforma*
puncture	*o furo*
repairs	*os reparações*
return (ticket)	*ida e volta*

service station	*a estação de serviço*
single (ticket)	*simples*
ticket	*o bilhete*
ticket office	*a bilheteira*
timetable	*o horário*
taxi	*o táxi*
taxi rank	*a praça de táxis*
train	*o comboio*
travel	*viajar*
travel agent	*a agência de viagens*
weekly (each week)	*semanal (cada semana)*

The Africans say, 'Patience is power.' Mozambique imbues patience in the tourist: it is a difficult country to get around. The majority of Mozambicans simply do not own cars; they travel on foot or by bike or, if they have to make a longer journey, wait for a lift. All the major cities have airports, and buses serve the main routes, but sooner or later you will certainly find yourself sitting on the side of a road as the hours pass, contemplating your shoes and wondering if you will ever get away. In the rainy season many roads are impassable – if you're thinking of doing any exploring at that time of year (November-April), take care to add several days to your estimated time of arrival.

When planning any trip always take into account that Mozambique is a coastal country in which a considerable proportion of the population live near the sea. Sometimes the quickest way to go north or south is by boat. All necessary details are given in the sections below, or in the relevant sections of the book.

For the purposes of this book, 'public transport' means any vehicle that is not your own, and includes buses, *chapas* and anybody that will give you a lift. Hitching in Mozambique is common and safe: most drivers see giving lifts as a useful way of making a bit of petrol money.

MAPS

You should buy a map before you go. The best map of Mozambique is the Ravenstein Verlag 1:2,000,000 road map. A few places are missing but overall it's the most accurate and up-to-date. There is also a Globetrotter map, and another published by Direcção Nacional de Geografia e Cadastro – both are reliable enough. You won't find any other maps beyond the occasional street plan you'll pick up while in Mozambique. See *Further Reading* p.45 for addresses of travel bookshops.

Place names

Except for Maputo, names of towns generally haven't changed since independence, but street names have. After 1976 there was a race to rename streets after heroes of the struggle rather than 19th century empire-builders. Every town now has an Avenida Eduardo Mondlane instead of a Rua Paiva de Andrade. This might cause some confusion if you have an older version of a street plan. Depending on the outcome of the 1999 elections, the new government might well decide to do away with some of Maputo's communist associations – it will be a shame when you can no longer take a stroll down Avenida Ho Chi Min. Many of Maputo's unnamed streets are now numbered (a practice we've ignored for the purposes of this book, since it seems to make little difference and in any case the project is by no means finished).

Pronunciation can cause headaches: the pronunciation guide (see *Language* p.39) gives basic information. Remember that 'x' is pronounced 'sh' so Xai-Xai is 'shy-shy' and Maxixe is 'masheesh'. Double 'ss' is also given a very soft inflection, so Quissico becomes 'kishiko'. Take note of accents – missing them out could mean you end up in entirely the wrong place. Závora has to be stressed on the first syllable – if you get it wrong you'll be met with headscratching and blank looks, and you might be put on a bus to Sofala by mistake. Mozambicans also miss out the last vowel if it is unstressed. Maputo becomes 'Mapoot', Tete is 'Tet', Quelimane is 'kelliman'.

AIR

LAM (Linhas Aéreas de Moçambique) fly regularly between Maputo, Beira, Lichinga, Nampula, Pemba, Quelimane and Tete. There are also flights available from Maputo to Vilanculos (for the Bazaruto Islands) and Inhaca Island. Flights are relatively expensive – Beira to Nampula for example costs around $150, but bear in mind that the overland journey on public transport takes three or four days, and would not work out much cheaper than a flight. A number of air charter companies operate from the main airports and city centres in Mozambique, these are detailed in *Maputo*.

It is important to remember that domestic flights are almost always overbooked, so it is wise to get to the airport in good time, and to reconfirm all onward flights. Also bear in mind that most destinations are not served every day by LAM: while there are ten flights a week between Beira and Maputo, there are only three a week between Maputo and Pemba, and one a week from Pemba to Beira.

Linhas Aéreas de Moçambique (LAM) offices

Maputo	Ave Karl Marx 220; tel 01-426001/4.
	Mavalane Airport; tel 01-465827/9.
	Ave Mao Tse Tung 19; tel 01-490590/496101; fax 01-496105.

	Central reservations tel 01-495810/8.
Nampula	Ave Francisco Manyanga, 4-D; tel 06-218001/212623.
Pemba	Ave 25 de Setembro 291; tel 072-2434/5.
Quelimane	Ave 1 de Junho; tel 04-212801/2; fax 04-212802.
	Airport; tel 04-212801.
Lichinga	Rua de LAM; tel 2434.
Tete	Tel 052-2055/6.
	Airport tel 052-20011.
Beira	Rua Costa Serrão 85; tel 03-324141/325573.
	Airport; tel 03-301024; fax 03-302627.

PUBLIC TRANSPORT

Bus and Chapa

There are two types of public transport by road in Mozambique: bus (called *autocar* or, more commonly, *machimbombo*) and *chapa*. On main routes bus serVices are frequent and reliable, with most towns being served at least once a day by mainline bus companies like Transportes Oliveiras and Virginia in the south, and in the north by Transnorte. Most buses leave very early in the morning, usually between 5 and 6am; bear in mind that in many places there is only one bus a day. Fares are inexpensive, but not as cheap as in neighbouring countries. A two to three-hour journey will be about $5, going up to $10 for longer routes. In many towns there is no central bus station, instead buses leave from a spot along the main road, generally a few hundred yards outside the town centre. Where relevant this is mentioned in the text.

Away from the main highways, and north of Pemba, there is no conventional public transport. Instead, a network of unlicensed *chapas* operates. A *chapa* is any truck or station-wagon operating as a taxi between given routes. They can be desperately uncomfortable, and maddeningly slow and erratic – journeys frequently end with a breakdown in the middle of nowhere, or at a police checkpoint with the driver annnouncing he can go no further with passengers. Longer routes are usually served by larger trucks fitted with wooden benches. It is very difficult to give an idea of prices, although the more organised *chapas* will charge a set amount for each journey. As a rule of thumb a journey of one hour should cost around $2, whereas a 12-hour trip (say between Pemba and Mocimboa da Praia) would be about $10.

HITCHING

Hitching (which you do by moving the extended arm up and down with flat palm downwards,) is an accepted method of travel all over Mozambique. In the remotest parts of the country it is the only means of getting around, and you need to take whatever you can get. You should always offer to pay; your money will frequently be refused, but just as often accepted – and expected. Most drivers (in many areas only one vehicle will pass in a day) will pick up a passenger they think can pay, so you will never be left on the side of the road. The driver will tell you how much he wants for the lift – expect to pay around $1 for an hour's ride. Hitching is perfectly safe. In most areas where you are likely to hitch you will wait so long for a lift you won't be fussy about who is driving. In any case, at any given spot there is always a little knot of people waiting for a lift, so you will seldom be alone with a driver.

RAILWAYS

There are some splendid stations in Mozambique, relics of the 19th century when the Portuguese enlisted the help of the British in grand designs to have trains running from north to south and east to west. Few of those dreams were realised; of the railways that were built, few survive. The great baroque terminus in Maputo, or Beira's kitsch masterpiece, see only a couple of trains a day. At the moment you can catch the luxurious Trans-Lubombo Express from Maputo to Johannesburg, the delightful Nampula-Cuamba train, (and go on from there to Liwonde in Malawi), or the scruffy Beira-Mutare train, but nothing else. Trainspotters will enjoy visiting the 19th century stations in most small towns – there is one in Xai-Xai, another in Inhambane – and looking at the old engines rusting in the sidings while small boys play football on the sand-covered rails.

BOATS

The people that live along Mozambique's 2,500km coastline make their living from the sea. The most common form of sea transport is the Arab dhow, a sturdy sail-boat that has changed little in the past few hundred years. With Mozambique's road network being generally poor, and the sea often being the most direct route, you would expect to have easy access to sea transport, but this isn't always the case. There are regular ferries from Maputo to Catembe and to Inhaca Island, from Vilanculos and Inhasssoro to the Bazaruto Islands, and between Maxixe and Inhambane. But it is more difficult to find transport up and down the coast from Pemba to Ibo, for example (a tedious journey by road), or from Mocimboa da Praia to Tanzania. This is not to say it is impossible: it just requires ingenuity and patience. Details on where to find dhows are given in the relevant sections. You will find that it is difficult to spend any time in Mozambique without taking at least one journey by dhow. Between Inhambane and Maxixe you have the option of 20 minutes breathing diesel fumes wedged in the hold of a rackety motor boat, or 40 minutes in the open air listening to creaking timbers and the flapping of a threadbare sail. It is not difficult to choose. If you decide to find a dhow captain to take you from Pemba to Ibo, you should expect up to 18 hours on the open sea without shelter, sustenance or toilet. It is a memorable experience, but one that should be prepared for.

DRIVING

Many South Africans and Zimbabweans would not think of coming into Mozambique without their own transport. Given the vagaries of public transport it is something of a relief to have your own car, even if you do miss a lot of the life of the country as you race along over new blacktop, or judder from pothole to pothole on the roads that haven't yet been improved. There are less of the latter every year: Mozambique's road network is being done up with European and World Bank money at such a rate that the entire EN1 will soon be a gleaming ribbon of new tarmac.

Much of the south, and parts of the north, can be explored in a saloon car with reasonable clearance, but you would be far happier with four-wheel drive. A saloon will take you to the major centres – from Maputo to Inhambane, for example, and on to Vilanculos, but it will not allow you to take any sort of minor road. The track down to Závora would not be possible in anything but 4WD, and there are hundreds of similar resorts that you would not be able to reach. Furthermore, except for Maputo, saloons are very rare in Mozambique; spares for a Toyota Landcruiser are far easier to come by than for a VW Golf.

If you are bringing a vehicle into Mozambique remember to equip yourself with all necessary spares – tyres, bulbs, fuses, windscreen wipers, spark plugs and so on. Carrying an accident triangle is compulsory, as is the wearing of seatbelts. Police checkpoints are common; you will be asked to show all vehicle documentation, your driving licence, passport and vehicle import papers. Policemen always like to find a reason to levy an on-the-spot fine, so you should not give them any reason to find fault. If they demand money, stand your ground for as long as your indignation lasts, and then hand over $10.

Although road improvement is going ahead, most roads were heavily mined during the civil war and many are still pitted with jagged potholes. The trick is to go very slowly, watch for oncoming vehicles, and pump the brake before each pothole. Follow the tracks that have been made either side of the carriageway, but on no account be tempted into off-road shortcuts: landmines can still be a danger.

Never drive at night. Mozambican drivers are good mechanics and can keep a car going long after most westerners would have given up, but they tend to drive fast and dangerously. Barrelling along at 80km/h in an overloaded *chapa* with tyres not only showing their fabric, but actually *sewn* together, it's not uncommon to pass an upside-down truck in the verge, its wheels still spinning while dazed people stand around. In your vehicle they crane their necks and say, 'that must have happened last night', but your driver doesn't relax his speed. At night all dangers are exaggerated, mainly because half the cars don't have lights. Other drivers turn them off to preserve the battery, switching onto full beam as another vehicle approaches, blinding the oncoming car at the crucial moment. Other dangers include potholes rendered invisible by your headlights, and banditry, seldom a problem by day but something to be aware of at night.

CITY TRANSPORT

The only city in which it is necessary to take public transport is Maputo, and even there you can walk to most of the places you need to go. In most large areas, you'll generally need a taxi or *chapa* to get out to the airport. The only cities in which you will find licensed taxis are Beira (in the main square) and Maputo (outside the big hotels, the station and taxi ranks at major junctions). Agree a price beforehand – even if the taxi has a meter it's unlikely to work.
Outside Beira and Maputo to get to the airport it is a matter of locating the airport road and waiting for a *chapa* to come along. For details on public transport in Maputo see p.119.

EXCURSIONS

There are a number of travel agents running excursions of varying lengths in and around Maputo, as far north as the Bazaruto Islands, and into South Africa. Travel agents in Beira (see *Beira* p166) will also organise trips on an informal basis.

In Maputo the main hotels are fully geared to organise excursions. Otherwise contact the following agencies:

Mextur: Ave 25 de Setembro 1226, PO Box 1222, Maputo; tel 01-428427/8/9; fax 01-421908.
Prosol: Ave Felipe Samuel Magaia 809, Maputo; tel 01-304098/304642; fax 01-421908.
SET (Sociedade de Exploração Turística): Ave 25 de Setembro 1743, Maputo; tel 01-422363; fax 01-422369.
Expresso Tours: Rua Joaquim Lapa 95, Maputo; tel 01-431662/4; fax 01-431665, e-mail exptours@emilmoz.com
Tropical Airtours: (South African safaris as well as luxury yacht charters), Ave 24 de Julho 909, Maputo; tel 01-425078/431006/7; fax 01-425082. Also Johannesburg; tel 011-337 9169/8946.

accommodation	*o alojamento*
air conditioned	*ar acondicionado*
bed	*a cama*
(with) bathroom	*(com) casa de banho*
breakfast	*o pequeno almoço*
boss, manager	*o gerente*
cabin	*a cabine*
campsite	*o campismo*
to camp	*acampar*
double room	*o quarto duplo*
drinking water	*água potável*
fan	*a ventoiha*
floor (storey)	*o andar*
guest	*o hóspede*
hot water	*o água quente*
laundry	*a lavandaria*
lift	*o elevador*
mattress	*o colchão*
single room	*o quarto individual*
shower	*o chuveiro*
to have a shower	*tomar um duche*
reception	*recepção*
tent	*a tenda*
toilets	*o casa de banho*
toilet paper	*o papel higiénico*

Mozambique is only just getting itself geared for tourism, and hotel accommodation is not ideal in many parts of the country. While you will never have any problem finding somewhere to sleep, you should be prepared to accept some pretty basic accommodation from time to time. In Maputo there is a paucity of middle-range hotels; at the top end you have any number of choices, from the Polana to the Pensão Martins, likewise at the bottom, but there are not so many of the good, clean, basic budget hostels for backpackers that are common in neighbouring countries. The situation is the same in the rest of Mozambique, but things are changing fast. At the time of writing, entrepreneurs from South Africa, Zimbabwe and Europe are planning lodges, resorts and hostels all the way up the coast. In the most popular resorts, like

Tofo Beach on the Inhambane peninsula, new backpackers' hostels are springing up all the time.

HOTELS AND PENSÃOS

Except for the upmarket hotels in the main cities, do not expect hot running water in hotels. If you are told the hotel has *água quente*, it is likely to mean a bucket of hot water will be brought to your room – a perfectly serviceable way of washing. Where breakfast is included in the price of a room, this is indicated in the text. In most hotels this will consist of tea or coffee, toast and seasonal fruit.

Accommodation in Mozambique isn't cheap, but in most towns you should be able to get a room without breaking your budget. A decent double room with air-conditioning and hot shower in Maputo could be as little as $35 or as much as $250. In Beira you can get a clean double room with a fan for $20. At the bottom end of the scale things get very much cheaper: a rat-infested double with fan and shared bathroom in Mocimboa da Praia is about $8. Residential *pensãos* in small towns are often the best value of all, with basic single rooms with shared bathrooms going for about $4.

Some towns have little or no formal accommodation. Ilha de Moçambique is one (until the Hotel Pousada is completed), Ibo is another. Whatever possibilities exist are indicated in the text, but it is usually acceptable to ask around for someone who would be willing to put you up for the night for a suitable price.

CAMPING

For budget travellers, camping is frequently the best, cheapest and cleanest option. Many campsites provide tents if you don't have your own. In Beira, for example, Biques campsite has hot showers and is regarded as far superior than any of the shabby hotels the city has to offer. The same goes for Maxixe, and many other places. Campsites are usually guarded and quite safe (though it is less than reassuring to see the night guard at the campsite in Vilanculos carrying a Kalashnikov rifle). Campsites usually charge between $3 and $5 per person per night. Rough camping on beaches shouldn't be discounted. As long as there are two of you and you can watch your belongings at all times you should be fine – but always take local advice, and make up your own mind.

If you are caught on the road far from a town at nightfall, stop at a village and ask if they have a suitable spot for you to spend the night. You may also pass one of the special police encampments which guard the EN1 at major junctions; they should be willing to let you share a corner of their site. It does not need to be stressed that you should on no account head into the bush except on well-trodden paths: mines are still a very present danger.

Eating and Drinking

apple	*a maçã*
avocado	*o abacate*
beef	*a carne de vaca*
beer	*a cerveja*
brains	*miolos*
bread	*pão*
butter	*a manteiga*
cheese	*o queijo*
chicken	*o frango/a galinha*
chips	*batatas fritas*
coffee	*o café*
dessert	*a sobremesa*
dining room	*sala de jantar*
egg	*o ovo*
fish	*o peixe/o pescado*
fork	*o garfo*
fried	*frito/a*
fruit juice	*o sumo*
goat	*a cabra*
hamburger	*o hamburguer*
ice	*o gelo*
kidneys	*rins*
knife	*a faca*
lobster	*a lagosta*
loin	*lombo*
lunch	*o almoço*
(without) meat	*(sim) carne*
menu	*a ementa/a lista*
milk	*leite*
mussels	*mexilhões*
octopus	*o polvo*
orange	*a laranja*
plate	*o prato*
pork	*o porco*
potatoes	*batatas*
prawn	*camarão*
rice	*arroz*

roll (with meat)	*o prego*
salad	*a salada*
sandwich	*o sande*
seafood	*o marisco*
snack	*o petisco*
soft drink	*o refresco*
spoon	*o colher*
squid	*o calamar/lulas*
steak	*o bife*
swordfish	*peixe-espada*
tea	*o chá*
tongue	*o língua*
wine	*o vinho*
(mineral) water	*o água mineral*

FOOD IN MOZAMBIQUE

Mozambique is deservedly famous for its prawns. They may not be as cheap and plentiful as they were in colonial days, before Russian trawlers overfished the breeding grounds, but they are delicious and still on the menu of any middle-range establishment. Restaurants like the Costa do Sol in Maputo are famous for their *camarãos*. The method of cooking is to split the prawns – often as long as the palm of your hand – and fry them on a griddle till the juices spit.

In Mozambique you can eat better and with a greater choice of food than in neighbouring countries. The Portuguese influence is much in evidence in the smarter restaurants, particularly in the use of wine in cooking. The sea provides a plentiful supply of fish and shellfish in the form of crayfish, crab, prawns and squid, while away from the coast, chicken is the staple food, backed up by beef, lamb and goat. Inland you will also find river fish. Fresh vegetables can be more difficult to come by, although in season maize (corn on the cob) is readily available, as are sweet and savoury potatoes and tomatoes. Many people subsist on the unpalatable and nutritionally valueless mandioca root, eating it raw or boiled. You won't have any problem keeping up your vitamin C intake on fruit – depending on the season, tangerines, oranges, bananas, apples, mangoes and other tropical fruits are piled up in the markets and sold by the bucketful for next to nothing.

After some time in the country you may get tired of the lack of variety offered in any restaurant outside Maputo. But as bored as you get with chicken you'll always be surprised by the flavour of a healthy bird cooked over a wood fire – the only form of stove for 90 per cent of the population. This is the authentic barbecued flavour that smart establishments in the capital go out of their way to achieve.

Where maize and sugar cane are cultivated, locals eat mongoose (cane rats), which they spit on a stick and roast over the fire. It's an acquired taste, something between tough chicken and pork. Not surprisingly, it's not a highly prized dish, and you won't find it on any restaurant menu.

Bread is baked daily in clay ovens and is delicious if you buy it early in the day. Rolls, either on their own, as *pregos*, or with a variety of fillings such as vegetable patties or spicy sausage, are readily available in markets and street corners. You'll find you can get through the day, especially if you are on the move, snacking on bread, fruit, corn on the cob, hard-boiled eggs, chicken legs and whatever else happens to be on offer.

Backpackers working to tight budgets should not find it difficult to be self-sufficient on the coast. If you are camping on the beach you will always be able to buy fish from the local fisherman, and you can get hold of fruit, vegetables, rice, beans and other staples at the market.

RESTAURANTS

As with hotels in Mozambique, there are few mid-range establishments, and what passes for upmarket is often overpriced and pretentious. In Maputo you will find restaurants to cater for every palate. Mozambican and Portuguese places serve chicken *piri-piri* (see below) or the best seafood, Americanised burger bars like Mundos do mouthwatering steaks and beefburgers along with a wide variety of international dishes; there are some excellent Chinese restaurants, as well as several fast-food outlets.

Outside Maputo and the main cities only standard Mozambican fare is available, although you can still eat well on a fairly modest budget. In the bigger towns – Beira, Nampula, Quelimane and Pemba – there is the usual scattering of classy-looking establishments, but you'll often find the best meals are to be had in the most ordinary places. Restaurants on the coast serve a variety of seafood dishes accompanied with rice or chips and salad. Chicken will also be on the menu, and north of the Zambesi you will find beef, lamb, pork or goat on offer. Steak (usually boiled and served with a fried egg) is often very tough; goat usually comes in the form of a tasty stew. Worth trying is chicken *piri-piri*, chicken served with a very hot sauce of crushed chilis. Most restaurants also serve *petiscos* and sandwiches, and in the big towns there are *pastelerias* selling such delicacies as cakes, pastries and imported chocolate.

CAFÉS

The Portuguese influence in Mozambique is most noticable in the café culture that exists in the larger towns. Maputo especially has some wonderful cafés, with street tables under awnings, and supercilious waiters in bow ties. In any sizeable town you should never be at a loss for a cup of tea of coffee, although establishments which will serve you a decent espresso can be counted on the fingers of one hand (one is the *Stop Café* in Maxixe, another is *A Tasca* in Pemba). The most common method of preparing instant coffee is to energetically mash the granules and sugar in the bottom of a cup with a dash of hot water, then to pour the boiling water on top of that. It makes a remarkably tasty – if very sweet – drink.

DRINKING

Soft Drinks

Soft drinks such Coca-Cola and Fanta are sold throughout the country, both imported and locally-made. Tap and pump water are definitely not safe to drink – there is a real danger of picking up the amoeba responsible for dysentry. You can find bottled water (much of it imported from Iran) in most towns, although in rural areas it can be a problem. The wisest course is to stock up on a couple of litres whenever you are going on a journey. Most bars will keep a jug of boiled *água de beber* in the fridge, which should be perfectly safe to drink.

Beer is readily available all over Mozambique in bottles and cans, and on draft in the most upmarket bars in Maputo. In even the remotest hamlets the importance of keeping it cold is recognised; wherever there is electricity you won't have to suffer the misery of a warm lager.

Beer, Wine and Spirits

South African Castle beer in cans and bottles is the most widely-sold foreign brand, now brewed under licence in Mozambique. As the price is the same and the labels identical (apart from the small print), it's difficult to tell the difference, although connoisseurs demand the South African variety when they order. Lion beer and Carling Black Label can also be found quite easily. A 450ml can costs between $1 and $1.50. The local Mozambican beers such as 2M and Manica are very good and widely available, though not much cheaper than imported beers.

Portuguese wine is available in Maputo and in the larger cities, as is the full range of spirits. Local spirits are popular and often worth trying, particularly a 40-per cent-proof banana liquor called *Enhica*. You will also see men (and women) drinking home-brewed cane spirit, which is usually extremely strong.

SMOKING

Mozambicans are heavy smokers, and not just the men; this is one of the few African countries where you will see women smoking in public. Camel,

Marlboro and Peter Stuyvesant are available in the south but are more difficult to come by north of the Zambesi. They retail at slightly more than local brands. Mozambican cigarettes have alluring names like Life and Grande Turismo, and are not unpalatable. You can smoke just about anywhere; long-distance buses are usually non-smoking, a rule that is strictly adhered to. If you are a smoker you'll find yourself handing out cigarettes on a regular basis. It is perfectly natural, and you shouldn't be shy of asking someone for a smoke if you are without.

HISTORIC MOZAMBIQUE

Many people come to Mozambique for the beaches and diving, forgetting it has some wonderful architectural remains, including the oldest European building in the southern hemisphere (the church of Nossa Senhora Baluarte on Ilha de Moçambique), and the most formidable fortress in Africa (São Sebastião, also on the island). The north of the country is a treasure-trove of colonial history – the island of Ibo is a museum of itself, Quelimane and Beira have some fine old buildings. Just to walk around these cities is to feel the ghosts of the Portuguese colonisers, who after all were still in situ just decades ago.

Although it recognises the importance of preservation, the government is hard put to earmark funds for the upkeep of old buildings, and many of them are falling apart. On Ibo, a literal backwater, the decay is palpable. The town's handsome colonnaded buildings – built with slave-money – are collapsing. It's not like an ancient European city, or one of those cowboy ghost towns in the Utah desert, so perfectly preserved it's impossible to imagine anyone ever living there. On Ibo you can almost see the *senhor* stepping off his verandah in polished boots, waiting a moment before climbing into his sedan chair.

In a few decades there will be little left of Ibo's Portuguese past. It's unlikely that the provincial government will embark on a regeneration programme now, and equally unlikely that the islanders regret losing the concrete reminders of so cruel a regime. Ilha de Moçambique will not suffer the same fate. It is already benefitting from tourist money, and will soon be Mozambique's prime tourist venue after the Bazaruto Islands. It is a fascinating place and should be on any traveller's itinerary no matter how little time you are spending in Mozambique.

There's little left of other historic towns. Zumbo, on the far western tip of Cahora Bassa lake in Tete province, was once one of the wealthiest towns in Portuguese East Africa. Now it's very difficult to get to, and is well off the tourist trail, but it could be an interesting route to take if you are coming into Mozambique from southern Zambia. Livingstone visited Zumbo on his 1858-64 Zambesi expedition, and found it in ruins even then. 'The chapel...commands a glorious view of the two noble rivers (the Zambesi and the Luangua), the green fields, the undulating forest and the pleasant hills,' he wrote, depressed. 'It is an utter ruin now, and desolation broods around. The foul hyaena has defiled the sanctuary.'

Sofala, one of Portugal's first strongholds on the coast, has long sunk into the ocean – but President Chissano still visits, believing it to be part of the historical heart of his country. Some places are guardians of little gems of history: Mary Livingstone's grave at Chupanga (see *Quelimane* p.194), or the town of Chai, where Frelimo fired the first shots in the war of independence (see *Cabo Delgado* p.245). However keen you are on the hedonistic life of the beach, don't forget Mozambique has a fascinating and turbulent history, and one that is still evident all over the country.

MUSEUMS AND GALLERIES

There are few museums outside Maputo, and they tend to be fairly dusty affairs, but always worth a visit. Most of the bigger towns have a collection of carvings, masks and local artefacts, often curated by a local enthusiast. Maputo has the best museums. Don't miss the complete set of elephant foetuses in the newly-restored Natural History Museum, or the fascinating range of historical documents in the Museu da Revolução. Of course, a visit to Ilha de Moçambique is not complete without a visit to the Palace Museum and its colonial and post-colonial exhibits.

Visual arts

Mozambican artists are prolific and world-renowned – Mozambique was the only African country represented in the Contemporary Art section of Expo 92 in Spain. As is to be expected, many of them work and exhibit in Maputo, where there are several excellent galleries and workshops (detailed in the text). Look out for the works of Naguib, Malangatana, Robert Chichorro and Bertina Lopes. You should also note the proliferation of murals in Maputo and around the country. One of the best known is the 95m panorama celebrating the revolution and independence just outside Maputo's Mavalane Airport. Another in the Cabo Delgado town of Chai, commemorates the beginning of the revolution.

One of the most famous of Mozambique's art forms is of course Makonde sculpture. How to find and buy Makonde works is detailed in *Shopping* p.84.

BEACHES, SNORKELLING AND DIVING

Mozambique's beaches are the best-kept secret in Africa. The 2,500km coastline is fringed with perfect, deserted expanses of pristine sand, fringed with coconut palms on one side and an azure sea on the other. The best, most accessible (and inaccessible) beaches are described whenever relevant in the text. There are those like Pemba which are rapidly being developed but are still exquisite, and others like Pomene (see p.154 *Inhambane*), where you won't see a soul.

It is not just the beaches: Mozambique has some of the best diving and snorkelling in the world, as well as superb game fishing. The coral reefs that line the coast are pristine, because they have faced none of the threats that bedevil reefs in more developed areas – tourism and its byproducts, ignorant diving techniques and pollution. Various NGOs are working to make sure they stay that way, carrying out surveys, and teaching local people how to preserve the coral. (For more information visit the British NGO Frontier's website www.mailbox.co.uk/frontier).

What this means for the snorkeller or diver is miles of gorgeous and accessible reef, shoals of luminous fish, and the exquisite colours of living coral. To snorkel off Pemba, Závora, Bazaruto, Ibo or any number of beaches up and down the coast is pure indulgence. For those who want to go deeper and further, the diving is unparalleled. From Ponta Malongane in the south, to the Tanzanian border, there are hundreds of islands, reefs and wrecks. Divers report seeing dolphins, humpback whales, ten species of shark including hammerhead, tiger, silvertip, nurse and whale shark, hawkshead turtles, potato bass and many other species.

If you are proficient and have your own equipment you can dive anywhere: the resorts mentioned below are reckoned to be some of the best, as well as Ibo and the Querimba islands, which are readily accessible by boat from Pemba. Beaches with facilities for beginners are Ponta Malongane and Ponta do Ouro, Xai-Xai, Vilanculos, Bazaruto and Pemba. In order to hire equipment you will need to have a certificate approved by PADI (Professional Association of Diving Instructors), which any dive school (detailed in the text) will train you for. Courses start at around $35 for one dive, leading up to $120-$150 for five-dive package.

Entertainment

beach	*a praia*
cinema	*o cinema*
concert	*o concerto*

dance	*o baile*
to dance	*dançar*
disco	*a discoteca*
to dive	*mergulhar*
festival	*a festa*
film	*o filme*
fishing	*a pesca*
fishing rod	*a cana de pesca*
gallery	*a galeria*
golf	*o golfe*
golf course	*o campo de golfe*
museum	*o museu*
nightclub	*a boite*
snorkel	*o tubo de ar*
sold out	*esgotado/a*
sport	*o desporto*
to swim	*nadar*
swimming	*a natação*
swimming pool	*a piscina*
tennis	*o ténis*
tennis court	*o court de ténis*
theatre	*o teatro*

CINEMA

Maputo has seven cinemas which show a range of American action films, Indian films (Mozambique has a sizeable Indian population), kung-fu and other imported 'B' movies. There are also a number of porn cinemas which are naturally best avoided. Beira has two or three cinemas with the same sort of fare on offer, and there are small cinema clubs in Quelimane, Inhambane and other larger towns. Films cost around $3.50 – it's probably wise to get there early if you want to see the latest American import. Outside Maputo and Beira you're unlikely to find a working cinema; instead, bars which have a television are usually packed inside and out, even for the latest showing of something sadistic from the Chuck Norris back-catalogue. Addresses of cinemas are listed in the text.

THEATRE AND DANCE

Maputo – and to a lesser extent Beira – have a thriving theatre and dance scene. In Maputo you can see *Mapiko* dances, and student and youth groups performing pieces which bring together traditional Mozambican dance with more modern elements. Venues are listed in the text; check the local press for details of what's on.

MUSIC

Mozambican music covers everything from the ancient tribal rhythms that you will hear in Cabo Delgado and the north, to hugely popular Mozambican rap. A typical Mozambican musical form is *Marrabenta* – a light fusion of African and Mediterranean rhythms. The Orquestra Marrabenta was a state-funded band who came together after independence during Samora Machel's drive to promote local African culture. They split in 1989, and several former members, including Pedro Lange, formed the Afro-Jazz group Ghorwane. Named after the lake in Gaza province which is supposed never to dry up, sleeve-notes on Ghorwane albums talk about how the group embodies the resilience of the human spirit in adversity, and how music was a unifying and healing influence during the war. They play regularly round the country, and have released a number of CDs which you'll be able to find in Maputo record stores.

Mozambican rap artists have a massive youth following; they also tour regularly and are worth seeing just to get an idea of the global nature of rap music, although the lyrics are a far cry from American or British rap. Keep an eye on the movements of MC Roger (who routinely sells out from Maxixe to Beira), Doctor Gato or Mombass. Other big names to look out for on the modern music scene are girl groups Female Move, Justina Delgado, Maya Cool and Juka.

Away from the cities, and especially in the north, traditional music still flourishes. The Makonde play wind instruments known as *lupembe*, made from animal horns, wood or gourds, which are used for Mapiko dances. In the south, Chope musicians play a form of xylophone called *marimba* and are known for their marimba orchestras.

NIGHTLIFE

If four hundred years of Portuguese colonial rule can be said to have bestowed any good at all, one of its positive aspects must be the essence of the Mediterranean that runs through the character of Mozambique like the writing in a stick of rock. Namibia may be run with a strong sense of Teutonic efficiency, and former British colonies are certainly haunted by the ghosts of gramophones and afternoon tea – but Mozambique has salsa.

Nightlife in Mozambique – in the cities at least – is very good indeed. Maputo has a selection of stylish, brash, trendy and downright seedy nightclubs that stay open till dawn and are frequented by everyone from local teenagers to wild Finnish aid workers, getting a fix of the big city before flying back to Pemba or Nampula. Just as there is a wide choice of venues, there is also a choice of music, from live jazz to African bands, often fused with a Latin rhythm that only a stone could resist wriggling its hips to.

Maputo has the best nightlife, Beira has some interesting places, but as the towns get smaller so the nightlife decreases. You'll always find a rowdy bar or even a disco on a Saturday night no matter how far from the road you are – but perhaps the 'Miss T-Shirt' competition in the dining room of the only hotel in town is not the real Africa you had dreamt of finding. North of the Zambesi, especially away from towns in Cabo Delgado, you will find things are quieter – often by virtue of the simple fact there is not enough electricity to make a decent noise with. In Cabo Delgado the Mapiko dance (part of the initiation ceremony for Makonde boys) takes place throughout the year, and is worth seeing if you hear of one.

baker	*padaria*
barber	*barbeiro*
battery (car)	*a bateria*
batteries	*as pilhas*
bookshop	*a livraria*
butcher	*o talho*
to buy	*comprar*
cake shop	*a pasteleria*
cassette	*a cassete*
closed	*fechado*
clothes	*a roupa*
compact disc	*o disco compacto*
film (camera)	*o rolo/a película*
footwear	*calçado*
furniture	*os movéis*
hairdresser's	*cabaleireiro/a cabaleireira*
ironmonger's/hardware store	*a loja de ferragens*
jeweller's	*a joalharia*
market	*o mercado*
optician's	*o óptico*
pharmacy (chemist)	*a farmácia*
present	*o presente*
sandals	*as sandália*
sanitary towel	*o penso higiéico*
to sell	*vender*
shoes	*os sapatos*
shop	*a loja*

sunglasses	*os óculos de sol*
supermarket	*o supermercado*
toy	*o brinquedo*

Souvenirs

Mozambique's most famous artefacts are the ivory and wood carvings of the Makonde people. The Makonde tribe – supposedly descended from a forest hermit who carved himself a wife and begat children, only one of whom survived – come from Cabo Delgado, close to the Rio Rovuma and the Tanzanian border. They are a proud people, unsubdued by the Portuguese until well into the 20th Century, and even then making life very difficult for tax-collectors and local garrisons.

Their carvings are intricate and beautiful. Only men practice the art, their skills handed down from father to son. Carvers are given a great deal of respect: it is considered that by their mastery of natural materials they are in closer touch with the spirit world than ordinary people.

Carvings can be divided into four main groups. The first is traditional artwork such as the masks used in Mapiko dances, part of the initiation ritual for young men. These used to be kept in secret hiding places, and women were forbidden to see them, but they are now openly displayed. *Binadamu* ('human beings' in Swahili), depict people in traditional roles, an old man with a pipe, or a woman carrying water. *Ujamaa* ('brotherhood' or 'unity') carvings take the form of totem poles – family groups, teachers with pupils, acrobats with monkeys and so on. Finally, *Shetani* ('spirit') carvings, which some commentators believe originated as the result of alcohol- or drug-induced hazes, show mischievous spirits, fertility figures with enlarged sexual organs and numerous breasts, and dancing imps.

There are carving cooperatives in several cities, notably in Pemba and Nampula, where you can watch the carvers at work and buy the finished products. It is a living art, and changes with the times. During the early days of Frelimo (whose first strongholds were in Makonde country) carvers introduced themes of repression into their work, and since the 19th century they have changed the nature of their statuettes and totems in accordance with what they think tourists and travellers want. As a result, purists will argue there is very little 'true' (ie traditional) Makonde workmanship around. Many of the 'Makonde' carvings in the curio shops and airports of southern Africa are not Makonde at all, but mass-produced in workshops in Malawi, Tanzania and as far afield as Kenya. Only if you visit a Makonde cooperative in Cabo Delgado can you be sure of getting the real thing.

Batik prints are also widely produced and available in the Maputo street markets. You should also look out for traditional ceramics, jewellery and items carved from malachite and other semi-precious stones, and modern

Mozambican art and sculptures. In Maputo, Beira and Nampula there are shops, cooperatives and galleries specialising in traditional and modern African fabrics. Details of all these are given in the relevant sections.

Books

If you have a mortal fear of travelling without books, stock up on paperbacks before you leave for Mozambique, and rely on swapping with other tourists. Good books are very hard to come by – it is far better to add a couple of pounds weight to your backpack than to find yourself faced with an 18-hour bus ride and nothing to read. Maputo has the only reliable bookshops (see p.130 for details) and even those stock very few books in English. Backpackers' hostels such as Fatima's in Maputo, Pachiça Lodge in Inhambane and the lodges in and around Tofo, keep libraries of dog-eared Danielle Steels and John Grishams which can be swapped for whatever you have in your pack.

Health and Hygiene

arm	*o braço*
AIDS	*a SIDA*
allergic to	*alérgico/a a*
antibiotics	*antibióticos*
appendix	*o apêndice*
asthmatic	*asmático*
bandage	*o penso*
bathroom/toilet	*a casa de banho*
to bite	*morder*
blind	*cego/a*
blood	*a sangue*
blood group	*grupo sanguíneo*
cortisone	*cortisona*
deaf	*surdo/a*
dentist	*dentista*
diabetic	*diabético/a*
diarrhoea	*diarreia*
doctor	*médico/a*
emergency services	*serviços de emergência*

epileptic	*epiléptico/a*
fever/high temperature	*a febre*
head	*a cabeça*
health	*a saúde*
hearing aid	*o aparelho de surdez*
heart condition	*cardíaco/a*
help	*a ajuda*
high blood pressure	*tensão alta*
hospital	*o hospital*
I feel unwell	*sinto-me mal*
injection	*o injecção*
injured	*ferido/a*
leg	*a perna*
malaria	*a malária/paludismo*
medicine	*o medicamento*
needle	*a agulha*
pain	*a dor*
painkiller	*o analgésico*
penicillin	*penicilina*
pharmacy (chemist)	*a farmácia*
pill	*o comprimido*
contraceptive pill	*a pílula*
poison	*o veneno*
pregnant	*grávida*
private parts	*as partes íntimas*
to sting	*picar*
stomach	*o estômago*
sunburn	*a queimadura solar*
sunstroke	*o insolação*
swollen	*inchado*
throat	*a garganta*
tongue	*a língua*
tooth	*o dente*
to vomit	*vomitar*
X-ray	*o raio-X*

As long as you take sensible precautions and make sure you are up to date on all your immunisations, you shouldn't get anything worse than mild diarrhoea while you are in Mozambique, and that only as a result of eating foods and spices that your body is unused to. Malaria is of course the greatest danger, but there is a range of prophylactics on the market which reduce the risk to negligable. Any advice given here is intended only as a guide and should not be relied upon exclusively: you should get a qualified medical officer's advice before you go. Doctors, hospitals, health clinics and pharmacies are listed where possible in the text. If no medical help is available, contact your nearest embassy or consulate. Many embassies keep supplies of drugs such as anti-rabies vaccinations.

VACCINATIONS

Vaccinations you are likely to need are: Diphtheria (usually combined with Tetanus), Hepatitis A, Polio, Rabies, Typhoid and Yellow Fever. Cholera is not regarded as a risk. The Foreign and Commonwealth Office (see p.93) regularly publishes guidelines on vaccinations needed around the world. Your GP will have these and should be your first contact. They will have records of your previous vaccinations and be able to advise what you need according to your present state of health, any allergies you may have, or whether you are pregnant. Your GP will also provide vaccination certificates if necessary. Useful addresses and helplines are given at the end of this section.

MALARIA

At best, malaria is incapacitating. At worst it can kill. In Mozambique, where good healthcare is hard to come by, you need to do everything in your power to avoid it. Seasoned travellers love talking about malaria and the various strategies they take to avoid it. People will tell you that if you do get an attack while taking antimalarials, there is nothing else you can be treated with; they will tell you they have been in the country five years and have never taken a thing, or that chloroquine makes you go blind, or your kind of antimalarial doesn't work in Mozambique. It's best to ignore everything except the advice of qualified medical officers.

Precautions

Antimalarials will *probably* stop you getting malaria if you are certain never to miss taking them. If you do get it, it's likely to be less severe if you have been taking tablets. The main types of antimalarial are (common trade names in brackets) chloroquine (Nivaquine), proguanil (Paludrine), and mefloquine (Lariam). Other types are pyrimethamine with dapsone (Maloprim) and doxycyline.

You will probably be recommended either chloroquine and proguanil, or mefloquine. The advantage of mefloquine is that it is stronger, is supposed to give better protection, and you only have to take one a week, whereas with chloroquine and proguanil you have to take two per day and a further two once a week. There have been reports of side effects with mefloquine, including irritability, insomnia, vivid dreams and anxiety, but most people take it with no problems at all.

You may get malaria despite taking antimalarials, so you must also do your best to stop mosquitoes getting at you. They bite mainly at dusk and at dawn, and sometimes through the night. Sleep with a mosquito net soaked in permethrin if possible, or cover all exposed skin with strong insect repellent. Mosquito coils, vapourising mats and electrical repellents are also effective.

Symptoms

Malaria can seem like a very bad dose of flu. Symptoms include fever with and without headache, aching bones, diarrhoea and vomiting. If you think you have malaria you should get to a doctor or qualified nurse within eight hours and ask for a malaria smear.

Treatment

It is a good idea to take a self-treatment kit, which you can use yourself or give to a doctor if no treatment is available. Chloroquine is regarded as ineffective for treatment of malaria in Africa, so you should take Fansidar (although not if you are pregnant or allergic to sulpha drugs), and/or quinine, which should only be taken under medical supervision, especially if you have been using mefloquine.

DENGUE FEVER

Dengue is one of the most common tropical diseases affecting travellers. It is a flu-like illness caused by a virus and spread by the Aedes mosquito, which almost always bites during the day. It is more common during the rainy season, and as likely to be caught in the city as in rural areas.

Precautions

Antimalarials can protect against dengue fever. There is no vaccine at present, and the best way to prevent it is to keep covered and use insect repellent – not an easy option in a hot climate. If you are in a badly affected area, spray your clothes with DEET insect repellent.

Symptoms

Severe muscle and joint ache, headache, fever and rash. The worst symptoms are over in a week; dengue rarely leaves lasting problems.

Treatment

Because it is similar to malaria, get to a doctor and have a malaria smear. If a dengue diagnosis seems likely, keep drinking fluids and take analgesics.

RABIES

Rabies is an extremely dangerous viral infection transmitted in the saliva of mammals such as dogs, foxes and bats. It kills around 75,000 people a year worldwide, and Sub-Saharan Africa is one of the rabies danger zones, although it's extremely rare for a traveller to get it.

Precautions

You should be immunised against rabies before you go, with Human Diploid Cell Vaccine (HDCV). These injections are painless and give a high degree of protection. Avoid all contact with dogs unless you are certain they have been immunised. Consider any animal rabid that is behaving strangely, or is unknown, or which suddenly disappears.

Treatment

If you can observe the animal you have been in contact with for at least ten days, and it is still alive after that time, you can consider it safe. If you are bitten, scratched or licked by an animal of which you are suspicious, wash the wound carefully with soap and water, preferably under a running tap to remove infected saliva and dirt. Apply iodine, disinfectant or alcohol (gin or whisky will do). Do not scrub the wound. If possible get to a doctor to have the wound sutured, and start a course of rabies injections – these are no longer given into the stomach.

DIARRHOEA

You're certain to get diarrhoea at some stage in your trip: to avoid it altogether you would have to keep off too much delicious local food. You will constantly find yourself in situations where it would be rude to refuse something, so you must make up your own mind whether you want to offend your host or risk a dose of diarrhoea. It is normally nothing to worry about if you keep up your intake of fluids. In rare cases you might have to see a doctor.

Precautions

Rule number one is, of course, avoid drinking water that is not boiled or sterilised. You should try to stick to this, because you might pick up an amoeba, and amoebic dysentery is an extremely unpleasant and debilitating affliction that will take the best part of a year to get over. The following can also give you diarrhoea: unboiled water or milk; salads, shellfish (especially uncooked); uncooked or unpeeled fruit and vegetables; inadequately-cooked meat, fish and eggs; ice and ice-cream; reheated food, and cold food left uncovered. Canned drinks are safe, as are tea and coffee, tinned foods, and fruit and vegetables you peel yourself.

Symptoms

The obvious ones. If you have a fever, find blood in your stools, begin vomiting, or if your diarrhoea doesn't improve within a week, you should see a doctor. In extremely rare cases diarrhoea can be caused by cholera, in which case there will be a rapid onset of uncontrollable diarrhoea with stools that look like rice water. Equally rare amongst travellers, typhoid gives diarrhoea in its later stages. In both cases you should keep drinking fluids and see a doctor.

Treatment

Dehydration is the main danger. Drink as much weak tea, coffee, soup, boiled water or mineral water as you can. For a do-it-yourself rehydration mixture, add 6 teaspoons of sugar and one of salt to one litre of water. Make sure you have at least one cup of fluid per session in the toilet. Eat only the blandest foods. You shouldn't need them, but medicines you can take are Imodium (Loperamide), or in severe cases Ciproflaxin.

HIV and AIDS

Sub-Saharan Africa is the worst affected area in the world. In Mozambique between one in seven and one in nine adults is HIV positive. Frightening though these figures are, Mozambique is less affected than neighbouring countries such as Zimbabwe and South Africa, not because people are any more careful but because the population is less mobile. As the country becomes more developed and people travel around more, the incidence of HIV and Aids is likely to increase. The risk to travellers, however, is slight. You should not be in any danger if you take the simplest precautions.

Precautions

The HIV virus is spread through sex with an infected partner, through infected blood transfusions, through dirty needles and anything else which pierces the skin, occasionally through infected blood and other body fluids coming into contact with mucus membranes or injured skin, from mother to child at birth, and through infected breast milk. You cannot pick up HIV from normal social contact, shaking hands, sharing plates, dishes or glasses. There is no evidence that mosquitoes or other insects can pass on the virus.

Make sure you complete all your immunisations before you go (to avoid the risk of an infected needle); have a dental checkup to avoid the need for emergency dental treatment, take a record of your blood group with you, take a needle and syringe kit. Don't have any sort of sex with strangers. You should also avoid blood transfusions if you can possibly help it, as even screened blood is not necessarily safe. Some people consider taking a kit containing an intravenous transfusion set and plasma substitute - see *Medical equipment* below for details. Also take every possible precaution to avoid malaria, as that can mean hospitalisation and a blood transfusion.

SUNSTROKE, HEATSTROKE AND PRICKLY HEAT

Mozambique's beaches are some of the most tempting in the world; you want to strip off and expose yourself to the sun as soon as you arrive. But remember that too much sun can increase the risk of skin cancers, and permanently damage your skin. You can also be in danger from overheating, especially in humid areas. You will spend a lot of your time exposed to the sun on the back of open chapas: the wind will cool you and deceive you into thinking you're not burning, so make sure you wear a hat. These journeys are debilitating enough without adding sunstroke to the equation.

Precautions

The basic rules are: limit your exposure to 10-15 mintues at a time when you first arrive, and try to avoid the strongest sun between 10am and 3pm. While you are acclimatizing avoid too much exertion. Keep your fluid intake up and keep off the alcohol. If you are worried about the available drinking water, drink coconut milk, Fanta or Coke. Remember that you can still overheat even if you are not exposed to direct sunlight.

Symptoms

Heatstroke is the failure of your body's heat control mechanisms. If you have a headache or feel dizzy or lethargic, you probably have a mild case. In severe cases you will have headache and delirium as your body temperature continues to rise. Heatstroke can be fatal if not treated immediately. Symptoms of sunstroke are similar, and will also include burnt skin. Prickly heat – intensely irritating itching – results from the blockage of sweat ducts. It is one of the most common heat complaints affecting travellers.

Treatment

If you are burnt or have sunstroke, drink plenty of non-alcoholic fluids, treat the affected areas of skin with calamine lotion, baby lotion or yoghurt, and rest for a couple of days. If you feel even the mildest symptoms of heatstroke, get into the cool, drink lots of fluids, and rest. You also need much more salt in the heat, so take salt tablets or add it to your food. If your temperature continues to rise have a cold shower or bath, or remove all your clothes and cover yourself in a wet sheet. If there is no improvement, seek medical help. The best way to avoid prickly heat is to wash frequently, keep your skin dry, wear loose-fitting non-synthetic clothes, and try not to sweat too much.

DANGEROUS ANIMALS

The civil war has decimated Mozambique's animal population, so you're in little danger of even seeing a wild animal, let alone being attacked by one. Nevertheless, there is big game in Mozambique, and in certain situations basic precautions are advisable.

Hippopotami cause more human deaths in Africa than any other mammal. It is not that they are overly aggressive, but short-sighted and single-minded. If they are surprised while grazing their first response is to head for the safety of the water, trampling anything that gets in their way. Never get between a hippo and the river. There are also **crocodiles** in many rivers, so you should take a modicum of care if you are bathing in remote places.

Poisonous snakes kill only about ten people a year in South Africa, and less still in Mozambique. You should be careful if you are scrambling around in rocky areas, especially if you are using your hands. If you are walking in the bush wear good boots, thick socks and long trousers. If you should be bitten, remove any restricting jewellery in case of swelling, clean the wound and bandage it, splint the bitten limb if possible, keep it below the level of the heart, and seek medical attention. Don't try and cut open the wound and suck out the venom – this never works.

Many different species of **shark** are found in the Indian Ocean. None of Mozambique's beaches have shark nets, but the incidence of shark attacks is very low. The danger is reduced in waters that are protected by reefs, which is where you are likely to be snorkelling or diving anyway.

MEDICAL EQUIPMENT

If you have an accident and need to be stitched up, it's as well to be certain of the sterility of the needles and sutures being used. MASTA (address below) supply a kit containing syringes, hypodermic and intravenous needles, sutures, sterile wipes and dressings. You will probably think it unnecessary, but you can also get a kit containing plasma substitute in case you have to have a blood transfusion. MASTA can advise on this. You should also take a first-aid kit containing DEET mosquito repellant, band-aid, aspirin, calamine lotion and a small bottle of antiseptic.

Useful addresses and websites

MASTA (Medical Advisory Service for Travellers Abroad): London School of Hygiene and Tropical Medicine, Keppel Street, London, WC1E 7HT; tel 0207 631 4408; fax 0207 323 4547; Website http://www.masta.org. For a health brief tailored specifically to your journey you have to call the Travellers' Health Line on 09068 224 100 (this is a premium line available from the UK with calls charged at £0.60 per min).

London School of Hygiene and Tropical Medicine: address above. Travel Clinic Healthline 0839 337 733.

Scottish Centre for Infection and Environmental Health: Tel 0141 946 712220.

The Foreign Office: Travel Advice Unit, Consular Division, Foreign & Commonwealth Office, 1 Palace Street, London, SW1E 5HE; tel 0207-238 4503/4504; fax 0207-238 4545; Website http://www.fco.gov.uk/travel. Country reports and advice for travellers – detailed if a little alarmist – also available on BBC2 CEEFAX p.470.

World Health Organisation (WHO): Website http://www.travelhealth.com/index.htm (up-to-date vaccination and health advice for travellers, country by country.)

army	*o exército*
bandit	*o bandido*
to be under arrest	*preso*
cocaine	*cocaína*
drugs	*as drogas*
drug addict	*viciado/a em drogas/drogadicto/a*
drunk	*bêbado*
fine	*a multa*
gun	*a arma*
help!	*socorro!*

leave me alone!	*deixe-me em paz!*
police	*polícia*
police station	*esquadra (da polícia)*
prison	*a prisão*
thief	*o ladrão*
wallet	*a carteira*
witness	*testigo/a*

CRIME AGAINST TOURISTS

Mozambique is one of the poorest countries in the world, and as a western tourist you almost certainly come from one of the wealthiest. Mozambican university lecturers – among the highest-paid people in the country apart from government ministers – earn around $230 a month. The money you have spent on your air fare is more than the average Mozambican will see in a lifetime.

It is impossible not to advertise the fact that you are, relatively speaking, extremely rich. However scruffy and unwashed you look, everybody knows you're carrying a couple of hundred dollars at least, and there's a lot of eminently stealable equipment on your back. Remember also that the civil war displaced and traumatised millions of people, and orphaned hundreds of thousands of children. There is no such thing as social security in Mozambique, and two-thirds of the population live in extreme poverty. Add to this the fact that only a tiny percentage of the weapons and ammunition thought to be in the country at the end of the war have been recovered, and you have a situation in which crime could flourish.

But anecdotal evidence suggests the worst crime most tourists in Mozambique suffer is theft. Campers have their cooking pots stolen, money disappears from hotel rooms, cars lose their windscreen wipers. Unless you are driving in certain areas (see below) you are highly unlikely to be the victim of a violent mugging. Some reckon that after 17 years of civil war, Mozambicans have no stomach for any more aggression. It's an attractive, if psychologically flawed idea. Violence begets violence, and the legions of mentally and physically damaged people left over from the war are certainly harbouring enough personal demons to visit them on anyone who gets in their way. Far more plausible is the theory that Mozambicans live so frugally and have seen so few tourists over the years that they have no reason to covet their wealth. As soon as tourist money starts pouring in, things will change. The big cities and tourist centres like Bazaruto and Vilanculos, already a prey to petty thieves, will become more and more unsafe. Maputo will take on the character of any other African capital, and will lose some of its charm.

How to avoid crime

You should take all possible precautions against theft, but it is also essential not to appear paranoid. Some manuals and guide books suggest such anti-slashing measures as lining your backpack with chicken wire (camping shops actually supply lockable steel-mesh covers), or reinforcing your moneybelt with guitar string. Those who look and behave like victims will become victims. If you are that worried about thieves you would do better to stay at home.

One of the problems of travelling in Mozambique is the fact that you're obliged to carry large amounts of cash at all times. Travellers cheques (see *Money*) are very difficult to change, and you could be far away from a city when they're stolen. They may be insured and replaceable, but that's scant comfort if you're five days away from any bank that can deal with your problem. The only recourse is to be very careful about your money. Keep it in a money-belt under your shirt and don't flash wads of notes around. You should keep a supply of 'mugger's money' – say, $30 – in a pocket, and nine-tenths of the rest, and your passport, in a moneybelt under your shirt. Keep an emergency supply in your backpack – enough to tide you over for a couple of days until you can get to a bank or your embassy to arrange for more funds.

Don't walk alone at night in unfamiliar areas. Many towns have no street lighting, and if you have to walk at night dark streets are unavoidable, in which case try to keep to the more frequented areas. Don't leave your bags unattended. Make sure you can lock your hotel room door, but don't leave your valuables in there anyway.

Most theft happens in markets, stations and other crowded places. Keep a tight hold of your bags and be careful of pickpockets.

CAR CRIME AND BANDITRY

In certain parts of Mozambique, especially the areas most frequented by South African and Zimbabwean drivers – the Mutare-Biera road, and the side roads around Vilanculos and Inhambane – carjacking is a possibility. During the civil war banditry was a definite hazard, and a decent vehicle, particularly a 4WD, is still a magnet for thieves. Over the last few years the incidents of carjacking have declined, and if you keep to the main roads as much as possible and absolutely avoid driving at night you should be in no danger. The Mutare-Beira road is now well guarded with army posts and is considered safe. Needless to say, you should not allow yourself to be flagged down by anyone but a uniformed policeman. In the unlikely event that you are carjacked (the usual method is to flag down the vehicle, reach through the driver's window and take the keys, order everyone out and steal the car) you should offer no resistance. It is better to be left on the side of the road without your car than to provoke violence.

You should on no account camp alone on quiet stretches of any highway. If you are unable to reach your destination, find a village and ask where you can camp, or look for an army encampment, introduce yourselves to *o comandante* and ask if he will find you a space.

The main danger for drivers is theft of unattended vehicles, and losing windscreen wipers, mirrors, headlamps and anything else removeable. You will notice that cars parked in towns often have no wipers: the drivers remove them and lock them in the boot. You should not leave your vehicle unattended for long; if it is unavoidable, find someone responsible who you can pay to look after it. Whenever you park you'll find a gaggle of small boys who will offer to look after your car. Make up your own mind whether to pay them or not.

THE POLICE

Popular confidence in the police is low. Over the past few years hundreds of policemen have been sacked for corruption, and hundreds more have faced disciplinary hearings. Human Rights groups regularly get reports of detainees being maltreated and beaten up, especially in Maputo. Police are routinely suspected of gun-running, buying and selling some of the hundreds of thousands of weapons that went missing when peace was declared in 1992. At the time of writing the police force is the subject of a major anti-corruption drive. A $12million programme aims to retrain more than 4,000 policemen by 2000, in the law, human rights, ethics, and techniques and tactics.

Part of the problem is lack of any coherent structure to the security forces after the war. The police and the army (FADM) never knew who was responsible for what, and the formation of elite units – like the Lightning Battalion which guards roads – made things even more complicated.

Unless you get yourself into trouble with drugs or other contraband, you're unlikely to have much to do with the police. At the numerous police checkpoints around the country, you'll usually have to show your passport and nothing else. The occasional policeman will try to squeeze a bribe out of you: see *Driving* for advice on what to do. Always bear in mind that officials at remote posts are not particularly accountable, and don't get paid very much. Treat them with respect.

You will come across special units on key roads like the Beira Corridor and the EN1. These battalions are invariably highly disciplined. The army is responsible for national security, guarding important installations, governors' palaces and so on. If you try to walk past a government building without crossing to the other side of the road, a hard-faced young soldier will motion you across the road with his AK-47. That's all the contact you're likely to want with the army.

DRUGS

Mozambique's drugs laws used to be among the most lenient in the world. As late as 1995, convicted heroin traffickers could expect a sentence of two to eight years – practically nothing when compared to the death sentences and life imprisonment handed down in some Far Eastern countries. But since Mozambique's borders have opened to a hugely increased amount of tourist and freight traffic, ministers have become concerned that the country is becoming a conduit for illegal drugs. Heroin, cocaine, marijuana and other drugs are being smuggled into Swaziland and South Africa by road from Maputo, which, along with other major cities like Beira and Nampula, are being used as transit points for illegal shipments from Malawi, Zimbabwe and as far afield as Kenya. In 1995 the government announced it was going to stiffen penalties for drug trafficking, although how draconian the new sentences have turned out to be is a matter for debate: in 1999 sixty foreigners were simply deported after being convicted in Nampula in connection with the seizure of large quantities of heroin, marijuana and morphine.

Whatever the penalties, it is wiser not to have anything to do with drugs in Mozambique. All 'street' drugs, from marijuana to heroin, are illegal, and to be found in possession will at the very least render you liable to the extortion of a very large bribe. At worst, you will be locked up for of days or weeks, and anyone who has seen a Mozambican police cell would not want to linger there.

Marijuana is available all over Mozambique, and you'll frequently be offered it at campsites and in the street. Make up your own mind how safe it is to accept, and remember, if you get into trouble with the police, you may not even be able to contact your Embassy for days. When you do get through to a vice-consul, they will be able to do very little for you beyond ringing your parents and telling them you won't be home for Christmas.

MINES

Thirty-five per cent of all accidental deaths in Mozambique are the result of motor vehicle accidents. Three per cent of accidental deaths are due to landmines.

Tourists in Mozambique need be in no danger whatsoever from mines. You must be aware that mines exist, and you must take precautions, but the likelihood of your seeing or hearing of a mine is remote. For various reasons – chief among them the huge publicity given the late Princess Diana's patronage of mine-clearance charity the Halo Trust – Mozambique is associated with landmines, and gradually the western world has built a largely exaggerated picture of a country paralysed by uncleared minefields. Mines have taken a terrible toll on the country, but it is important to keep them in perspective: in Mozambique you are many times more likely to be injured or killed by a motor vehicle than you are by a mine.

The problem may have been exaggerated, but it must be stressed that thousands of Mozambicans have been devastated by landmines. Alongside Angola, Afghanistan and Cambodia, Mozambique is considered one of the nations worst affected by mines. Since the first landmine exploded in Mozambique in 1965, some 10,000 people, mostly civilians, have been maimed or killed. Immediately after the war, around 500 people a year fell victims to mines. Those figures are certainly much reduced today.

Around 20,000 mines were planted, 99 per cent of them of Soviet origin, the rest from Eastern Europe, Britain, the United States, Belgium, China, Italy, France and Portugal. Mines were planted by Frelimo guerillas and by the Portuguese army, by Renamo and its South African and Rhodesian backers, by Tanzanians supporting Frelimo, and by Malawians. Renamo used them extensively to destabilize the civilian population and to render their land useless. Mines were planted to block major supply routes and rural tracks. Frelimo laid minefields to 'protect' villages considered Renamo targets, and to protect vital installations, garrisons, and Mozambique's borders with South Africa and Malawi.

Two types of mine were used, anti-tank and anti-personnel. The first, about the size of a cake tin, will destroy a vehicle. They are so devastating that only 100 are needed to paralyse a country; forty have been found in Mozambique. Anti-personnel mines are usually about the size of a large tin of shoe polish, and come in two main forms. Pressure mines are buried in the ground, explode with the pressure of a foot, and are designed to take the leg off (it is considered strategically better to wound a soldier than to kill him, because a wounded man needs two others to help him, thus taking three combatants out of action instead of one). The second type of mine, the 'bounding fragmentation' or anti-group mine, is also buried, and detonated by trip wire. On detonation it jumps one metre into the air and explodes. It is lethal within a 10-20 metre circle.

It is very easy to plant a mine, but clearing is expensive and time-consuming. A 30-man team and its equipment costs about $200,000 per year, in which time it would hope to clear one square kilometre of land in total. The problem is heightened by the fact that minefield charts – especially Renamo's – are hopelessly inadequate. Clearance teams generally identify problem areas by reports of human or animal casualties, and set to work with high-powered metal detectors and occasionally dogs. It is dangerous work – most squads have had members killed, and all have reported casualties.

At present there are around 2,000 people involved in mine-clearance. The best-known organisation is the Halo Trust, which has its headquarters in Quelimane and operates in the north of the country. The Norwegian NGO People's Aid operates from Tete, another group called Handicap International is based in Inhambane, and the United Nations and other groups are based in Maputo. Other countries are involved: in June 1998 a French non-governmental organisation began clearing mines in the Moamba district of

Maputo province. In the first three months they cleared 2,500 anti-personnel mines planted by Frelimo to protect power lines bringing electricity from South Africa.

Since the end of the war, around 60,000 mines have been cleared. The country will never be entirely free of them – just as unexploded World War Two bombs are still turning up in London, Mozambicans will be finding mines in 50 years' time – but all major roads have been de-mined, and experts estimate that in five to six years, deminers are going to stop finding work.

Of the thousands of Mozambicans that have lost limbs to mines, most are thrown back on their own resources. There are three or four prosthetic clinics in the country fitting false legs and arms. The Quelimane clinic treats around 20 patients a month, and reports that it could treat more but many people do not have the money or resources to travel to the clinic. There are two national organisations that help mine victims, the Mozambican Association of Disabled People (ADEMO) and the Mozambican Association of Disabled Soldiers (ADEMIMO).

Avoiding Mines

As stressed above, you are in no danger from mines on any main road, or much-frequented track. If you see danger signs – a skull and crossbones and the words *Perigo Minas* – you should take them very seriously indeed. In any case you should never walk anywhere that is not well-trodden. When your bus makes a rest-stop, don't go forging into the undergrowth to relieve yourself. Experts are reluctant to point to any one area of the country that is more or less dangerous than another, but most agree it would be very unwise to walk on any verge alongside the Ressano-Garcia – Maputo road, off the path near any of Mozambique's borders, or around satellite dishes, water towers and military installations.

WHAT TO TAKE

Clothing

If you're camping it's difficult to keep your backpack weight down, but remember you'll be humping it around day after day, on and off trucks, buses and dhows, and keep your clothing to a minimum. Women should take a couple of pairs of light cotton long trousers and cotton wraps (or buy a *capulana* when you arrive). You should take a fleece for cold nights (it also makes a good pillow), one lightweight kagoule (showerproof is sufficient), three or four T-shirts, one long-sleeved shirt, shorts and lightweight trousers. Boots should be tough and light. Probably your most essential item is a pair of good strong sandals. You will live in them, so make sure they are the best quality.

Camping equipment

A good two-season tent is essential for Mozambique – there are campsites in most resorts which are cheaper and often cleaner than any of the hotels. Sometimes you'll find no other accommodation. A two-season sleeping bag is sufficient, and a foam sleeping mat (which can double as a cushion on long journeys). You might think of taking two light pans, and a cup. A stove would be useful but not essential – you can always find firewood. A Sigg water bottle is essential, as is a torch and spare batteries, and naturally you'd no more travel without a Swiss Army Knife than you'd leave your right arm at home.

Other useful items

In no particular order you should include: a cotton money belt, gaffer tape for repairs, a squash ball to use as a sink plug, spare toilet paper, sewing kit, a Portuguese phrase book, a snorkel and mask, sunglasses, novels, spare films, and, most important of all, a first aid kit (see *Health and Hygiene* for details). Women should take a good supply of tampons (see also *Women travellers* below).

TOURIST INFORMATION

The official Mozambican government tourist agencies are *Futur* (Fundo Nacional de Turismo) and *Dinatur* (Direcção Nacional de Turismo). Both have offices in Maputo (addresses below). Futur is the more helpful of the two, but if you need up-to-date information you would be far better off going to the Polana or Cardoso Hotels and asking their travel agency staff. There is no national network of tourist offices: where a town has an information point this is marked in the text. The best course to take in any of the larger towns is to find a travel agent for the latest information on flights, buses, trains and so on. There are also a number of hotels and backpackers hostels which are good for swapping information: Fatima's in Maputo, Pachiça Lodge in Inhambane, and any other popular tourist lodging will furnish you with more reliable news than any official source.

In South Africa a useful source is the Mozambique National Tourist Company (address below). They are basically a travel agent, organising bookings in hotels and camps as far north as Vilanculos, but they are also happy to supply information on the current state of tourist facilities in Mozambique.

Futur, Ave 25 de Setembro 1203, Maputo. Tel 01-307323; fax 01-307324.

Dinatur, Ave 25 de Setembro 1502, Maputo. Tel 01-420147; fax 01425275.

Mozambique National Tourist Company, PO Box 31991, Braamfontein 2017, Johannesburg. Tel 011-339 7275; fax 011339 7295.

WHEN TO GO

It is best to visit in the winter months of May to October, when coastal temperatures do not get higher than 20-25°C, but many tourists visit all the year round – Christmas in Pemba is a particularly busy time. During the summer months of November to April – the rainy season – temperatures are much higher and conditions can be oppressively humid, especially on the north coast and inland. Pemba, for example, is extremely hot and windy. The main roads in the south should not be affected by rain, but many dirt tracks, for example down to beach resorts like Závora, become very difficult indeed. Main roads north of the Zambesi are generally in much worse condition and are badly affected by rain. Travelling in the north in the rainy season is even slower than it is in dry conditions. Remember that during the rainy season there is also increased risk of malaria.

The coast as far up as Vilanculos is very popular with South African and Zimbabwean tourists, so you should try to avoid the most popular resorts, like the Bazaruto Islands, Xai-Xai and Inhambane, during school holidays. Hotels are often fully booked at these times, although you should have no trouble getting a place in a campsite. School holidays in South Africa and Zimbabwe vary from province to province but are roughly as follows: four weeks at Christmas, two weeks at Easter, three weeks at the end of June and one week at the end of September.

Travelling with babies and young children

In many ways Mozambique is a wonderful place for children. It is clean and relatively free of disease, Mozambicans love children, and in many areas any white child would be seen as an adorable oddity. Food for older children is not a problem – a fish diet is highly nutritious. Many South Africans and Zimbabweans holiday in Mozambique with very young families, but they almost always drive their own vehicles and bring everything they need with them, and most would not consider trying to get around on public transport. Usually only the most intrepid of travellers contemplate taking their baby or small child to Mozambique. It is not that your child runs an increased risk of disease, simply that it is one of the poorest countries in the world, with a very high infant mortality rate, and if they should fall ill it would be difficult to get prompt medical attention outside Maputo or Beira. Furthermore, unless you have your own vehicle, travelling is an exhausting business. Many of your journeys are made on the open back of a truck, which is something that many western kids would not submit to with the forbearance of local children. Remember also that nappies, baby food, formula milk and other essentials are unknown outside Maputo.

Women travellers

Women travelling in Mozambique are no more at risk than men – crime and banditry are on the rise but this is not directed towards women any more than men. You should be aware that in the eyes of many African men it is unusual for western women to travel alone, so you should be careful not to give out unconscious signals in the way you dress, for example. Shorts and t-shirts are acceptable in the cities but in smaller towns and rural areas it is respectful to cover up your legs. The *capulana* – the brightly-coloured, all-purpose cotton wrap that Mozambican women wear and use as a bag or baby-carrier – is useful to cover up if you are wearing a swimming costume. If you are travelling alone in the more remote rural areas of the country, people are understandably inquisitive but women are unlikely to be threatened. In the cities, the obvious safety rules apply (see *Crime and Safety*). There have been instances of jewellery and watches being snatched from wrists and necks in the cities during the daytime, so dress plainly. Essentials such as tampons can be bought in Beira and Maputo but are very expensive. You are unlikely to find them in any other parts of the country.

Disabled travellers

There are many amputees in Mozambique, and thousands of partially-sighted and blind people, but they are thrown very much on their own resources. Wheelchairs are practically unknown, no form of public transport has wheelchair facilities, pavements are fraught with hazards such as gaping holes and tree roots, and there are no ramps anywhere outside Maputo. Mozambique is therefore not promising territory for disabled people without their own transport. But many wheelchair users and other people with disabilities have travelled all over Africa, usually in their own transport, but sometimes without. For more information visit the excellent website at www.geocities.com/Paris/1502/. It has nothing specific on Mozambique, but has accounts of wheelchair journeys through Africa, helpful links and lists of further reading.

Electrical equipment

Mozambique's electricity supply is sporadic and power cuts are a fact of life. Don't take any piece of electrical equipment that you need to rely on. If you have a laptop computer check the transformer and make sure it is compatible. Current is 220V AC at 50 cycles, with two-pin plugs. Make sure you have an adaptor for anything using 110V.

Student and Youth Concessions

Take an ISIC student card if you like, but you'll find very few concessions for students. In any case, museums and the like are so cheap you should simply pay the full price as a gesture of support.

Time

Mozambican time is two hours ahead of Greenwich Mean Time and one hour ahead of British Summer Time. The 24-hour clock is used extensively.

Weights and measures

Mozambique uses the metric system, although in practice fruit and vegetables are sold by the panful or by quantities. Anything in season (the only time you will find it) is so plentiful that prices are negligible to a western pocket.

EMBASSIES AND HIGH COMMISSIONS

If you run into any sort of trouble, whether through crime, ill-health, or for any other serious reason, your first port of call should be your embassy. Staff are used to dealing people's problems and will do all they can to help you. Bear in mind that if you break the law or get involved with drugs, your embassy will be able to do very little for you.

The following is a list of main Embassies and High Commissions in Mozambique.

UK	Ave Vladimir Lenine 310, Maputo; tel 01-492011; fax 01-421666.
USA	Ave Kenneth Kaunda 193, Maputo; tel 01-492797. Ave Mao Tse Tung 548, Maputo; tel 01-491916 (Consulate).
Australia	Ave Julius Nyerere 794, Maputo; tel 01497328.
Brazil	Ave Kenneth Kaunda 146, Maputo; tel 01-490986.
Canada	Ave Julius Nyerere 1128, Maputo; tel 01-492623.
China	Ave Mártires Machava 1309, Maputo; tel 01-491462.
Denmark	Ave 24 de Julho 1500, Maputo; tel 01-429052; fax 01-303526.
Finland	Ave Julius Nyerere 1128, Maputo; tel 01-490518; fax 01-491612.
France	Ave Julius Nyerere 1419, Maputo; tel 01-495111.
Germany	Rua Damião Góis 506, Maputo; tel 01-492714; fax 01-492888.
Holland	Rua Mukumbura 285, Maputo; tel 01-490031; fax 01490429.
Italy	Ave Kenneth Kaunda 387, Maputo; tel 01-492046.
Malawi	Ave Kenneth Kaunda 75, Maputo; tel 01-492676; fax 01-490224.
Norway	Ave Agostinho Neto 620, Maputo; tel 01-429411; fax 01-429410
Portugal	Ave Julius Nyerere 720, Maputo; tel 01-490316.
Russia	Ave Julius Nyerere 1612, Maputo; tel 01-490901.
South Africa	Ave Eduardo Mondlane 41, Maputo; tel 01490059; fax 01-493029.
Spain	Ave Kenneth Kaunda 140, Maputo; tel 01-490565.
Switzerland	Ave Julius Nyerere 1213, Maputo; tel 01-492744.
Tanzania	Ave Mártires Machava 852, Maputo; tel 01-490110.
Zambia	Ave Kenneth Kaunda 1286, Maputo; tel 01-492452.
Zimbabwe	Ave Mártires Machava 1657, Maputo; tel 01-490404.

USEFUL WEBSITES

The following is a short list of useful sites you could visit before you go. Where relevant the URLs are repeated in the text.

News agencies

http://www.africanews.org/
South African news agency with extensive coverage of Mozambican issues.

http://www.lusa.pt/lusanews/
Lusanews, the Portuguese news agency's website. Quite extensive coverage of Mozambican issues.

http://www.poptel.org.uk/mozambique-news/
AIM – the official Mozambican news agency's website. Political, economic and general news, in English.

Political, economic and development issues

http://www.ccmusa.co.mz/elinks.html
Useful links to a variety of sites, from the Mozambique News Agency (see above) to the University of Eduardo Mondlane in Maputo.

http://www.tcol.co.uk/index.htm
The Commonwealth Online – useful links to a variety of official and unofficial Mozambique sites.

http://www.undp.org/
The website of the United Nations Development Programme covers Mozambican development issues in detail

General

http://www.fco.gov.uk/
The UK Foreign Office official site. Well-organised, but somewhat alarmist.

http://www.geocities.com/Paris/1502/
An informative site with nothing specific on Mozambique, but many accounts of wheelchair journeys through Africa, helpful links, lists of further reading etc.

http://travelhealth.com/index.htm
World Health Organisation travel health advice – an excellent and informative site.

http://travel.state.gov/
Website for the Travel Department of the US State Department, well organised with information and warnings for travelling Americans and others.

Flight finders

http://www.bargainholidays.com
Sometimes has bargains to Africa

http://www.city2000.com/travel
Linked to Galileo, the reservation system that most travel agents use. Can be useful for last-minute bargains to South Africa.

http://www.deckchair.com
This is the brainchild of Bob Geldof. It asks where you want to go and when, and then trawls the airline reservation systems for the cheapest options. Uncluttered and highly efficient

http://www.excite.com/travel
Excite's travel section takes you through to Thomas Cook and other agents.

http://www.lastminute.com
A wealth of last-minute bargains, from rock concerts in Madrid to flights from London to Dar es Salaam. Don't be put off if you don't get what you want the first time.

http://www.statravel.co.uk/
Same service as above.

http://www.thomascook.co.uk
Constantly-updated selection of the deals offered in Thomas Cook's thousands of high street branches. Colourful and easy to find your way around.

http://www.trailfinders.com
The well-established UK long-haul backpackers' travel agent. A handy site with lots of good visa information.

http://www.travelocity.co.uk
This site can scan 95 per cent of all airlines for the best prices. Check for South Africa bargains splashed on the homepage.

http://www.usitcampus.co.uk/
Flight finding service. No Mozambique fares but you might pick up a cheap one to SA or Tanzania.

PUBLIC HOLIDAYS

New Year's Day	1 January
Heroes' Day	3 February
Women's Day	7 April
Workers' Day	1 May
Independence Day	25 June
Victory Day	7 September
Revolution Day	25 September
Christmas Day	25 December
Good Friday	
Easter Monday	
Maputo Public Holiday	10 November

Day commemorates the death of the first Mozambican president, Eduardo Mondlane, in 1969; Womens' Day commemorates the death of Josina Machel; Victory Day celebrates the signing of the Lusaka Accord in 1974. Islamic holidays are not officially recognised but are kept by Muslim communities.

Maputo City and Province

Downtown Maputo

Most tourists see practically nothing of Maputo Province beyond the capital. It is Mozambique's smallest and most southerly province, bounded in the south and west by South Africa and Swaziland, and in the north by Gaza province. Except for the diving resorts to the south of the city, there's little for the tourist beyond the (very considerable) attractions of the capital. It is a region of low-lying grassland and acacia and miombo woods, with temperatures that can rise to 40° in the summer months, and sink to 20° in winter, when grey skies and dispiriting drizzle are not uncommon. Over half the population of the province live in the city; the majority of the rest – just under a million people – are subsistence farmers or fishermen.

If you have your own transport, or a good deal of time to spare, it would be worthwhile exploring the freshwater coastal lakes of the province: Lagoa Piti and Maundo in the Maputo Elephant Sanctuary (see p.135) and Lagoa Páti in the north. These are a feature unique to southern Mozambique, and are havens for a great variety of rare birds – ospreys have been spotted – and other wildlife including monkeys and several types of gazelle. Further north, lakes like Poelala are being developed in a low-key fashion (see section on Závora in *Inhambane*) but the coast to the immediate north of Maputo city is untouched. It is very difficult to get to as there are few roads, and landmines are an ever-present danger, but if you are interested in wildlife you might be surprised by what you find.

It should be mentioned of course that if you're not equipped (either mentally or practically) for exploration, the lakes of Gaza and Inhambane provinces – Uembje, Nhanzume, Inhampavala, Quissico and others – are much more accessible. Furthermore, it's not as if they are surrounded by souvenir shops: in this stretch of the Mozambican coast, 'developed' usually means a couple of intrepid South Africans running three canoes and a ramshackle bar. They are not swamped with tourists.

To the south of Maputo city are the Maputo Elephant Reserve and the resorts of Ponta do Ouro and Ponta Malongane. These are very popular with South African game fishermen. Although you can swim there, if you don't intend to fish or water-ski, and you're heading up the coast anyway, you'll find far better swimming and snorkelling further north.

MAPUTO CITY

Maputo is not what you expect. When you first arrive it might seem like any other African city, with high-rise blocks and teeming streets, a bustling business district and thriving street life. But as soon as you get into the rhythm of the place you realise it has a unique character. Centuries of Portuguese domination have imparted a tangible Mediterranean air to the city, and you can almost feel you're in a slightly raffish part of Lisbon or Barcelona as you sit sipping coffee or a beer at one of the hundreds of cafés that line the wide boulevards.

The city has the natural advantage of a beautiful setting, built on the hills overlooking Maputo Bay with the deep blue of the Indian Ocean beyond. It is compact, occupying an area of about 20 square kilometres and with a population of less than a million. It is very easy to find your way around, and with its café life and profusion of restaurants it is a remarkably pleasant city to explore on foot.

A walk around Maputo (called Lourenço Marques, or LM, until 1976) uncovers some gems, from nineteenth century colonial buildings like the recently-renovated railway station and Natural History Museum, to the botanical gardens and the Museu da Revolução – complete with Eduardo Mondlane's VW Karmann, the gym clothes of Josina Machel (once married to Samora but killed during the civil war), and a wealth of photographs and papers documenting the revolution.

The unique mixture of African and Latin has also blessed Maputo with the most vibrant nightlife in southern Africa. In a long night you can sample a range of restaurants, bars, nightclubs, jazz dives, discos and seedy beer shacks that you will certainly not find anywhere else in Mozambique and are unlikely to encounter in any of the neighbouring countries.

History

The Portuguese trader and navigator Lourenço Marques first visited Delagoa Bay in 1542, on the instructions of the Captain of Mozambique and Sofala. Struck by the large number of elephants around the bay, he reported favourably on the possibilities for the ivory trade, and in the following years he made a large number of semi-official voyages south. Marques was by no means the first – Delagoa Bay appears on maps as early as 1502, and he made his exploratory journeys at the same time as a general drift southwards of independent Portuguese and *mestizos* – Afro-Portuguese intent on escaping the jurisdiction of the northern forts.

Shortly after Marques' first visit, Portuguese ships began to visit the bay. Its extensive system of waterways and estuaries, into which four major rivers flow, were navigable well into the interior. The Portuguese made no effort to establish a permanent presence, but used the small settlement on the bay as a base for trading visits into the interior.

Sometime in this fruitful period King Joao III of Portugal named the bay after Marques. By the 1560s Portuguese ships arrived on a regular basis, laden with ivory from as far south as Natal. By the middle of the 17th century, although ivory was the principal commodity – the Portuguese held five different trading fairs in the bay in 1647 – other goods were bartered for. According to one captain they also bought 'ambergris, ivory, slaves, honey, butter, horns and hoofs of the rhinoceros, and tusks and hoofs of the hippopotamus' in exchange for beads and cloth.

In the second half of the 18th century the Portuguese shifted the centre of their operations, finding it more profitable to trade with the Makua and Kilwa people of the north and not have to make the dangerous voyage to the south. Their ships visited the bay less and less often, and the British and Dutch moved in on the trading possibilities. But after 1700 – perhaps because of the increasing strength of the Dutch in the area – trade was abandoned by the British as well.

Throughout the 18th century various trading posts and factories were built. While the town of Lourenço Marques was never more than an unremarkable outpost, trade in the area did not die. It was considered important enough for the Dutch to built a fort there in 1721, which was attacked and destroyed by British pirates the next year. They rebuilt it and tried to establish a European colony but couldn't make it work and pulled out in 1730.

It wasn't until the end of the century that trade picked up again. The British came back, using the bay as a way station for their ships from India. The Austrians also established a factory there, and the Portuguese revived their interest in the area. Whalers began to arrive to stock up on fresh meat and supplies. As economic activity picked up, imports entered the country in much greater quantities which in turn prompted a richer flow of ivory and other commodities from inland. Cattle were driven from the rich grasslands of Swaziland and Natal. It was an economic expansion that affected the south more than anything – any European ships coming to the area looked there for their needs rather than to the drier, more barren north.

But it was the relationship with South Africa that was to have the greatest effect on the development of southern Mozambique – particularly the arrival of the Boers. When they began to settle the Transvaal in the 1830s one of their first acts had been to try and forge a route to the sea. In 1838 Louis Trichardt and his fellow trekkers had reached Delagoa Bay, keener than ever to establish a base on the sea after experiencing the ravages of malaria and sleeping sickness. But the British and Portuguese resisted any idea of a Boer presence in the bay. For the next two decades the Boers had to look to Durban and the ports of the Cape as trading outlets, until in 1861 President Pretorius declared the Transvaal's frontiers extended to the coast. That set off a protracted period of political wrangling which culminated in an uneasy treaty between the Transvaal and Portugal, recognising the latter's possession of Delagoa Bay and a section of the coast.

The discovery of diamonds in the Vaal river in 1867 and gold at Lydenburg in 1869, and the opening of the great gold reef at Witwatersrand in 1886 was the catalyst that set off a period of large-scale industrial expansion in South Africa. This in turn affected southern Mozambique, with the building of railways, roads and the development of all the service and consumer industries needed to support gold and diamond mining. Transport links to Lourenço Marques were all-important, and the Portuguese and Transvaal governments pressed ahead with their plans to build a rail link. This proved too much for the British, who saw such a link as directly contrary to their efforts to control the Boer republics.

Accordingly Britain sought to contain the Transvaal once again - by annexation. In 1877 Natal police occupied Pretoria and formally declared the Transvaal a British colony. This annexation was to radically transform the economy of the area. Now the idea of a rail link to Lourenço Marques from British-controlled Transvaal became extremely attractive, and Britain and Portugal drew up a treaty in which the building of a railway was the central objective.

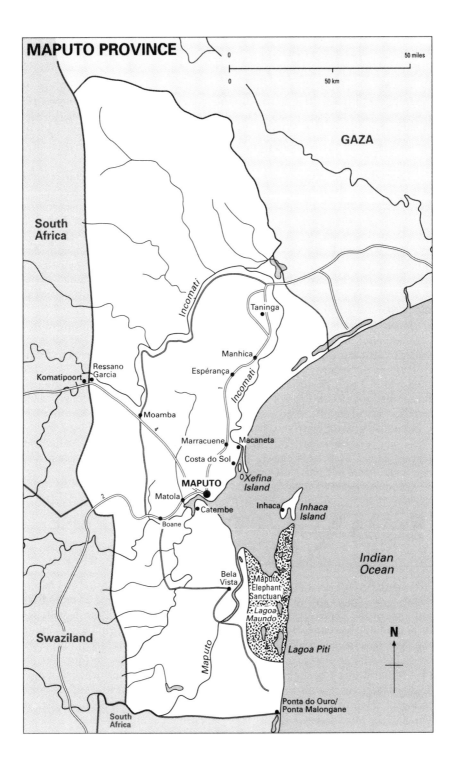

MAPUTO PROVINCE

0 [ ] 50 miles
0 [ ] 50 km

GAZA

South Africa

Taninga

Manhica

Incomati

Espérança

Ressano Garcia

Komatipoort

Incomati

Moamba

Marracuene

Macaneta

Costa do Sol

MAPUTO

Xefina Island

Matola

Inhaca

Inhaca Island

Catembe

Boane

Indian Ocean

Bela Vista

Maputo Elephant Sanctuary

Lagoa Maundo

Swaziland

Lagoa Piti

Maputo

N

Ponta do Ouro/ Ponta Malongane

South Africa

It was the completion of this line in 1894 that assured the future of Lourenço Marques. Ilha de Moçambique, thousands of kilometres to the north, had been the impregnable capital of the Portuguese East African empire since the 16th century, but with links with South Africa becoming stronger its remoteness from the economic and political centre became obvious. In 1902 Lourenço Marques was designated capital.

Throughout the 20th century the town continued to grow – in 1928 it had a population of 40,000, of which 9,000 were European. In the 1930s, Portuguese banks and industrial interests were encouraged to invest in Mozambique, which they did principally in Lourenço Marques (or LM as it was known) and Beira. By the end of the Second World War LM was a thriving industrial city, producing building materials, consumer goods and household plastics, chemicals and refined oil. Tourism also developed, the lure of a Latin culture proving attractive to South Africans, who came there to make the most of the black prostitutes and nightlife they couldn't get under the puritanical apartheid regime.

In the period leading up to independence in 1975 – when the capital was renamed after the river which flows south from the bay – Lourenço Marques was considered one of the most beautiful of southern African cities. Portuguese residents and South African visitors would stroll its wide boulevards and take coffee in its many cafés, surrounded by the elegant houses and grand buildings of the colonial capital. After independence, as the Frelimo government allied itself with the Soviets and the Eastern bloc, communist missions arrived, Marxist slogans began to be painted on the walls, and street names were changed to reflect the government's ideological stance. Today, Maputo is one of the only cities in the free world where you can walk down Avenida Ho Chi Min, have a beer in Avenida Mao Tse Tung, or get your shoes shined on Avenida Kim Il Sung.

Getting Around

ARRIVAL AND DEPARTURE

Air

Mavalane Airport is about 8km north of the city on Ave Acordos de Lusaka. There is no regular bus to the airport although it is easy to find a *chapa* from any one of the main streets. On arrival you can get a taxi from outside the terminal into the centre of town. You should pay $10-$12, although many of the taxis have meters which could climb to as high as $16. Maputo is served by South African Airlines (SAA), Sabinair, Lineas Aereas de Moçambique (LAM) and Air Portugal. LAM flies direct to Lisbon once a week, Johannesburg nine times a week and Harare twice a week. It also flies direct to Beira, Lichinga, Nampula, Pemba and Tete, with connecting flights to Quelimane. Most internal flights leave three or four times a week. Sabinair flies to Inhaca and Punto do Ouro at weekends, and Vilanculos and Bazaruto on Mondays, Tuesdays and Fridays.

It is possible to get charter flights to most tourist destinations in Mozambique – check with Sabinair (number below).

Departure tax is $20 on international flights and $10 on internal flights. It is essential you confirm your flight 72 hours before departure. Flights are regularly overbooked and unconfirmed passengers stand a good chance of being bumped.

Airline offices

LAM, Avenida Karl Marx 220, Maputo; tel 01-426001/4. Avenida Mao Tse Tung 19; tel 01-490590/496101; fax 01-496105. There is also an office in the airport (tel 01-465827/9); reservations by phone also (tel 01-465810/8).

South African Airlines, Praça de Junho 16, Ave Samora Machel, Maputo; tel 01-420740/42; fax 01-422481.

Sabinair tel 01-465108.

Prosol tel 01-425322.

Train

All train times are subject to alteration: they are correct at the time of going to press but should be checked. For all train information call 01-431269, or go to the main station at Praça dos Trabalhadores.

The finest train to leave from Maputo is the Trans-Lubombo Express. The 24-hour ride to Durban is luxurious and spectacular, and costs around $30 payable in rand. Run by a South African company it travels between Durban and Maputo, stopping at Empangeni, Golela, Mpaka, and Goba. The train leaves Durban at 7.30pm Tuesdays and Fridays and arrives in Maputo at 6.15pm the following day. It leaves Maputo at 9.30am Thursdays and Sundays and arrives in Durban at 7.30am the following day. Booking is essential: call or visit the main railway station in Maputo (number above), Johannesburg 011-773 2944, Durban 031-361 7621 or Swaziland 09268-52872/52983.

Trains for Johannesburg leave from the main station at midday on Mondays, Wednesdays and Fridays, and arrive at around 6am. Trains from Johannesburg leave on Tuesdays, Thursdays and Sundays at 5.30pm and arrive in Maputo at 10.30am the following day. The train stops at Nelspruit, Middelburg, Witbank, Germiston and Pretoria.

The timetable for trains leaving for the Zimbabwean border is irregular but at the time of writing they are leaving at 8am on Saturday mornings. Check on the number above for confirmation.

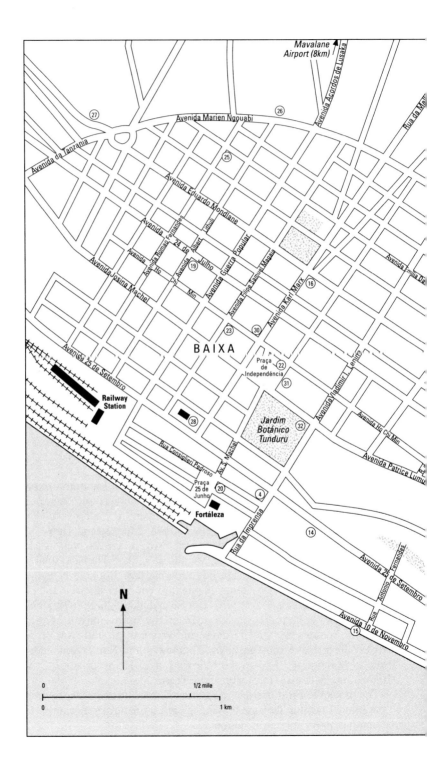

MAPUTO

1 Hotel Polana
2 Hotel Cardoso
3 Terminus
4 Hotel Tivoli
5 Vila dos Pescadores
6 Pensão Martins
7 Costa do Sol
8 The Burger Inn
9 Fatima's
10 Bar Mundos
11 Jardim Quadrado
12 Sheik
13 Piri Piri
14 Feira Popular
15 Ferries to Inhaca/Catembe
16 Hotel Universal/Transportes Virginia (to Xai-Xai & North)
17 Panthera Azul buses
18 Natural History Museum
19 Museu da Revolução
20 Museu da Moeda
21 Museu da Geologica
22 Centro Cultural Franco-Moçambicano
23 Museu Nacional de Arte
24 Núcleo de Arte
25 Mercado Estrela
26 Mercado Xipamanine
27 Mercado Fajardo
28 Mercado Central
29 Mercado Janeth
30 Bazar de Pono
31 Cathedral de Nossa Senhora de Concepcion
32 Clube Radio Moçambique
33 UMD Clinic

Bus

Long-distance buses depart from several different places – there is no central bus station in Maputo. The two main bus companies are Oliveiras and Transportes Virginia, which both go north to Xai-Xai, Maxixe, and Beira. There's little to choose between them in terms of comfort and speed, but Transportes Virginia leave from a far more convenient spot, in front of the Hotel Universo on the corner of Ave Karl Marx and Ave Eduardo Mondlane. You can buy your ticket from the office in the basement of the hotel the day before you leave. Oliveiras leave from the top end of Ave 24 de Julho. The bus to Vilanculos leaves at 6.30am and arrives at 5pm, stopping at Xai-Xai, Inhambane and Maxixe.

Most buses leave at between 5am and 6am – it is important to be there as early as five because buses will leave as soon as they are full. Buses which go all the way to Beira often leave at 1pm and spend the night in Maxixe or Xai-Xai.

There are one or two companies that offer tours of Maputo and further afield. Expresso Tours (tel 01-431662/4; fax 01-431665, e-mail exptours@emilmoz.com) do one, two and three-day tours to Inhaca Island, Bazaruto Islands, Xefina, Xai-Xai for between $50 and $200.

International buses

Several companies provide transport to and from South Africa and Maputo. Panthera Azul (tel 01-494238; fax 01-498315) leave from Julius Nyerere in front of the Piri-Piri restaurant for Johannesburg (daily 8am, Sundays 9am), Durban (Thurs and Sat 7.30am) and Nelspruit (times as Jo'burg). Expresso Tours (see above) also go to South African destinations such as Kruger National Park and Nelspruit. Tropical Air Tours (tel 01-425078 or 431006/7) run daily buses to Johannesburg and Nelspruit, leaving at 8am from Ave 24 de Julho 909. Lastly Translux leave daily for Johannesburg from near the SAA offices in Praça 25 de Junho.

Hitching

If you want to hitch into South Africa the best place to start is Matola, just outside Maputo going west. Walk or pick up a *chapa* on Ave 24 de Julho or Ave 25 de Setembro and ask to be set down in Matola. If you're going north take a *chapa* to Benfica or Infulene and start from there.

Car Rental

The major international car rental companies Avis, Hertz and Europcar operate in Maputo, as well as Imperial and Rent-a-Car. Travel agents have details, or contact the companies direct. Addresses below. Most have offices at the airport and can be contacted from major hotels.

Car hire companies

Avis	tel 01-465140
Hertz	tel 01-491001 (in the Polana Hotel) or 494982
Europcar	Ave Julius Nyerere 1418, tel 01-497341, fax 01-497334
Imperial	tel 01-493543, fax 01-493540
Rent-a-Car	tel 01-422506.

CITY TRANSPORT

Public transport

Chapas – which in Maputo are usually 20-seater minibuses – can be flagged down anywhere. They are unofficial, ubiquitous, frequent, cheap, and almost always packed to capacity. There is a conductor who will take your money (around 5 cents depending on the length of the journey), wedge you into any available space and give you the nod when you need to get off. Official city buses run on the major routes, tending to go to the city limits and beyond. Bus stops can be found outside the main station, the major squares, the Natural History Museum, and the larger markets. They are recognisable by white signs with all the letters of the alphabet on them, a complicated system denoting the route of the bus, which does not need explaining here. They are slightly more expensive than the *chapas* – around 10 cents a journey.

Taxis

Taxis are widely available in Maputo, mostly from outside the airport, the bigger hotels, in front of the railway station, and the major squares and markets. Some have meters that should not necessarily be trusted – you should expect to pay $3-$4 for a journey within the city centre. Most hotels will book a taxi for you. Polana Taxis (01-493255) is one of the most reliable firms.

Private Car

Driving in Maputo is a good deal safer than anywhere else in Mozambique. Remember to drive on the left and watch out for potholes. Driving at night should not present a problem in the better-lit thoroughfares, but be very careful in unlit streets.

Maputo's traffic police are as zealous and as potentially dishonest as they are in any major city. Traffic police wear white shirts and blue trousers (or skirts) and only they are authorised to stop you for traffic violations. You may also be stopped by national police (in grey uniforms) who may ask you to drive to the nearest police station. You should carry all the necessary documents with you in the car at all times – insurance, vehicle registration, drivers licence and import papers. It is not uncommon for police to try to supplement their incomes with on-the-spot 'fines'. If you are sure your papers and safety gear are in order, stand your ground. You may decide it's easier in the end to pay – after all they won't be asking for more that $10 – in which case make sure you get a receipt. Remember always to be scrupulously polite and patient with any uniformed official.

Car crime

You need not be a victim of car crime if you take simple precautions. Always leave your car in a guarded parking lot during the day as well as at night (any restaurant or hotel with customers who arrive by car will employ a full-time guard). You'll notice that cars parked in the street seldom have windscreen wipers – it's a good idea to remove them, and your hubcaps, or somebody else will. Obviously never leave anything in the car that will tempt someone to break a window and help themselves. Whenever and wherever you stop, a small boy will appear and ask you if you want him to look after the car for a small fee. Visitors to the city usually cough up half a dollar. Locals send him away with nothing.

Ferries

Ferries to Catembe, Inhaca, Macaneta, Ponta de Ouro, Ponta Malongene and other resorts around Maputo are covered in *Inhaca* on p.133.

Maputo suffers from a shortage of mid-range accommodation, and you'll find prices a good deal higher than in other southern and east African capitals. But there are plenty of hotels and you shouldn't have any difficulty in finding a fairly decent room for your stay. There are no campsites in Maputo itself: the nearest place to camp is Macaneta, 37km north of Maputo (see below).

Top of the range

Hotel Polana, Ave Julius Nyerere 1380; tel 01-491001/7; fax 01-491480; e-mail mail@hpolana.uem.mz. Double $130-$250, single $115-$235, breakfast included. Billed as one of the finest hotels in Africa the Polana has been lavishly restored and has all the facilities expected of an international five-star hotel – pool, duty-free shops, bars, conference rooms, gym, casino, bakery. If you're not staying, pay a visit – the setting is quite beautiful. You could even have a cup of tea on the terrace overlooking the bay. More practically, hotel reception will organise speedboat trips and charter planes to Inhaca and other resorts. You can also make international calls from the tiny business centre in the lobby at reasonable cost, as well as send faxes and e-mails, and log on to the Internet.

Hotel Cardoso, Ave Mártiries de Mueda 707; tel 01-491071; fax 01-491804. Double $145-$240, single $115-$210, breakfast included. Almost as luxurious as the Polana, with the added advantage of an even more beautiful position facing west over the bay. A sundowner from the Cardoso gardens is a delight.
Terminus Ave Francisco Orlando Magumbwe 587 and Ave Sekou Touré; tel 01-491333; fax 01-491284. Double $95, single $65-80. Modern, pleasant and central, with all the facilities from satellite TV to swimming pool. Provides pick-up service from airport.
Hotel Tivoli, Ave 25 de Setembro 1321; tel 01-4244353; fax 01-424966. Double $100-$110, single $80-$90. One of the few good hotels in the business district; very handy if you're in Maputo simply for business. All modern facilities.
Hotel Escola Andalucia, Ave Patrice Lumumba 508; tel 423051/4; fax 01-422462. Double $110, single $65, breakfast included. Air conditioning, swimming pool and conference facilities. The hotel is also the training school for the hoteliers of Maputo, and the service and food has an excellent reputation.
Residence Kaya Kwanga, Rua D. Joao de Castro 321 (next to Mini-Golf complex on the Marginal); tel 01-492215/492806, fax 01-492704. Double $105, single $100, breakfast included. Pleasant thatched bungalows, restaurant, pool, tennis court, children's play area and conference centre. Meals served outside by the pool.
Rovuma, Rua da Sé 114; tel 01-305000; fax 01-305305. Double $120-$210, single $95-$185, breakfast included. At the time of writing the Rovuma is still undergoing extensive renovation. One of the best-known hotels in Maputo.
Vila dos Pescadores, Ave de Marginal 12020 (just after Costa do Sol); tel/fax 01-450301. Double $65, suite (6 beds) $120, luxury double suite $250. Just built, very clean and pleasant. Also has large self-contained reed-roofed apartments with kitchen. The complex is perfectly-situated for trips out to Inhaca, which can be arranged for around $100 for 20 people. There is also the fishing village nearby and a daily fish market.

Mid range

Pensão Martins, Ave 24 de Julho 1098; tel 01-424930/5/8; fax 01-429645. Double $60-$70, single $35-$65. Central, recently renovated, friendly staff, clean, spacious rooms. Gets booked up with conferences and aid workers. Swimming pool, excellent restaurant attached to the hotel.
Hotel Moçambicano, Ave Filipe Samuel Magaia 961; tel 01-429252. Double $85, single $65, breakfast included. Recently renovated with bar and pool.
Residencial Hoyo-Hoyo, Ave Francisco Orlando Magumbwe 837; tel 01-490701; fax 01-490724. Double $55, single $35, breakfast included. Private parking, TV in all rooms. One of the newest hotels in Maputo.

Costa do Sol, Ave de Marginal; tel 01-455115; fax 01-455162. Double $20-30, breakfast included. Part of the Costa do Sol restaurant, the hotel rooms are old-fashioned and a bit on the small side.

The Burger Inn, Bairro de Triunfo (just before Costa do Sol). Tel 01-455211. Double $20-30. Good large double rooms with fan, communal bathrooms, 'English' breakfast included in the price. Restaurant attached.

Budget

Fatima's, Ave Mao Tse Tung 1317, near corner of Ave Vladimir Lenine. Doubles and singles around $10. Fatima is a local woman who has set up a hostel in her spacious detached house in an upmarket residential district. The rooms, around a central courtyard, come with and without bathrooms. Now one of the most popular backpackers' hostels in Maputo, it's a convivial place and good for swapping information with other travellers, even if you're not staying there. Cooking facilities and fridge stocked with beer and Fanta, limited safe parking, English-speaking staff.

Pensão Continental, Ave Felipe Samuel Magaia, near Mercado Central. Nice clean rooms, dining room and bar. Good value.

Hotel Turismo, Ave 25 de Setembro, corner of Ave Karl Marx; tel 01-305284. Double $35-50, single $30. Old-fashioned and shabby but clean. Useful for the business district. Close to the railway station and Praca dos Trabalhadores.

Tamariz, Rua Consiglieri Pedroso 102; tel 01-422596. Doubles and singles $30-50. Near the Turismo, convenient and tidy but not particularly good value for money.

Hotel Universo, Ave Eduardo Mondlane, corner of Ave Karl Marx. Double $25 with bathroom. Decrepit but handy, with the main office of Transportes Virginia in the lobby, and the buses leaving from outside the door.

Pensão Central, Ave 24 de Julho, near corner of Ave Vladimir Lenine; tel 01-424476. Double $18. Good big doubles, clean but fairly noisy. Very central.

Pensão Africana, Ave Romao Fernandes Farinha, near corner of Ave Eduardo Mondlane. $12 per bed in dormitory of four. Restaurant and bar downstairs. Chaotic and dirty, but friendly and lively. Excellent atmosphere, good value.

Hotel Santa Cruz, Ave 24 de Julho, near corner of Ave Amilcar Cabral. Double $20-30. Recently renovated, clean but uninspiring.

Pensão Nini, Ave Julius Nyerere, near corner of Ave Eduardo Mondlane. Double $36, single $18. Limited safe parking. Near Mundos Bar and other popular restaurants and bars. Fairly clean rooms, no ensuite, decrepit bathrooms.

Pensão Alcobaca, near Mercado Fajardo in Ave de Trabalho. $7 for shared room. Residential pension with bar. Dingy.

Hotel Girassol, Ave Patrice Lumamba, near corner of Amilcar Cabral; tel 01-421644. Double $8-10 with bath. One of Maputo's cheapest. Dingy but easy on the pocket.

Eating and Drinking

You need never be bored in Maputo. The city has a heady Mediterranean feel and a sophisticated club scene. There are bars and restaurants to cater for every palate and pocket. Whether you're interested in the finest international cuisine or chicken piri-piri, if you like your beer straight from the can or from a glass with a little paper doily, if you want a strip show or an American jazz band, Maputo has it. Things don't get going until late at night – it's not uncommon to eat at 10pm or later, and then go on to a bar or club.

A good place to start is the Ave Julius Nyerere, at the south end near the junction of Ave 24 de Julho. Some locals call this the Golden Mile because of the wealth of restaurants and bars. Later on you might head up to Mini-Golf on the Marginal, where, along with Maputo's beau-monde you can practice your golf putting, have a meal and then swing a shoe at one of the disco nights. If your taste runs to slightly more earthy pleasures, head down to the Feira Popular. As the sun comes up, you can stroll along Ave 25 de Setembro, have a continental breakfast at the Café Continental, and watch the businessmen going off to work.

Polana district

Hotel Polana, (see *Accommodation* above) the Polana has several restaurants, a couple of which do very good value set meals for around $18 per head. The coffee shop sells excellent pastries and cakes made on the premises.

Hotel Cardoso, (see *Accommodation* above) recommended for three-course blow-outs for $16-18 per head. Check out the restaurant's international theme weeks.

Bar Mundos Ave Julius Nyerere 657, on the corner of Ave Eduardo Mondlane; tel 01-494080. This is the place to go if you feel you need to get acclimatised to Maputo. The owner, Albert, keeps his bar well-stocked with imported beers, and offers a varied menu of excellent burgers, meat and pasta dishes, and weekend breakfasts. A popular hang-out for expats and locals, Mundos is a good central meeting place.

Jardim Quadrado, Ave Julius Nyerere, next to Mundos. Upmarket open-air restaurant specialising in Mexican and Portuguese dishes.

Pequim, Ave Julius Nyerere 822, opposite Mundos; tel 01-493899. Main courses of seafood and steaks average around $8. Pequim has an excellent reputation.

A Grelha, Ave Julius Nyerere 967; tel 01-494095. Steak and seafood with an Italian slant. Average price $10 main course. Highly recommended by all who have eaten there.

La Bussola, Ave Julius Nyerere 866. $10 average. Good music. Portuguese dishes served on the terrace.

Green Rabbit, Ave Julius Nyerere. A nice, very clean little terrace restaurant in a residential area. General, good quality burger-based meals and a decent wine and beer list.

Sheik, Ave Mao Tse Tung, corner of Ave Julius Nyerere; tel 01-490197. Very upmarket international cuisine, night-club and disco. $10 to get in on Fridays and Saturdays, less on Thursdays.

Mini-Golf, Marginal; tel 01-490382. You can eat at Mini-Golf's restaurant but the place's reputation is as *the* premier disco for Maputo's beau-monde. Generally open till 4 or 5am Tuesday to Saturday, tea dances Sunday afternoons. Men pay $8, women $4.

Clube Maritimo, Marginal; tel 01-496345. Very good seafood and an excellent Sunday lunch buffet for around $15. You should also try eating in the bar/restaurant at the back of the fish market opposite the Clube Maritimo on the Marginal, until around 7pm. Decide what fish you want and somebody will fetch it for you. If you don't go with someone who knows what they are doing, make sure you know the price of the fish you're buying.

Cristal II, Ave 24 de Julho 554; tel 01-497595. Main courses for $6-7. Wide range of Portuguese dishes.

O Petisco, Ave Francisco Orlando Magumbwe 837; tel 01-480701. Part of the Hoyo-Hoyo complex, near Piri Piri (see below), O Petisco is rapidly gaining a reputation for its Indian food. Worth a look.

Costa do Sol, Ave da Marginal; tel 01-455115. Main courses around $10. Accessible by bus (take it to the very end of the Marginal, to where the road becomes a track. The restaurant is on your left). Costa do Sol is one of the oldest restaurants in Maputo and does excellent seafood, with prawns a speciality. Especially good at lunchtime. Well worth a visit.

Piri Piri, Ave 24 de Julho 3842; tel 01-492379. Piri Piri has the atmosphere of a buzzing European fast-food joint. The chicken is excellent and it can be interesting to sit outside on the busy intersection of 24 de Julho and Julius Nyerere, watching the happenings in the street.

Ungumi, Ave Julius Nyerere 1555; tel 01-490951/11. Near the Polana Hotel, Ungumi nurtures its reputation as the finest restaurant in Maputo, and you should have a look even if you can't afford to eat there. It is housed in the beautiful early-20th-century residence of a wealthy colonial family, which at independence became the Vietnamese Embassy. The walls of Ungumi's three small dining rooms are hung with modern Mozambican art. The average meal costs from $80-100.

Villa Italia, Ave Friedrich Engels 635; tel 01-497298. $8 Average. This attractive restaurant has been set up in a private house with garden, pool and terrace. Wide variety of Italian dishes, take away service, desserts a speciality.

Restaurant 1908, Ave Eduardo Mondlane, corner of Salvador Allende; tel 01-424834. Housed in the former hospital of Lourenço Marques (the pillars carry the stamp of a Glasgow forge) before it moved to its present premises next door, Restaurant 1908 serves Italian, Mozambican and Indian dishes. The waiters wear starched white uniforms and the decor is colonial, and there's a less formal eating area outside. Worth a visit.

Pensão Martins, Ave 24 de Julho 1098; tel 01-424926. The restaurant attached to the pensão has a pool and a barbecue area. Very pleasant, Mozambican dishes. Good bar selection.

Baixa District

Feira Popular, Ave 25 de Setembro, near corner of Vladimir Lenine. The atmosphere of the Feira Popular is something between a fairground and the 'village' at the end of a rock festival when most people have departed, leaving only the hard core behind. This isn't to say it doesn't get lively – it does, but it's a kind of sozzled liveliness that leaves you longing for your bed. The Feira was conceived by Samora Machel in the first heady days of independence as a playground for the underprivileged children from the Maputo slums. Now the children and their climbing frames have long gone (though dodgems and a clutch of other rides and sideshows still remain) leaving a square kilometre or so of shack-like bars and clip-joints minded by tough locals, beery ex-pats and brassy women, and a couple of high-quality eateries it's worth the taxi-fare to visit. There is a secure car park outside where you can leave your car for around 50c.

If this makes Feira Popular sound seedy, it's meant to. But seediness is fine in its place and if you're in the right mood you can have an excellent evening – far more of the real Maputo experience than the svelte jazz bars in the centre of town. If you've only got a couple of nights in Maputo, spend one of them here.

There are 61 bars in the Feira, and the best thing to do is simply wander around and see what takes your fancy. One of the best places to eat is *A Cegonha* (tel 01-425561) a Mozambican-Portuguese restaurant with a reputation for its Zambesi dishes, or *Restaurante Escorpiao* (tel 01-302180), which has reasonably-priced, excellently-cooked dishes. Closed on Mondays. Also have a look at *O Coqueiro*, *Lua* (Chinese), *Esplanada Oriental* (Indian), and *Quisquo Portugália* (Portuguese).

Other restaurants in Baixa include:

Tai Pan, Rua Consiglieri Pedroso 343; tel 01-425534. Reputed to be the best Chinese food in Maputo, as well as having excellent views over the city at night.

Cafe Lily Ave Ho Chi Min, opposite the Immigration office. An Ethiopian restaurant with a good reputation.

Macau, opposite Feira Popular. Smart Chinese restaurant.

Radio Mozambique Restaurant at the top end of the Jardim Tunduru Botànico is a very agreeable place for a meal or an ice cream, overlooking the gardens and a stone's throw from the tennis courts.

Other restaurants around the city:

A Tasquinha, Ave de Angola 2770; tel 01-465628/9. Quite a long way out, near the Praça 21 de Outubro in the north-west of the city, A Tasquinha is recommended. Specialises in beef cooked on a hot stone, and crab. $8 average.

Ze Verde, Ave de Angola 2952; tel 01-465084. Near A Tasquinha, this is a Portuguese restaurant. Bacalhau (salt cod) and caldo verde are a speciality. Average $8. Closed Sundays.

Micael, Rua da Resistencia 185. A jolly Brazilian place with live music on Saturdays.

Ivana, Ave dos Presidentes; tel 01-418554. Zambesian food. Closes around 9pm but worth a visit if you're in this part of the city.

Pont Final Takeaway, Ave Eduardo Mondlane and corner of Ave Guerra Popular. This buzzing fast food restaurant is very popular with locals. All the usual chicken dishes, very reasonably priced.

Cafés

Maputo gains a lot of its Mediterranean atmosphere from its café life. On Ave 25 de Setembro, just down from the Jardim Tunduru Botànico, the *Café Continental* is a fine place to have a beer or a coffee and watch the street life, especially as just over the road is a decent little street market selling batiks, wooden and ivory carvings and other curios. The *Café Djumbu* nearby does good breakfasts. Other places for a coffee are the bars in the big hotels – the *Polana* and the *Cardoso* especially – and any number of little dives round town. There are also some good ice cream shops, notably *Ti'Palino* on Ave 25 de Setembro, *Beijo Gelado* on Ave 24 de Julho, *Esquimo Sorvete* on Ave Julius Nyerere and *Gelados Tropical* also on Julius Nyerere, near Piri Piri.

Exploring

You are likely to spend almost all of your time in two main districts of Maputo, **Polana** and the **Baixa**. The former is the area to the east of Ave Amilcar Cabral and south of Ave Mao Tse Tung. It has wide, tree-lined residential streets, lots of smart bars and restaurants, and the two best hotels in Maputo, the Cardoso and the Polana. Some of Maputo's smartest addresses are in this part of town, especially around Avenida Julius Nyerere, overlooking the bay. In the Baixa, the area to the south of Ave 24 de Julho and more or less to the west of Ave Amilcar Cabral, is the main business district, strung out along Ave 25 de Setembro, where you'll find some excellent cafés and bars. Most of the foreign embassies are here, as well as government buildings, and some of the busiest markets.

Except for the streets that follow the curve of the bay – the arterial Avenida Marginal and its neighbouring roads – Maputo is laid out in a grid pattern. It is easy to orient yourself by following one of the four main streets, Ave Eduardo Mondlane and Ave 24 de Julho which bisect the city west to east, and Ave Vladimir Lenine and Ave Karl Marx, running south to north.

You may come up against the new system of road numbering, recently introduced by Maputo city council on the grounds that only 450 of the city's 2,400 roads have names. Each number is in two parts, the first digit – 1-5 – representing one of the five business districts, and the second three digits referring to the road. Ave Karl Marx, for example, is 1.177. At present the system doesn't seem to impact on house or building numbers, and for the purpose of this book we have ignored it.

Maputo is very easy to explore on foot: you can traverse the centre in an hour. A good place to start is the **Cathedral of Nossa Senhora de Conceição** off the Praça da Independencia in the Baixa. It is extraordinarily ugly, the original 'whited sepulchre', completed in 1944 and built mainly with forced labour. The **Conselho Municipal**, built around the same time, stands at the top of the square. One block south-west of the square is the **Jardim Botánico Tunduru**, an oasis in the middle of Maputo, whose gardens were designed by an Englishman, Thomas Honey. At the top of the gardens is the **Café Radio Moçambique**, where you can watch Maputo's smart set as they amble out of the tennis club next door. The main entrance to the gardens is on Ave Samora Machel, near the **Casa de Ferro**, a bizarre house made entirely of iron plates, and designed by Gustav Eiffel (of Eiffel Tower fame). It was built in 1892 for the Governor General of Mozambique but, chic as it must have seemed to live in an iron box, it soon became clear it wasn't compatible with the African climate. Now civil servants have the pleasure of working there – if you peer through the windows you can see them perspiring at their desks. Also at the entrance to the gardens is a bronze statue of Samora Machel, donated by the late North Korean president Kim Il Sung.

Just to the west of the Praça da Independencia, on the corner of Ave Josina Machel and Felipe Samuel Magaia, is a **memorial** to Great Trek leader Louis Trichardt, erected at the very spot where the intrepid Boer is supposed to have dropped dead from malaria after walking from South Africa.

One block south of the Jardim Botánico is Praça 25 de Junho, which has a thriving **curio market** at weekends (get there before 3pm), the **Museu de Moeda**, and the **Fortaleza**. Due south is the port, which once unloaded 500 ships a year and accounted for half the entire commercial activity of Mozambique. Moribund during the war it is now considerably more active, and well worth a visit if you like to watch busy docks. From Praça 25 de

Junho you should go west up Rua Consiglieri Pedroso for five minutes, until you get to the **railway station**, built at the end of the 19th century as the railway opened to South Africa and sent Mozambican trade soaring. It's a magnificent building, a gorgeous confection in green and white, and one of the great sights of this surprising city.

If you're interested in statues you might decide to have a look at Eduardo Mondlane's, at the western end of the Ave Eduardo Mondlane. If not, you could take any one of the main streets (Patrice Lumumba, 24 de Julho, Eduardo Mondlane) and either get a bus or walk all the way to the east of the city, and the Polana district. Going down these generous avenues, lined with shops, restaurants and banks, gives you a good idea of the scale of Maputo.

In Polana don't miss walking along Ave Friedrich Engels, which looks onto the perfect natural harbour of Maputo Bay. This is the smartest part of Maputo; the road takes you past the Cardoso Hotel, the **Natural History Museum** and the **Presidential Palace**, then snakes up to the north and the ultra-smart Polana Hotel. It then goes into Ave Julius Nyerere, where you will find most of the best restaurants (*Mundos* is a focal point) and bars.

 # NIGHTLIFE

Depending on your tastes, there are several areas that shouldn't be missed. Rua de Bagamoio, which runs between Praca dos Trabalhadores and Praca 25 de Junho, used to be known as the Street of Sin but it's calmed down a bit. It still has a few very seedy bars which are worth a look – one of the most lively is the bar in the *Central Hotel*. Nearby on Ave Zedequias Manghanela is *Eagles Bar*, packed at the weekends and allegedly open until the last customer leaves. Behind that is the *Clube Desportivo*, which has live music most weekends (check the local papers for details). It can get very full and people tend to demonstrate their opinions of the bands by throwing glasses, often at each other and anyone who happens to get in the way.

A few blocks east is the Feira Popular (as described above, p125), where you can eat quite cheaply. Before about 11pm the Feira is a little quiet, but you'll always find a pool game or someone to talk to until things get going.

The more salubrious bars and restaurants are to be found in the Polana area. *Mundos* (address above) is a good place to start an evening: walking up Ave Julius Nyerere towards Ave Mao Tse Tung you'll find *Joy's Piano Bar* (Ave Julius Nyerere 945; tel 01-497325) which is exactly what you'd expect a piano bar to be, and *Sheik* (address above), with a disco downstairs, a jazz bar upstairs frequented by Maputo's smart set, and a stiff entrance fee. There must be thousands of places like it round the world, where professional couples go to relax in 'classy' surroundings. They are characterless places, but agreeable nonetheless. Also on Ave Julius Nyerere is *La Bussola*, a favourite hangout for the Portuguese community.

Other bars and clubs include the sophisticated (and expensive) *Clube 7* (Ave Vladimir Lenine 2236), and the small but vibrant *Khwana*, near the Xipamenine market in the Mafalala district.

CINEMA, THEATRE, DANCE AND MUSIC

Any of Maputo's daily newspapers – in particular *Savana* – lists cinema programmes. Films on offer include imported 'B' movies, kung-fu, the latest Hollywood releases, and Indian movies. Almost all are dubbed into Portuguese. The main cinemas are the Xenon (Ave Julius Nyerere) which shows mainstream American movies, Gil Vicente (Ave Samora Machel) and the Scala (Ave 15 de Setembro 1514). Other cinemas are the Olimpia, the Império, Cinema Matola and Cinema 700. See local press for details. Tickets cost $1.50 to $3.

Maputo has a thriving theatre and dance scene, often with students and young people mounting shows which fuse traditional dance (such as Mapiko) with more avant-garde elements. Check the daily press for details of what's on at Clube Matchedje (Ave 24 de Julho and Travesia de Varieta; tel 01-402153) where small professional companies put on performances of modern and traditional African dance, music and theatre. Other theatres are Teatro Avenida (Ave 25 de Setembro) which is a good place to see a Mapiko dance and Casa Velha (Ave Patrice Lumumba).

Mozambican groups such as Ghorwane and rappers like MC Roger regularly play in Maputo. Keep an eye on what's on at the Pavilhão de Desportivo (behind Eagles Bar on Ave Zedequias Manganhela).

MUSEUMS AND ART GALLERIES

You should not miss the gothic splendour of the **Natural History Museum** (Rua dos Lusíadas, opposite the Cardoso Hotel; tel 01-491145) with its stuffed monkeys (all wearing slightly peeved expressions) and complete collection of elephant foetuses. At the time of writing it is being renovated but should be open to the public by 2000. If it seems closed, find a caretaker or one of the workmen and ask if you can have a look around. If you are at all interested in the recent history of Mozambique you should make a point of visiting the **Museu da Revolução** (24 de Julho and Albert Luthuli; tel 01-400348, open daily from 9am-12pm, 2pm-6pm, closed Saturday morning). As well as Eduardo Mondlane's VW, the museum's four floors house the most comprehensive collection of documents, photographs and militaria depicting the history of the revolution. Another interesting visit (again, closed to the public at present but it shouldn't be difficult to get someone to let you in) is the **Military Museum** in the Fortaleza (just off Praça 25 de Junho). The 19th century fort is an impressive sandstone building, worth a look even if you can't get into the museum. The **Museu da Moeda** (Praça 25 de Junho; tel 01-420290), might not have the most fascinating of displays – the history of money in Mozambique – but the building it is housed in is the oldest in Maputo and should be seen. Lastly, if you are interested in geology the **Museu de Geologia** (24 de Julho 355; tel 01-498053) is lovingly curated and gives a detailed history of the geology of the country.

There are one or two art galleries and cultural centres that are worth visiting. The **Centro Cultural Franco-Moçambicano** (Praça da Independencia; tel 01-420786) runs cultural events, theatre, music and dance, film festivals and art exhibitions. The **Museu Nacional de Arte** (Ave Ho Chi Min 1233; tel 01-420264) is the best place to get an idea of the variety of Mozambican painting and sculpture, with a permanent display featuring artists such as Naguib, Malangatana, Alberto Chissano and Mucavele. The **Núcleo de Arte** (Rua da Argélia 194, off Julius Nyerere, open daily except Sundays), is a cooperative workshop which mounts displays by local artists, and is also a popular meeting place for the more bohemian locals and ex-pats.

Maputo's street markets are a delicious assault on the senses. Like all the best markets they are cacophonous, and smell pungently of ripe and rotting fruit, fish, birdshit, sweat and alcohol. They draw you in and keep you till you emerge the other end with filthy feet and ribs bruised by jostling elbows. The best place to start is the **Mercado Central** (Ave 25 de Setembro, two blocks east of the railway station), in a fine turn-of-the-century building. One of the busiest markets in Maputo, it has everything from fresh fish and fruit and veg to soap and candles. Further north is the **Mercado Estrela** (Albert Luthuli and Emilia Daússe), where you can buy clothes, shoes and household electricals. Other markets include the **Xipamanine Market** in the Mafalala (at the northern end of Albert Luthuli), a massive affair known for its traditional medicine stalls selling dried monkey paws and the like. South-west of Xipamanine is **Mercado Fajardo** (Ave de Trabalho, off Praç 21 de Outubro) a completely chaotic outdoor market where you'd be wise to keep a tight hold of your bag. Several of the markets are good for a meal or a drink. One of these is **Mercado Janeth** (at the eastern end of Ave MaoTse Tung); another is the Bazar do Povo (Ave Karl Marx and Ho Chi Min).

Bookshops

The best place for books in English is *Sensações* (Ave Julius Nyerere 657, next door to Mundos), which has a good selection of new and second-hand novels, children's books, magazines and stationary. *Minerva Centrale* (Rua

Pedro Goso) and *Interfranca* (Ave Julius Nyerere) have good selections of Portuguese books and magazines, though nothing in English.

Changing money

It is unnecessary to list the banks in Maputo. You will be able to change dollars and travellers cheques at most branches of Banco Comercial de Moçambique and Banco Internacional de Moçambique. There are banks in the Baixa along Ave 25 de Setembro and along Ave 24 de Julho. See *Money* p.59 for more information.

Help and Information *i*

For serious matters – if you are robbed or get involved in any other sort of crime, if you are arrested (either for the right or wrong reasons), or if you fall ill – you should contact your embassy. Consular officials are trained in dealing with such matters, and know the ins and outs of Mozambican local politics and diplomacy. If you are arrested for drugs-related reasons, don't expect them to be able to do very much for you beyond explaining what, and how serious, your situation is. Addresses for the embassies in Maputo can be found in *Help and Information* on p.104.

Tourist Information

Your best bet is the information offices of the Cardoso and the Polana, where they speak excellent English and have up-to-date information on what's on in the city, excursions etc. The Empresa Nacional de Turismo (1203 Avenida 25 de Setembro; tel 01-425011) is not quite so reliable.

Travel agents. For a list of LAM offices and tour operators in Maputo see *Getting Around* p.115.

Post Office and Telecommunications

The main post office is at Ave 25 de Setembro 30, opposite Café Continental. Open weekdays 7.45am-12pm, 2pm-5pm, closed Saturday pm and Sundays. TDM (telecom) offices are at the main post office, and at Ave 24 de Julho 239, and Ave Filipe Samuel Magaia. Public phones can be found in many cafés, bars and kiosks around the city. For shipping parcels, there is a DHL office in Ave 25 de Setembro.

Medical treatment

If you're going to get ill in Mozambique, Maputo's the best place for it to happen, but it can't offer the sort of specialised health care that you will find in South Africa or Zimbabwe. If you really are in trouble you should contact your embassy. However, there are a number of clinics where English is spoken and the standard of care is high. If you go to one of the private clinics, double check your insurance – medical care is extremely expensive. The **Central Hospital** on Ave Eduardo Mondlane has a 24-hour Special Clinic (tel 01-424633) and pharmacy; **Clínica de Sommerschield** (Rua Pereira do Lago 52; tel 01-493924) is a private clinic, also with a pharmacy. Another private clinic is **Urgencias Médicas Domiciliárias** (24 de Julho 823; tel 01-431736/8, or 222 for emergencies), which also has an ambulance available. There is also now a **Blue Cross Clinic (Clínica Cruz Azul)** (Ave Karl Marx 414; tel 01-430213), and a dental clinic at the Hotel Polana.

Libraries and information centres

The British Council Library (Rua John Issa 226; tel 01-421574/5, open 10am-5pm Tuesdays to Fridays, 9am-12.30pm Saturdays) stocks a selection of UK papers; US Information Centre (Ave Mao Tse Tung 542; tel 01-491916) has American literature etc, and a video library; other main libraries are the Mozambique National Library (Ave 25 de Setembro) and the Portuguese Library (Ave Julius Nyerere).

Churches

The Catholic Seminário Maior Pio X (Ave Kim Il Sung) has mass in English at 9am on Sundays; the Anglican Church of St Stephen and St Lawrence (24 de Julho 1516) has mass on Sundays at 10am. There is a synagogue on Rua Tomás Nduda 235, and mosques at Rua de Mesquita, Ave de Angola and Rua de Alegria.

AROUND MAPUTO

The main points of interest around Maputo are the beach resort of Macaneta, the dam at Boane, the islands of Inhaca and Ilha Portuguesa, the Maputo Elephant Sanctuary, and the resorts of Ponta do Ouro and Ponta Malongane. All are accessible by public transport from Maputo.

MACANETA

This is the closest beach to Maputo, 37km north on the EN1. It's easily reachable for a day trip. Expresso Tours (tel 01-431662/4), the Polana or Cardoso Hotels organise trips out there. The beach is attractive but the sea isn't particularly good for swimming or snorkelling. You can camp at *Complexo Turistico Macaneta*, which also has chalets for $60, or stay at the

Incomati River Camp (reservations Maputo on 01-425322), a smart 'barefoot' lodge built from local materials. Accommodation per person per night is $75 (full board) or $40 (self-catering). You can also camp at *Jay's Beach Lodge* (for reservations call Jay on 082-30143), which also has chalets for $100. There are a couple of restaurants and bars, the best being the *Macaneta* at the Complexo Turistico.

BOANE/BARRAGEM DOS PEQUENOS LIBOMBOS

The dam at Boane, 55km from Maputo on the Ressano Garcia/Komatipoort road, makes a good day-trip. You can swim in the lake and the dam (Barragem dos Pequenos Libombos) is an arresting sight. Accommodation is available at *A Palhota* (tel 01-775006), self-catering bungalows for $60, rooms for around $30. There is a restaurant and bar, pool, volleyball and disco. Expresso Tours (01-431 662/4) run day trips, or you could pick up a Johannesburg bus (see *Getting There*) and ask to be set down at Boane.

INHACA

Inhaca Island was of strategic importance during the 16th century reign of Chief Inhaca, who offered hospitality to Portuguese traders and frequently aided shipwrecked sailors - for which he was rewarded with gifts of beads and cloth. He accumulated considerable wealth and political power, dominating an area as far inland as the Lebombo mountains, and controlling all the access routes from the south. Inhaca's ascendancy lasted until 1621, when he quarrelled dramatically with the Portuguese, with the result that they shifted their allegiance north to Xefina Island and the rival chieftain Tembe, who became their principal trading partner.

Inhaca today has a population of about 5,000, which subsists almost entirely by fishing. There are breeding colonies of dugong (sea cow) and turtles around the island, which, although they are protected species, are quite often caught and the meat distributed amongst the island communities. The islanders use the catching of a dugong and the resultant plenty (the enormous mammals render about 300kg of meat) as an excuse for fairly wild celebration.

The island is ringed with gorgeous tropical beaches and has excellent snorkelling, diving, and deep-sea fishing – trips can be arranged from the Inhaca Hotel (see below). Much of the island is protected as a wildlife reserve, and scientific research is carried out from a marine research station to the south of Inhaca Village, where there is also a decent museum of natural history. But the biggest draw for tourists are the island's beaches and coral reefs. Inhaca is easily explorable in a day, although a stay in the Inhaca hotel, recently-refurbished by the Pestana group (responsible for the Polana in

Maputo) is worthwhile if you can afford it. There are also a couple of campsites. Rough camping is not advised.

If you arrive by boat you will land on the west coast at Inhaca Village, a tiny settlement with a market and a couple of bars, and the highly-recommended *Lucas's Restaurant*. This place is very popular with South African tourists, and charges $8-10 for seafood dishes. If you've been fishing you can take your catch there in the evening and they will cook it for you. From the village you can walk to the northern tip of the island where there is a fine lighthouse. The best beaches are on the eastern coast of the island – make your way down the beach down from the lighthouse, a walk of a couple of hours. Locals run an informal tractor-taxi service all over the island, so you should never be stuck for a lift.

Arrival and Departure

The public ferry from Maputo takes three to four hours, costs around $5 and leaves at around 7.30am daily from Ave 10 de Novembro, near Rua Antonio Fernandes and the Fortaleza. To be sure to catch the morning boat, be at the jetty by 6.30am or even earlier. It is essential to check ferry times as they change frequently. The ferry returns the same day: it is quite possible to visit Inhaca in a day. The ferry is operated by Agéncia Marítima, (Ave Karl Marx, harbour end). Other more expensive options include plane and speedboat charter. Fatima (see *Accommodation* in Chapter 1, *Maputo*) arranges speedboats out to the island for $20-30, a good option as you're likely to find other people staying at her place who will be willing to split the cost. The main hotels in Maputo also arrange speedboats, as do *Nkomati Safaris* (tel 01-492612/493553) for $50 per person with a minimum of six people, *Free Spirit* yacht charters (tel 01-455002), and *Mozambique Yacht Charters* (tel 01-431713). Also contact Jorge on 01-494276, who runs boats for around $50 from Thursday to Sunday.

Sabinair does flights from Maputo airport on Saturdays and Sundays for around $50 per person (tel 01-465108).

Accommodation

The only formal accommodation on the island is the *Inhaca Hotel* in Inhaca village (tel 01-429277 in Maputo). Refurbished to international standards, a double costs $80-$160 depending on the season. Otherwise there are a couple of campsites: *Coconut Lodge* at Santa Maria on the southern tip, and another near the lighthouse on the north of the island. There is a small market at Santa Maria but you're advised to take everything you need. Also ask for *Ismael Backpackers*, a hostel/campsite recommended as clean, cheap and safe.

Eating and Drinking

If you're camping you can buy all the necessaries on the island: rice, fish, vegetables, drinks and bottled water. Otherwise there is the hotel (expensive), and *Lucas's* in the village, and a newly-opened bar nearby.

ILHA PORTUGUESA

It's possible to walk across to Ilha Portuguesa, just opposite Inhaca village, but you have to wait for a very low tide. Ask in the hotel for a boat across. The island is a former leper colony and is completely undeveloped, with some beautiful beaches. While it's possible to camp wild on the island it's generally not advised unless you are in a group.

XEFINA ISLAND

The centre of the 16th century chieftain Tembe's fiefdom, Xefina became an important trading link for the Portuguese, who have left their legacy in the form of ancient cannons. Just off the mainland, by the *Costa do Sol* restaurant near the Bairro dos Pescadores (see *Maputo*), it's a pleasant place for a picnic, a swim and a snorkel, and easily accessible by dhow. You can also camp there, but take everything you need – there is a well with fresh water but nothing else.

CATEMBE

Catembe is a fairly downbeat village that used to be a desirable residential area, a ten-minute ferry ride over the bay from Maputo. One of the best reasons for taking the trip (boats from Maputo leave every couple of hours from the jetty on Ave 10 de Novembro) is to visit the *Restaurante Diogo*, whose owner is originally from Goa and who has earned a deservedly high reputation for his prawn dishes. Near the restaurant is a decent-enough beach.

MAPUTO ELEPHANT SANCTUARY

When Lourenço Marques first visited Delagoa (Maputo) Bay in 1542 he found large numbers of elephants in the area. In the 16th century whole communities lived off the elephant herds that roamed the delta. Hunting was a staple part of a sophisticated commercial network, with young men employing a variety of dangerous and highly-skilled methods of tracking and killing, both for meat and for ivory. Trains of 1,000 porters and more were commonplace, wending their way throught the bush to the many ivory fairs that were regularly held.

Nowadays there is little enough wildlife anywhere in Mozambique, and the great wildlife reserves are especially denuded through a combination of the ravages of the civil war, and poaching. Of the great herds of elephant only about 60 are thought to remain, down from a population of 350 in the early 1970s. They migrate to South Africa's Tembe reserve and thus spend large parts of the year outside the sanctuary. A herd of 65 white rhinos introduced from South Africa has been decimated if not wiped out by poachers, and it is thought that only a few leopards, cheetah, buffalo and antelope remain. All are so shy it's highly unlikely you will see any.

There are various plans to restock the park. In 1998 New Orleans businessman John Blanchard – who allegedly lent his support to Renamo during the civil war – promised to raise millions of dollars to revive the area, building a hotel, floating casino and lodges. It remains to be seen whether the project will get off the ground.

At present the only place to stay is the *Msala Bush Camp* on Lagoa Maundo in the reserve (contact Polana Tours; tel 01-493533). For an organised tour you pay $120 per day for full board, and organised game drives both during the day and night. There isn't that much chance of seeing elephant, but other wildlife includes kudu, giraffe and hundreds of birds. The camp is in a wonderful location between the lake and the sea, and the snorkelling is good. If you have your own tent, camping within the bush camp costs $20 – but it shouldn't be difficult to get the price down a bit, depending on where you pitch your tent.

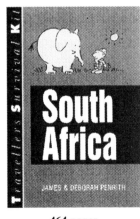

464 pages

Softback Price £10.99

ISBN 1-85458-175-9

Travellers Survival Kit South Africa

Now South Africa has rejoined the international community it is deservedly growing fast as a holiday destination. This guide by well known South African-based writers covers the whole range of the country's attractions, from the natural beauties of the game parks and nature reserves to the man-made pleasures of Sun City.

PONTA DO OURO AND PONTA MALONGANE

Set amongst rolling dunes and dune forest, these attractive beach resorts are about 120km south of Maputo, right on the South African border. They are more accessible from South Africa than Maputo, so if you're coming north you might consider stopping on the way. The area is completely undeveloped apart from the beach resorts, which are extremely popular with South Africans; if you want to stay in the resort during school holidays you should book in advance. The road is not good and requires a 4WD; there's no formal public transport from Maputo – the best way of getting there is to catch the ferry to Catembe and try to hitch a lift. The sea is good for swimming and surfing, but the area is best known for its big-game fishing. You can also hire ski-boats.

Ponta do Ouro is a small fishing village with a couple of shops and little else. The nearby *Centro Turistico Ponta do Ouro* has two- and four-bed chalets for $30-60, and camping for $6 per person. There is also a restaurant and shop. Ponta Malongane is 10km to the north of Ponta do Ouro, also set amongst dune forest. Camping is possible at the *Ponta Malongane Holiday Resort*, which also has beach chalets and a restaurant, and a dive camp where you can hire equipment or organise dive trips.

Gaza

Deep Sea fishermen
Xai-Xai

The province of Gaza borders both Zimbabwe and South Africa, and – inland – is one of Mozambique's most remote and inaccessible regions. Along its 150km coastline are excellent beaches at Xai-Xai and Bilene, and in the centre of the province is the Banhine National Park. There is very little reason for tourists to visit the interior of Gaza – transport is minimal and there is little to see. Banhine is entirely without tourist facilities.

Gaza takes its name from the powerful Gaza monarchy, ruled over by a succession of Nguni chieftains until the end of the 19th Century. Inaccessible though it is to the tourist, it is a well-populated region and produces cashew, cotton, rice and maize, particularly in the fertile Limpopo valley.

BILENE

About 100km north of Maputo, Praia do Bilene lies 33km off the EN1. The resort has a lovely beach on the Uembje Lagoon, which is protected from the ocean by a string of small islands and sand spits. This is the nearest resort to Johannesburg and is very popular with South African families; you shouldn't have any problem camping but you will find all formal accommodation is fully booked during school holidays.

Bilene is very easy to get to. See section on Xai-Xai (below) for details of buses from Maputo. Ask to be set down at the Bilene turn-off at Macia, from where there is frequent transport going down to the town. There are two campsites on the beach, both of them equal in terms of cleanliness and safety. *Campismo Palmeiras* charges around $5 per person and also has three- to four-person chalets for $35-40, and a restaurant and bar. The campsite is clean, well-shaded and safe. Further down the beach is the attractive *Complexo Parque Flors*, and the *Complexo Turistico Lagoa Azul*, which has two-bedroomed fully-furnished chalets for $40-50.

As well as the campsite bars and restaurants, there are a few convivial places along the beach road – check out *Tchin Tchin* and the *Pavilão Tamar* – as well as a market and grocery shops.

ZONGOENE

Set in a vast expanse of rolling sand dunes at the mouth of the Limpopo is the small resort of Zongoene. The river mouth has created a wide area of flat sands which are excellent for 'safari tours' on quad bikes (ask at the Zongoene Lodge for details), and there is good snorkelling, diving and game fishing in the area. The Limpopo flood plain is a fascinating area to explore, bounded by immense casuarina forests. You can also visit the Monte Belo lighthouse, inaugurated in 1914. Zongoene lies about 200km north of Maputo, 36km from the EN1 down a dirt road which is only suitable for 4WD. The turn-off is just before Xai-Xai, in the village of Chimbiane. There is an airstrip which takes charter flights from Maputo.

The only formal accommodation is the recently-opened *Zongoene Lodge*, which consists of individual thatched bungalows, bar, restaurant, terraces and games room. There should be no problem camping either in the grounds or outside, if you ask permission.

XAI-XAI AND PRAIA DO XAI-XAI

Three hours up the coast from Maputo on the excellent EN1, the capital of Gaza province is an unremarkable, dusty but thriving little town with an excellent campsite and a good beach nearby. If you're not planning to stay, Xai-Xai (pronounced 'shy-shy') is also a very good stop-off point, with petrol

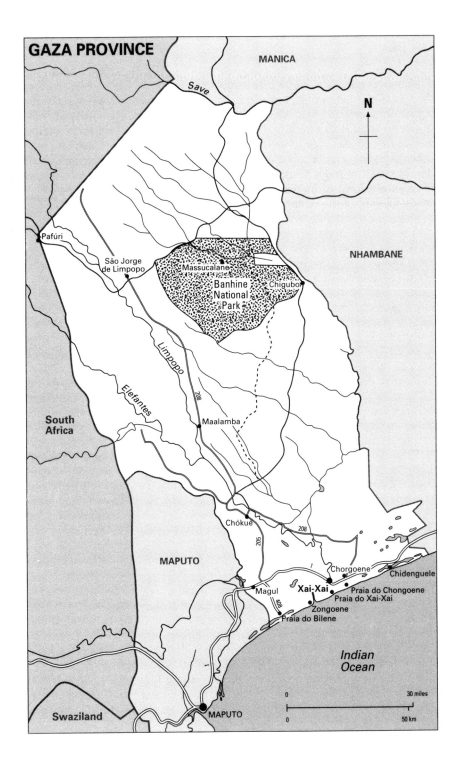

available, supermarkets, post office, telephone exchange, a bank where you can change money (although if you're going to the campsite you can pay for practically everything in rands or US dollars) a busy market, a variety of well-stocked shops (stationers, haberdashers), and a large furniture-making cooperative on the edge of town. There are also a couple of hotels in town, although by far your best bet is to take a chapa down to the beach and either stay in the clean and safe campsite or in the nearby *Halley's Hotel*. While in town have a look at the defunct railway station, just off the main street. A handsome turn-of-the-century Portuguese building, it hasn't seen a train since 1996, and no one is able to say when it will reopen.

The beach is a vast stretch of virgin sand leading down to a fairly rough sea that isn't good for swimming so much as cavorting in the waves. If you're not interested in game-fishing there is little to do except relax on the beach, but it's worth visiting the ruined Chongoene Hotel about an hour's very pleasant walk east along the beach, or 15 minutes' drive along the jeep track which skirts the campsite. The hotel closed fairly recently and its outbuildings are still in good condition, but most of it is in a state of total dereliction, the pool crumbling and the terraces pitted. It's an evocative place, redolent of a vanished and much wealthier era. At the time of writing there are signs of work going on – but it is impossible to predict an opening date.

Also worth seeing is the Wenela tidal pool, 2km west of the campsite. It has a certain reputation amongst the locals, who call it Jordan on account of the baptisms that are sometimes held there. What is interesting is the natural tunnel and blow hole that link the pool to the sea. On no account try to swim into the tunnel – the force of the tide is lethal.

Praia do Xai-Xai has a reputation amongst South African big-game fishermen for the excellence of its deep-sea fishing, and the area is abundant in rock cod and barracuda. The camp-site is usually crowded with laagers of Isuzu trucks and boats, and jolly fishing parties cooking the day's catch. If you want to fish contact Johann Möller, who operates a concession within the campsite. Trips cost $50 and take in the nine reefs around Xai-Xai.

Arrival and Departure

Xai-Xai lies on the EN1, 225 km north of Maputo. Buses leave from Maputo at 6am from the Hotel Universo in Ave Eduardo Mondlane and Ave Karl Marx, or earlier from Praça 16 de Junho on Ave 24 de Julho (see *Arrival and Departure* in *Maputo* for more details), arriving at around 9am. The fare is $5. The bus drops you at the main square in Xai-Xai, from where you can catch a *chapa* to Praia do Xai-Xai, about 12km away. If you are driving take the Maxixe road out of town and turn right just after a BP garage and the Motel Concha on the left. From there it's 10km to a big roundabout from which you should take the first exit, and then a dirt track to your left leads down to

Halley's and the campsite. To get back to the main road, head up to the roundabout and hitch a lift. Expresso Tours in Maputo (tel 01-431662/4, fax 01-431665, e-mail exptours@emilmoz.com) do two-day excursions to Xai-Xai, leaving Maputo at 8am and returning at 3.30pm the following day.

Accommodation

The best place to stay is the campsite, for $5 per site and $3 per person. It's clean and guarded, with plenty of shade, a decent bar and restaurant and good showers. Within the site the fishing concession (see above) provides 12-person reed bungalows for $10 per person and camping for $6 per person. Just before the camp is the pleasant *Halley's Hotel* (double $35-40), with a good restaurant that serves prawns, crayfish and chicken for reasonable prices. Next door to Halley's is a small shop for basic groceries. In town the *Pensão Africana* opposite the bus station has doubles with bath for $20-25, but it's fairly squalid. The *Motel Concha* just outside town on the Maxixe road is cleaner and a better option altogether, with doubles at around the same price. Finally, about 15 minutes walk east from the campsite is the Chongoene Holiday resort, a complex of 15 log cabins which at the time of writing is in the process of being built. Call Pretoria 012-252 4715 or 011-433 8216 for details.

CHIDENGUELE

Thirty kilometres north of Xai-Xai there are beach cottages to let at Chidenguele, and a very secluded campsite on the southern shore of Lagoa Inhampavala. It's probably not worth stopping here unless you're in your own 4WD and fancy a detour. Bring everything you need, although fresh water is usually available from a spring.

Inhambane Province

Dhows at Maxixe

THE COAST TO INHAMBANE

Inhambane Province is the best-developed region in Mozambique, with a string of idyllic palm-lined beaches and the country's greatest tourist attraction, the exquisite Bazaruto Archipelago. The well-surfaced EN1 sticks close to the coast throughout the province's length, and all the resorts are well-served by public transport. Just inland from the coast Inhambane is fertile, the landscape characterised by enormous coconut groves and cashew plantations, both of which are extensively cultivated.

But it is the coastline which captivates visitors. While northern Mozambique is rich in colonial architecture, ancient churches and forts, what lures visitors to the south is the string of unspoiled beaches and accessible coral reefs. Inhambane is famous for its game fishing, diving and snorkelling and is very popular with South African and Zimbabwean tourists, who take over the resorts and campsites during the school holidays. Even in high season, however, the small resorts that line the coast are uncrowded, and you will have no difficulty finding hotel rooms and camping spaces. Inhambane has more hotels than any other province and the main towns – Inhambane itself, Maxixe and Vilanculos – are well-supplied with budget accommodation and campsites. The only exception is the Bazaruto Archipelago: if you intend to stay in one of the islands' main resorts it is essential to book your hotel beforehand, although camping is not a problem on most of the islands.

Although the southern half of the province has some beautiful beaches and lakes, particularly Quissico and Závora, many travellers head straight for the provincial capital Inhambane and its sister town Maxixe. The former, one of the oldest settlements in Southern Africa, is a delightfully old-fashioned little town. It is very well-placed for the beaches of Tofo and Coconut Bay, which are becoming very popular with backpackers.

QUISSICO

The drive through Quissico is magnificent, with perfect views of the string of freshwater lakes that characterise this part of the coast. Except for Poelala (see below) none of the lakes are even remotely developed and so most are difficult to get to, but well worth the effort of asking around and finding out the best paths used by the locals. The lakes are very close to the road but on no account try to make your own way down – there is some danger of landmines. Lagoa Quissico is accessible via a 10km dirt track which goes off the EN1 just outside town. You can get fuel, groceries, fresh fruit and vegetables in the town itself, where there is also a pensão – the *Pousada de Zavala* – and a restaurant called the *Planet Ran Tan Plan* just opposite the bus stop on the EN1. Other than picking up supplies there's no reason to stay in Quissico.

ZÁVORA

Závora beach is as beautiful and unspoilt as any in Mozambique. While South Africans flock here for the game fishing, it is also an excellent place for snorkelling, with low-tide rock pools and some nice reefs. The sea is wide

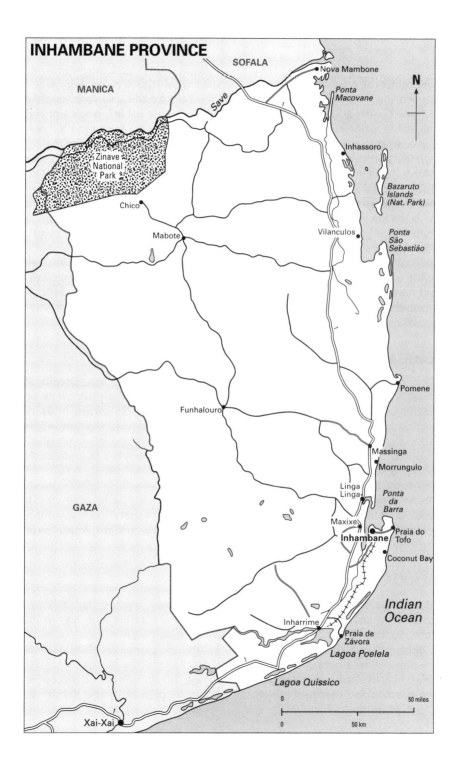

and calm with a coral reef which forms a sheltered lagoon at low tide, so it's a good place for families with children. There is no town as such, just the *Závora Lodge*, a South African-owned campsite with cabins, restaurant and bar, set in a beautiful position high over the beach. You don't need to book for camping (although it would be wise to check how full they are during school holidays) but for cabins it is essential to call in advance, via *Mozambique Connections* in Johannesburg (PO Box 3781, Kempton Park 1620; tel 011-394 8727 or 011-4554046/7). To get to Závora take the Maxixe bus from Xai-Xai, and get out at Inharrime. If it's after dark, there is a pensão at Inharrime where you can stay the night, unless you want to negotiate a taxi, which you can do in the bar on the main road at Inharrime. Otherwise, find a chapa to take you to the turn-off to Praia do Závora, a dirt track marked at the 17km mark north of Inharrime. From there it's about another 10km until you get to Závora Lodge at the end of the road. There is one fork, but the route is clearly signposted. After rain the road would be very difficult in anything but a 4WD. If dry, it's just about passable in a saloon, but it's not recommended.

LAGOA POELALA

One of the most beautiful of the freshwater lakes along this stretch of coast, Poelala – alleged to be Vasco da Gama's first landing place when he put in on Mozambique's southern coast in 1498 – is a haven for birds as well as monkeys, gazelles and other wildlife. A nesting pair of ospreys has been sighted, there are black and white kingfishers, red bishops, lilac-breasted rollers, bee-eaters, three different types of hornbill and hundreds of parrots and parakeets. You can get to the lake from Závora – take the left-hand turn about 700m on the track from the lodge to the main road. An enterprising English/Portuguese couple are setting up a lodge on the lake, and offering sailing and canoeing, watersports, birdwatching expeditions and river trips. Contact Sandy at Black and White Trucks near Pretoria (tel 011-316 4980).

MAXIXE

Maxixe (pronounced 'masheesh') is tough and dirty, bustling and thriving, making its sister town over the bay appear almost effete in comparison. Inhambane, a 40-minute dhow ride away, is altogether cleaner, nicer and more bourgeois than its upstart neighbour. But Inhambane (see below) is a beautiful town, and even if you only have a few hours in Maxixe, a 40-minute trip by dhow over the bay is essential. If you're staying, Inhambane is well-placed for the beaches and backpacker's hostels of the fat peninsular that forms the mouth of the river.

One of the reasons Maxixe has that hustling feel to it is that it is the only place in Mozambique where the EN1 touches the coast. Long-distance trucks rumble through at all hours of the day and night, the seedy hotels on the main road catering for their drivers. Although Inhambane should be your first choice if you're staying a while, if you're on your way up the coast, it's wiser to get a bed in Maxixe. You're perfectly placed for a lift, all the buses leave from here, and being a business area Maxixe has everything from banks to grocery stores.

All the action in Maxixe centres on the **Stop Snack Bar** on the main road. Run by the affable Abdula Hussein, it specialises in *casquinha* (stuffed crab), and also serves excellent seafood and chicken dishes. Next door to Stop is the landing stage for dhows and motorboats for Inhambane. At the end of the road opposite Stop is a large market – excellent for supplies of just about anything, and just before that is the bus station for all buses north and south. There are two or three banks where you can change dollars, a Mobil petrol station (on the left a couple of hundred metres out of town in the Beira direction), and a post office.

Accommodation

The best place to stay in Maxixe is the *Campismo de Maxixe* a hundred metres south of the Stop snack bar. If you're not camping you can rent one of the caravans for $6-$7, otherwise pitches are $3. The staff are friendly and speak some English, and the restaurant serves the best chips in the province. Otherwise there is a selection of fairly ropey hotels: the *Posada do Maxixe* opposite Stop has doubles for $11, as well as an uninviting restaurant. The *Hotel do Golfinho Azul* (tel 023-30228) has doubles for around $13. Outside town on the Beira road is the massive *Motel Palmar*, where buses stop for the drivers to have a meal on the way to Vilanculos. There can't be any good reason to stay, or indeed eat there. Another place slightly out of town on the Vilanculos road is *Residencial Tania*. Its doubles are around $15, and it's no more comfortable than anywhere else in town.

Eating and Drinking

The best places to eat are the campsite and the Stop snack bar. Stop has the bay on one side and the busy EN1 on the other, meaning you can turn away from contemplating the peaceful dhow traffic and the attractive low skyline of Inhambane, to enjoying the sight of overladen trucks and heaving chapas belting past on Mozambique's arterial highway. The food (at about $5 for a main course) is good. Otherwise there's little to tempt you in Maxixe, the *Restaurant Don Carlos* on the road running parallel to the EN1 being uninviting in comparison.

INHAMBANE TOWN

Inhambane is in the centre of coconut country, with groves and plantations lining the EN1 as you approach. Its old-fashioned atmosphere and large Indian population lend it a completely different atmosphere to most other Mozambican towns. Inhambane is one of the oldest settlements between Maputo and Beira. Portuguese traders had been visiting the area since the mid-16th century, and in 1560 a Castilian Jesuit named Gonçalo da Silveira arrived with six companions to set up a mission. This was short-lived: Goncalo himself was murdered on a visit to the Zambesi, attempting to convert the great Monomotapa dynasty to Christianity. Recognised as a trading centre in 1763, together with Sofala and Lourenço Marques it was one of the three garrisoned enclaves set up by the Portuguese. While Sofala fell into decay in the mid-19th century, Inhambane prospered on the proceeds of ivory and slaving. Portuguese domination of the area was informal and depended for its authority on a feudal system whereby the local chieftains paid tribute and supplied manpower when it was needed for any purpose. The trading alliances formed with the chiefs were unstable: in 1838 Inhambane was sacked by Gaza chieftain Soshangane and almost all the trading community killed, and ten years later it became involved in serious hostilities with local Tsonga chiefs. But the town rallied, and in 1858 had a population of 4,000, three-quarters of which were slaves. In the Inhambane area as a whole it is estimated that by the mid-1850s some 55 villages, 22 local minor chiefs and over 50,000 people were subject to Portuguese rule.

Inhambane has aged gracefully. It's as far from a bustling slave and ivory centre as you can imagine, with its dilapidated but elegant buildings and wide, tree-lined streets an evocative reminder of its prosperous past. It's easy to sit for hours on the palm-fringed sea-wall and watch the crabs scuttling on the beach, and up in town there's hardly much more going on. A good time to be in Inhambane is October, for the *Corrida de Barcos a Vela*, the annual dhow race which takes place in the bay.

If you drive in from Maxixe, an hour's journey around the mouth of the river, you see a different side of the town. As you approach you pass a couple of fish factories, and then come to a thriving market, where you can pick up cheap jeans, T-shirts and other useful items of clothing.

The dhows (there is also a motorboat) drop you off at the landing stage just down from the main square. Inhambane is such a pleasant town to walk around, the best way to explore is simply to amble up and down the streets. There is a dusty little **museum** in the Rua Vigilancia that's worth dropping into if you're passing. Just to the right of the landing stage is a telephone exchange where you can make international calls, and you can change money in the **Banco Comercial** at the crossroads halfway between the station and the jetty. Have a look at the station, at the end of the road leading into town from the jetty. At the

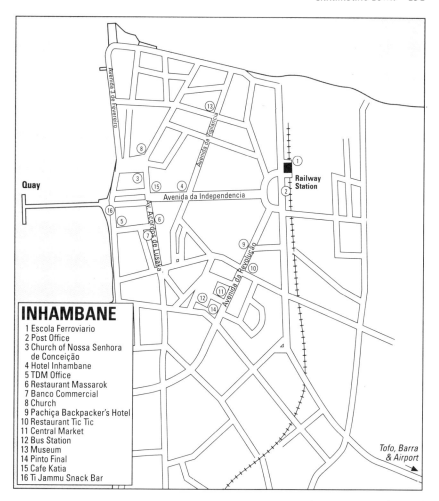

INHAMBANE
1 Escola Ferroviario
2 Post Office
3 Church of Nossa Senhora
  de Conceição
4 Hotel Inhambane
5 TDM Office
6 Restaurant Massarok
7 Banco Commercial
8 Church
9 Pachiça Backpacker's Hotel
10 Restaurant Tic Tic
11 Central Market
12 Bus Station
13 Museum
14 Pinto Final
15 Cafe Katia
16 Ti Jammu Snack Bar

time of writing it is completely defunct – local boys use the tracks as a football pitch. You should also make sure you visit the beautiful 18th century church of **Nossa Senhora de Conceição** to the north of the main square, where you can sometimes climb the bell tower for superb views across the bay.

ARRIVAL AND DEPARTURE

The turn-off to Inhambane on the EN1 comes just after Cumbana, about 30km south of the town. Long-distance buses go straight on to Maxixe, but you can ask to be put down and take a chapa up to Inhambane. The best way to get there is to go to Maxixe and take a dhow or motor ferry across the bay – it's very cheap and a delightful way to approach the town. If you don't want to get your feet wet when you arrive, the boatmen will carry you onto the beach. This is standard practice: men straddle their shoulders, and women (even the most matronly) ride side-saddle.

ACCOMMODATION

For backpackers – if you're not making immediately for the beaches described below – the best place to stay in town is the *Pachiça Lodge* (Ave do Revolução). Run by Isabella Bartlett and her son Richard, it's a neat and convivial hostal with dormitory beds for $6-$7. Cooking and washing facilities, barbecue, meals and drinks are provided. It's a good place to swap information (and books). Otherwise the only other accommodation is the *Hotel Inhambane*, on the corner of Ave Independencia and Vigilencia, which is clean and good value with doubles for $15-$20. Also check the *Escola Ferroviario* next to the railway station, which has 4-bed dormitories for around $16.

EATING AND DRINKING

One of the nicest places to eat in Inhambane used to be the *Ti Jamu Snack Bar* overlooking the bay just by the jetty, but at the time of writing it was closed as it has an idiosyncratic existence. There are a number of cafés and restaurants which are worth a try – the *Café Katia* near the city square, and the *Punto Final* near the market in Ave Revolucão. The best-known restaurant is the *Tic Tic*, also in Ave Revolucão, which has a good reputation for fish, and outside tables on a fairly quiet street. Otherwise try the *Primavera* to the south of the jetty in Ave 25 de Setembro, or the locally-recommended *Massarok*.

 If you have transport and fancy seeing the interior of Inhambane province, an interesting trip might be a visit to Funhalouro, about 120km due west of Maxixe. There are hundreds of baobab trees and very little else, but the stark landscape and tiny settlements are a contrast to the bustling coast. Ask around for a guide in Maxixe or Inhambane.

PRAIA DO TOFO

The northern and eastern part of the Inhambane peninsula has some of the most popular beaches in the area, and most backpackers who are planning a stay of any length in the area head out there at some stage. The snorkelling is reckoned to be the best in southern Mozambique. There are several places to stay up there, either camping or in more formal accommodation – Pachiça

Lodge in town is the best place to pick up the latest information on which of the lodges is open and which has folded. At Tofo the most established place is the *Complexo Turistico do Tofo Mar*, with double rooms for $30-$50, and a restaurant with a reputation for its lobster. There is a hotel behind it with slightly cheaper rooms. You can book in Maputo (tel 01-427352). The best bet for budget travellers is the *Americano*, which has safe camping for $4, dormitories for $6 and rooms for $8-$10. There is also Casa Barry's (tel 023-29007), with self-catering chalets for $40-$60.

PONTO DA BARRA

On the very northern tip of the peninsula, you can get to Barra by taking the sandy road off to the left just before the final turn-off to Tofo. There is a major resort here – *Barra Lodge* – with self-catering chalets, dormitories and camping. Prices vary depending on the season. Alternatively you could try the *Barra Reef*, which at the time of writing is in the process of construction. If there are no rooms available you can camp there.

NORTH OF INHAMBANE

LINGA-LINGA

This beach is best reached by dhow from Morrumbene, 30km up the coast from Inhambane. There is a camp there called *Funky Monkey* (though its continued existence is in some doubt – get an update at Pachiça Lodge) which supports local sustainable development. They also organise boat trips and take tourists out on manatee (dugong) searches.

MASSINGA

Drivers needing a welder recommend the workshop behind the filling station in Massinga, where there is also a restaurant called *Dalilo* which allegedly stocks a variety of imported beers. There is no formal accommodation.

MORRUNGULO

A beach that stands out in a coastline renowned for its beauty, Morrungulo is extremely popular with Zimbabweans and can get very full during the school holidays. The fishing and diving there is excellent, and there is a dive centre at the beach where you can rent everything you need. The resort is about 100km north of Maxixe and is served by a signposted 13km dirt road, negotiable in a saloon car, that branches off the EN1 a few kilometres north of Massinga. To get there by public transport, get off the bus at Massinga and look for a chapa, or ask to get down at the turn-off and try to hitch – not the best option as there's not that much traffic. There is camping on the beach for about $8 per person, and self-catering chalets with all mod cons including hot water for $100 a day. If you're camping you can also hire a barraca – a thatched shelter – for $15 a day. During school holidays it's essential to book, which you can do by calling Meridian Travel in Johannesburg (tel 011-783 7116, fax 011-783 5858), or Harare (tel/fax 04-303504).

POMENE

If you have the time to get there, Pomene could be described as the definitive paradise beach. You're very likely to have the place entirely to yourself, so take everything you need with you. Whale sharks have been sighted here – spending a few days doing nothing but look at the sea is a pleasure in itself, but to see the one of these vast – and supposedly harmless – beasts breaking the surface of the water would be glorious. If you have your own transport, take the unsignposted right hand road about 25km out of Massinga, and then take another right turn about 25km after that. Otherwise, ask at Nhachengue or Massinga (a better bet) if there is any transport going that way. In the end you might end up having to pay someone a few dollars to take you there. There are no facilities of any sort, though local fishermen will sell you their catch.

VILANCULOS

The night-guard at the campsite in Vilanculos carries a loaded Kalashnikov, which says something about this nondescript, sprawling town. What used to be a popular resort before the civil war retains few signs of glamour. There are some nice houses overlooking the beach, especially the palatial Casa Suleiman, which belongs to the local Frelimo member of parliament, but otherwise it's a pretty shabby place, with a reputation for thieving, and grasping locals who are fully aware of the value of every tourist that passes through.

And tourists do pass through, in their thousands. Vilanculos has all the facilities of a large town – a Banco Comercial where you can change dollars (head left along the main road from where the bus drops you off), a post office (opposite the garage – near the roundabout to the right of the bus-stop), supermarkets and a large and bustling market. The town is also served by an international airport, and is the main jumping-off place for the enormously popular Bazaruto Islands, visible from the beach.

Vilanculos is well-served with backpackers' hostels and cheap hotels, and has a couple of decent bars. There are also some diving concerns in the process of being set up – ask at John's Place or the Dona Ana for details. The beach is attractive, but any swimming and snorkelling is infinitely better on one of the islands.

Arrival and Departure

Vilanculos is well-served by all the main-line buses travelling between Maputo and Beira. If you're coming from Maxixe or Inhambane make sure you check bus times carefully – if you miss the early-morning bus you can pick up the Maputo bus on its way up to the Save river, which passes through Maxixe at around 2pm.

You can also fly with LAM direct from Maputo several times a week and from Johannesburg a couple of times a week (timetables change twice a year so you will need to check – see *Maputo* for contact numbers).

Accommodation

The *Campismo de Vilanculos* is cheap and central, but it has a terrible reputation for thieving, and with its dusty pitches and loud gangs of Zimbabwean students it's not a particularly attractive place. *John's Place* the other side of the market (ask for directions) is friendlier and safer, and you can rent a tent if you haven't got your own. Pitches cost $3 with your own tent and twice that without. At the time of writing there's nothing else at the market end of town, but lodges come and go so it's worth asking. Along the beach road there are a number of options. The *Hotel Dona Ana* is a massive bauhaus-style building at the far end of the beach (turn left out of the camping site) with a restaurant, clean but shabby rooms for $8-$20, and safe parking. On the same road, between the campsite and town, *Josefina's* is a complex of spotless two-room and four-room reed cabins, which cost $13-$15 per room, or $40-$50 for the whole cabin. A further 3km out of town past Dona Ana's are two tourist lodges, *Simbire* and the *Last Resort*, which have camping and reed cabins. It should be quite easy to hitch out there.

Eating and Drinking

If you're staying at the campsite the obvious course is to buy your fish or chicken in the market or direct from the fishermen on the beach, and barbecue your supper. Otherwise there is a restaurant that will do you a very decent fish meal with chips for a reasonable price. *Dona Ana* also has a restaurant (closed out of season) with meals for around $4. In town there's the *Bar Ti Zé*, with outside seating and a relaxed approach to service. *John's Place* has a bar and will cook for you, and down on the beach road there are a couple of bars, notably the *Quiosco Tropical*, which serves ice-cold beer and fish meals for around \$4. It has tables overlooking the sea and is a pleasant spot in the evening.

INHASSORO

The drive from Vilanculos to Inhassoro takes an hour along a decent stretch of the EN1. Inhassoro is a nice, relaxed little town, though tourists seldom stop there. It has the advantage of being only 15 km from the main road (down a track that is passable in a saloon, though 4WD would be advisable after rain), and it's also the closest town to Bazaruto, the biggest island in the Bazaruto archipelago. From Inhassoro the best place to organise a motor boat out to Bazaruto or Santa Carolina island is the Seta Hotel, which also has safe parking. There are two places to stay in Inhassoro: the Mozambican-owned *Seta Hotel* (on the main road into town; tel 0152-309 9842) is building bungalows which will go for \$70-\$80 for four people, and at present has clean double rooms for \$20. The campsite costs \$5 per person. Next door to the bus station, about 1km from the hotel, is the recently-renovated *Complexo Salema Mufundisse Chibique*, consisting of restaurant, shop and basic rooms.

THE BAZARUTO ISLANDS

The Bazaruto Archipelago – Bazaruto Island, Benguerra, Magaruque and Santa Carolina – lie 15-20km off the coast, just north of Vilanculos and south of Inhassoro. The most southerly islands, Magaruque and Benguerra, are visible from the beach at Vilanculos. Declared a national park in 1971, the archipelago was one of the few places in Mozambique which it was safe to visit during the civil war, and as a result they have developed a mainly South African-run tourist industry in isolation to the rest of the country. Each of the islands has its own airstrip; apart from the handful of visitors that arrive from Vilanculos or Inhassoro, most people fly in directly from Johannesburg.

With their white beaches, gently-leaning coconut palms, and abundant wildlife, the islands are exquisite. Because of their unusual gestation as a tourist centre they are radically different to the rest of Mozambique. As you sit in your tasteful lodge you could easily imagine yourself on any tropical island anywhere in the world. This might not be to everyone's taste, but the Bazaruto Archipelago is definitely worth a visit. Staying there doesn't have to be prohibitively expensive: there are cheaper lodges and hotels on Santa Carolina and Bazaruto Island. Otherwise, if you can afford the \$100-150 per night needed for the main lodges, you'll experience a level of luxury unheard of outside of the best Maputo hotels. You can also camp on Bazaruto and (at present) on Benguerra. In common with the rest of Mozambique, it should be possible to camp on the beach for free if there are enough of you and if you're far enough away from the hotels. The problem is that the islands are the biggest

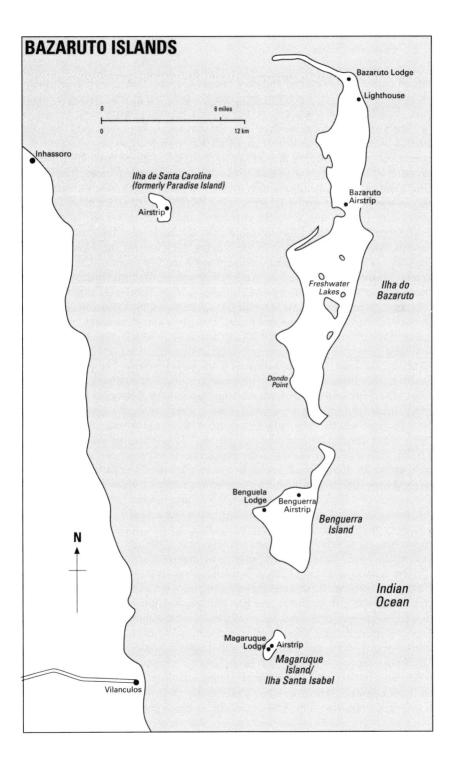

BAZARUTO ISLANDS

0   6 miles

0   12 km

Bazaruto Lodge

Lighthouse

Inhassoro

Ilha de Santa Carolina (formerly Paradise Island)

Airstrip

Bazaruto Airstrip

Freshwater Lakes

Ilha do Bazaruto

Dondo Point

N

Benguela Lodge

Benguerra Airstrip

Benguerra Island

Indian Ocean

Magaruque Lodge   Airstrip

Magaruque Island/ Ilha Santa Isabel

Vilanculos

tourist draws in the country, and they therefore attract their fair share of dodgy characters. If you really want to camp rough do it, but at your own risk. Make sure you listen to local advice, and never leave your tent unattended.

Quite apart from the beaches, fine swimming, diving and snorkelling, the islands are famed for their wildlife. Rich and varied vegetation supports 180 species of birds, including the crab plover, olive and blue-cheeked bee-eaters, green coucals, the narina trogon, and visiting colonies of lesser flamingoes (the next nearest nesting colonies are in Tanzania's Rift Valley). There are butterflies endemic to the islands, over 40 reptile and amphibian species, including five types of turtle can be found (one of which is the rare Loggerhead), and breeding crocodiles on the freshwater lakes of Bazaruto Island. Mammal types native to the islands include suni antelope, samango monkey, red duiker, four-toed elephant shrew and bushbuck. The protected waters support a wonderful variety of marine life: marlin, barracuda, humpback whales, several types of dolphin and sailfish. Most marvellous of all, the dugong or sea-cow can still be sighted around the archipelago. It is thought that this gentle sea-herbivore, with its vaguely human form, social nature and habit of suspending itself upright in the water, is responsible for the mermaid myth. This is why their classification is Sirinia, after the sirens of Greek mythology. The area between Ponta São Sebastião (the peninsula just south of Bazaruto) and the Save River is their ideal evironment, but dugongs have also been seen as far north as Angoche and the Tanzanian border. They are adapted for life in shallow water, feed in herds or family groups and mate for life. One of their most attractive characteristics is that the females nurture their young through several seasons: they are often accompanied by the young of the previous two births. Dugongs have few predators, but none so dangerous as man. There are now heavy penalties for killing them, but dugongs are still hunted, both for their meat and fat but also for the medicinal properties attributed to various parts of their bodies. Many are trapped accidentally in fishing nets, but many more deliberately killed. On Inhaca Island in the south, fishermen throw parties when one is caught: the 300kg of meat they carry will feed an entire community. They are regarded as highly endangered, but you still have a fairly good chance of seeing one.

The islands have long been a flourishing maritime community. Before the Portuguese arrived, Bazaruto Island and Benguerra were occupied by local tribes. In the 16th and 17th centuries they had a mainly Muslim population, who traded the ambergris and pearls for which the islands were famous, all along the coast, especially with the chieftaincies of Inhambane. As Portuguese influence over the coastal region increased, traders gradually began to settle on the islands, and in 1855 a trading post was set up on Santa Carolina which in its first two years sold 8,000lb of ivory. As the islands became more and more important, military posts were established (there is a ruined 19th century fort on Magaruque), and Santa Carolina, the smallest of the islands, briefly became a penal colony.

Bazaruto is Mozambique's main tourist destination. Both the provincial and national government are concentrating on making the most of their appeal while at the same time keeping the tourist influx to an acceptable level. Numbers of beds in lodges and hotels are restricted, and much of the profit from tourism is ploughed back into local communities. It remains to be seen if this form of sustainable development can work as Mozambique becomes ever more popular.

Arrival and Departure

You can get to the islands by light plane, motor boat or dhow. All the islands have airstrips but only Magaruque's has an all-weather surface. After heavy rain, flights will be diverted there from the other islands and transfers by boat arranged. You can book flights at the main hotels in Maputo (see *Maputo* for contact details) or through the travel agencies and charter companies listed on p.52-3. If you are staying in one of the main lodges (see the sections on each island below), they will arrange flights and boats from the mainland for you. Benguela Lodge on Benguerra, for example, organises transfers from Vilanculos as well as safe parking during your stay on the island.

You can also fly to the islands, via Vilanculos, from Beira. Asitur in Beira run charter flights which cost $1,210 for a 9-seater plane.

If you intend to make your way over to the islands from Inhassoro, see that section (above) for details. From Vilanculos you can hire a dhow for a visit to Magaruque or Benguerra – ask at the Last Resort, from where the dhows leave. The trip takes from two to four hours depending on prevailing winds and the season. Make sure you arrange it at least a day in advance – dhows also depend on tides and you may have to wait several hours or a whole day for a suitable time. A dhow and captain should cost around $15 for the round trip. Or for a real treat *Sail Away* (near the *Hotel Dona Ana* in Vilanculos) organise all inclusive trips by dhow around the islands for around $150.

BAZARUTO ISLAND

Best reached by boat from Inhassoro, Bazaruto is the largest of the islands. It has a grass airstrip in the north which is in the process of being upgraded; at present it takes charter flights from Johannesburg (contact *Mozambique Island Tours* tel 011-447 3528; fax 011-880 5364) or Maputo (contact the Hotel Rovuma or any of the main hotels). Points of interest are the now defunct lighthouse on the northern tip of the island, and the freshwater lakes to the south, which have a sizeable crocodile population. There are a number of places to stay: *Bazaruto Lodge* is the oldest hotel on the islands, and has bars, restaurant and swimming pool, and all the trappings of what is called 'barefoot' accommodation – luxury masquerading as the basics. Prices start at around $150. In Maputo you can book through Pestana at the Rovuma Hotel

(tel 01-427372), Polana Tours at the Polana Hotel (tel 01-493533, fax 01-493538) or Prosol (tel 01-425322). In Johannesburg call 011-447 3528 for bookings. *Sabal Bay Lodge* is an 'environmentally sensitive development' which means basic chalets with wooden verandahs. Prices start at $50-$60 a day. For bookings call Thomson Tours in Johannesburg (tel 011-788 2664). You can also camp on Bazaruto at Zenguelmo, the rangers' station. There are basic facilities and the rangers themselves are knowledgable about the wildlife and the surrounding area. Ask at one of the lodges for directions.

BENGUERRA ISLAND

The second-largest in the archipelago, Benguerra is 11km long, 5km wide and has a population of about 800. It has some of the most luxurious accommodation and excellent fishing, diving and snorkelling. The island is on the list of paradise destinations for the international jet-set: a well-known Irish newspaper tycoon recently threw a lavish wedding for his daughter there, with hundreds of guests flown in from all corners of the world. There are sandy beaches all round, and a reef which is excellent for snorkelling. Accommodation consists of *Benguela Lodge* (Benguela Island Holidays in Johannesburg; tel 011-483 2734/5, fax 011-728 3767), described as upmarket even for paradise, and the *Marlin Lodge* (Johannesburg; tel 011-543 2134), just as luxurious but slightly cheaper. There is a campsite on the west side of the island but it is illegal and its future is in doubt: if you want to camp make sure you ask on the mainland about availability. You can get to Benguerra by charter plane from Johannesburg, Harare or Maputo (call Benguela Island Holidays for details) or by boat from Vilanculos.

MAGARUQUE ISLAND/ILHA SANTA ISABEL

You can walk round Magaruque in about three hours. It's one of the smallest and nicest of the islands, and being the closest to Vilanculos it's also the easiest to get to. Magaruque also has a concrete airstrip which makes it more accessible by air than its neighbours. Contact Sabinair in Maputo (tel 01-465108) or Prosol (tel 01-425322) for charter flight details. There is one hotel on the island which charges $95-$110 per person per day, full board. Contact the numbers above for booking details.

ILHA SANTA CAROLINA

The smallest of the islands and the closest to the mainland, Santa Carolina is only 3km long and less than a kilometre wide. There is an airstrip and a newly-renovated hotel, from where you can arrange water-sports and diving. For more details contact *Maccon International* in Johannesburg (tel 011-447 3216).

Sofala and Manica

Ship's Graveyard, Beira

These two central provinces are the 'waistline' of Mozambique, with the vital Beira Corridor – the road from Zimbabwe to the coast – forming a tightly-buckled belt across the midriff of the country. Bordered by the Indian Ocean to the east and Zimbabwe to the west, Sofala and Manica may be of little interest to tourists but they have played an important part in the ancient and modern history of Mozambique.

In the 15th Century the region was first settled by muslims who traded and paid allegiance to local chiefs. The Zambesi valley had long been of strategic importance as the main conduit between the East African interior and the coastal port of Sofala, and the Portuguese had some of their earliest settlements in the province. During the 19th Century the Gaza monarchy, which extended from the Zambesi delta, through Sofala and Manica and at least as far south as present-day Swaziland, was dominated by the Nguni chieftains Soshangane, his son Umzila, and his successor Gungunhana. The power of the monarchy waned during the 'Scramble for Africa' at the end of the century. Umzila and Gungunhana negotiated and quarrelled with the Portuguese, the British and the South Africans, seeking treaties and protection from each in turn. By 1891, when Britain and Portugal were hammering out their own treaties for the partition of the lands they had been bickering over for the past decades, the power of the Nguni was negligible. Sofala and Manica were firmly in Portuguese hands.

During the civil war the region was of great strategic importance. Renamo had strongholds in Gorongosa National Park and controlled much of the region, using the Mutare-Beira road to mount raids on Beira and other key towns. After 1979 the road was protected by the Zimbabwean army and became one of the only routes in the country that guaranteed safe passage.

Any travellers coming in from Zimbabwe or on their way up the coast will visit Beira, the hub of the region. The city seems to have a bad reputation amongst travellers but is in fact a modern, sophisticated and fairly pleasant provincial capital. One of the few other reasons to stop long in these provinces is the birdwatchers' paradise of Gorongosa National Park. Once one of the best reserves in Southern Africa, Gorongosa has no big game left, but birds have survived. The park and the majestic mountain of the same name are firmly on the international twitchers' itinerary.

BEIRA

Beira is a modern working port; ships depart for and arrive from Durban, Maputo, Quelimane, Ilha de Moçambique and ports as distant as Lisbon and Madagascar. Since 1985 it has benefited from a series of projects set up under the SADC (Southern African Development Community). The port has been drained and deepened, modern container and oil terminals have been built, and the railway has been extended to allow for more freight traffic.

Don't be put off by Beira's reputation: it suffers from no more crime than any other southern African city of its size. Like all ports its highly mobile population can give the city an air of lawlessness, and there are no-go areas – basically anywhere unpopulated after dark, especially the beaches – but if you approach it with a modicum of common sense you'll find it a charming place.

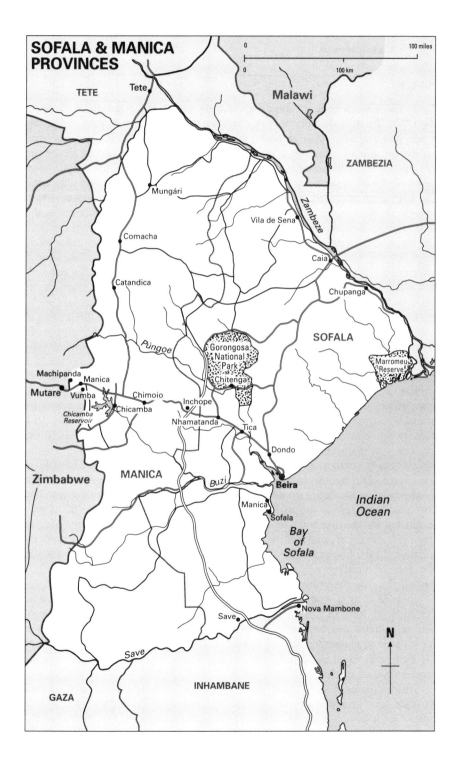

History

There has always been an important trading centre at the mouth of the Buzi river. The dunes and sandy bays of the river mouth provide convenient access to the sea, and there is fresh water and fertile soil around. The area has been settled for at least a thousand years, but the main centre has shifted as the sea has eroded the soft coastline. The old town of Sofala – which stood about 50km south of modern-day Beira – was the hub of a large trading area until the 17th century, ruled over by a muslim sheikh who claimed tribute from anyone, Portuguese or Arab, who wished to trade in the area. Sofala was the first town in Mozambique in which the Portuguese settled. They were quick to recognise the important role the town played in the gold trade, and in the early 16th century built a fort (with stone sent from Portugal) and established a trading post. Sofala and its satellite towns made up a complex trading network that was sometimes referred to as the 'Land of Sofala', and stretched as far south as the Save river and even incorporated the Bazaruto Islands.

During the 16th century gold gradually gave way to ivory as the principal commodity, and there was a corresponding shift northwards of the main trade routes to the interior. By the 1530s, while the Portuguese had extended their domination of the area by killing the sheikh and installing a puppet ruler, the Portuguese captaincy had been set up on Ilha de Moçambique. Sofala began to decline in importance and by the next century it was an isolated outpost, its few buildings being gradually overtaken by the encroaching bush, and wild animals roaming the streets. One historian recorded at the end of the 16th century that hyaenas had dug up all the corpses in the graveyard. In 1634 the captain lived alone in the fort, with no soldiers whatsoever. The only reason Sofala was manned at all was for fear it might be occupied by the English or the Dutch. During the following century the old Portuguese town almost disappeared as the dunes on which it was built were reclaimed by the sea. The fort itself played an important part in Sofala's history. In 1783 it was inundated for the first time, but managed to stay standing. At the beginning of the 19th century it sheltered the tiny Portuguese community from attacks by local warlords, but gradually its foundations became unstable and eventually the ancient building was dismantled, and its stones transported to build the cathedral in the burgeoning city of Beira.

In 1878 a sharp young Portuguese officer called Joaquim Carlos Paiva de Andrada – a kind of Latin Cecil Rhodes – was granted a huge concession of timber, mineral and land rights in Mozambique. In 1884 he established a base for himself in the newly-created district of Manica and Sofala, at the mouth of the Pungue river about 50km north of the old town of Sofala. This became the modern city of Beira.

Beira's growth was rapid. In 1891 it was formally incorporated into Mozambique after Rhodes himself tried to annexe it. In 1898 a railway was built – with British money – to connect Rhodesia to Beira. By the end of the

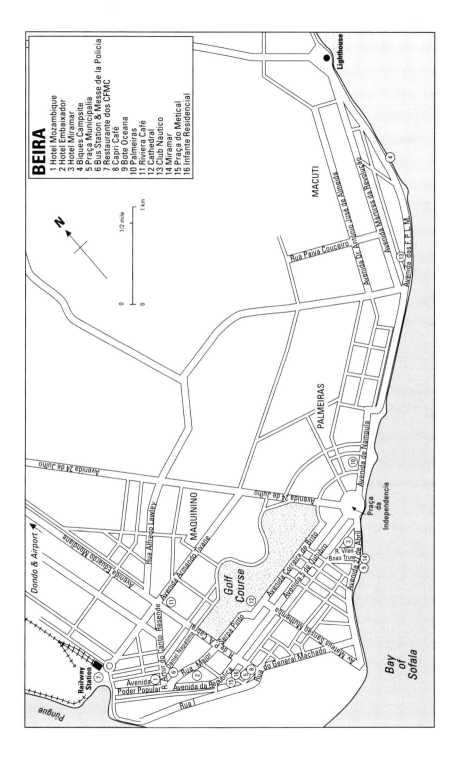

BEIRA

1 Hotel Mozambique
2 Hotel Embaixador
3 Hotel Miramar
4 Biques Campsite
5 Praça Municipalia
6 Bus Station & Messe de la Policia
7 Restaurante dos CFMC
8 Capri Café
9 Bote Oceana
10 Palmeiras
11 Riviera Café
12 Cathedral
13 Club Nautico
14 Miramar
15 Praça do Metical
16 Infante Residencial

N

1/2 mile
1 km

Lighthouse

MACUTI

Avenida Dr. António José de Almeida
Avenida Márques da Revolução
Avenida das F.P.L.M.

Rua Paiva Couceiro

PALMEIRAS

Avenida de Nampula

Avenida 24 de Julho

Avenida 24 de Julho

Praça da Independencia

Avenida Eduardo Mondlane

Dondo & Airport

Rua Alfredo Lawley

MAQUININO

Avenida Armando Tivane

Golf Course

Avenida Correia de Brito

Avenida 1 de Quibiro

Avenida 7 de Abril

R. Vilas Boas Truer

Rua Artur do Canto Resende

R. de Serpa Pinto

Rua do General Machado

Av. Mateus Sansão Muthemba

Av. Daniel Napatima

Rua Major 2 de Cab

Rua Major

Avenida da República

Rua T

Avenida Poder Popular

Railway Station

Punhe

Bay of Sofala

century it was the second most important city in the colony, with a population of over 4,000 (of which 1,172 were European). Andrada's Mozambique Company – with huge injections of British capital – constructed the port and harbour with stone quays, cranes and warehouses, sea-defences and a lighthouse.

By 1910 Beira had become a town with a distinctly British character, with hotels and bars built to serve the large British population. Even the currency, circulated by the Banco de Beira, was sterling. The town had stopped growing but it was easily the most important city in Mozambique after Lourenço Marques. The census of 1928 records a population of 23,694, of which 2,153 were European. Lourenço Marques had then a population of 43,000.

In its early days the town must have been a wild and unhealthy place. The land around was so untamed that lions sometimes came into the streets, and while the railway line was being constructed scores of workers fell victim to dysentery and malaria. During the first half of the 20th century it developed fast – by 1928 it had a population of 23,000, half the size of Lourenço Marques. Beira today is Mozambique's second city, a thriving metropolis with a population of half a million.

AIR

LAM flights connect Beira directly with Harare, Johannesburg, Maputo, Nampula, Pemba and Quelimane. At the time of writing Beira-Quelimane (5 times a week) costs $100, Beira-Nampula (4 a week) $155, and Beira-Pemba (every Sunday) $190. Flights are usually overbooked and without careful planning you could find yourself cooling your heels for a week if, for example, you miss the weekly Pemba plane. The LAM office is in Rua Costa Serrão (tel 03-324141 or 325619 for reservations; fax 03-328632). Staff are friendly and speak good English. There is also an office at the airport. Sabinair (tel 03-301392: fax 03-301393) run daily charter flights to Vilanculos and the Bazaruto islands, as do Asitur (Ferreira de Almeida, tel 03-327497/327498). A 9-seater plane costs around $1,500 to hire. The airport is to the north of the city. You can get a chapa from the bus station or a taxi, which should cost no more than $6-7.

PRIVATE CAR

If you have been in the north of the country you will be used to bad roads, but if you're coming up from the south this will be your first taste of some of the worst driving conditions in Mozambique. The stretch from Inhassoro to Inchope is good and presents no problems to a saloon car. But there is a 30km section just south of Inchope that was heavily mined during the civil war, is passable only in a 4WD, and even then can take over two hours. In dry weather a rugged saloon might get through but it's not advisable. Note that at the time of writing there are extensive road-repair programmes all over Mozambique, especially in the north. Although there are no immediate plans to resurface this stretch of road, ask other drivers for an update before you set off.

The roads north of Beira are very bad: the 264 km to the Zambesi is pitted with deep potholes, has unbridged rivers and streams, and is frequently impassable in the rainy season. If you intend to cross the Zambesi, you need to get to Caia where there is a sporadic vehicle ferry (you can stay the night there if necessary – see *Public Transport* below). The journey can take ten or more hours. There is a lot of war-wreckage scattered on the way, including rusting tanks and landmine warning flags. This part of Mozambique was heavily mined during the war, so do not be tempted to wander off the track.

At present the only other way across the Zambesi is the three-kilometre road bridge at Vila de Sena (60km upstream from Caia). It was sabotaged during the war, and has just been reopened. But it's a very rough mud track (only passable with 4WD) from Caia to Vila de Sena. Once over the bridge the first town on the north bank is Mutarara, from where a track takes you to the Shire/Chire river, where there is another vehicle ferry on a pulley system. After that, head towards Morrumbala, and about 20km north of there you can either take a track to the right which joins the Quelimane road, or carry on north, bypassing Quelimane and going to Mocuba, up to Alto Molócuè and on to Nampula. See the *Public Transport* sections below for details on getting to Zimbabwe.

PUBLIC TRANSPORT

There is no formal public transport north from Beira. You have the choice of either taking a series of chapa rides to cover the 1,055km to Nampula via Quelimane – a journey that would take at least five days but could be interesting, if exhausting – driving your own car, flying, or seeing if you can hitch a lift on a boat going up the coast. See the sections below for details on all these options.

From Maputo, Transportes Virginia leave from outside the Hotel Universo (see p.118 *Maputo* for details) between 5am and 6am, and arrive in Beira around midday the following day after overnighting at the Save River. The trip costs $20. The other national bus company, Transportes Oliveiras, leaves from Praça 16 de Junho on 24 de Julho in Maputo at 1pm, stays the night in Maxixe and arrives in Beira after dark the following day.

The **main bus stop** in Beira is in Ave Artur Canto Resenda and Daniel Napatima, in front of the enormous oval building. Buses south leave at

4.30am, stay the night at Maxixe and arrive in Maputo at around 2pm the following day. As always, check times thoroughly. At the time of writing there is no midday bus.

Going west to Zimbabwe

The Beira corridor – the road that runs from Beira to Mutare in Zimbabwe – is in good condition and well-served by public transport. The journey can take anything from 4 hours to a day, depending on where the bus stops. During the rainy season the road is prone to flooding around the River Pungue, so be aware of this before you set off. The road cuts through beautiful scenery and a number of villages, becoming increasingly mountainous towards Zimbabwe. If you're travelling in summer, you'll notice much cooler temperatures and a welcome drop in humidity.

There are buses which go from Beira to the border post at Machipanda on a daily basis, for around $5. The buses usually leave a couple of times a day, but the border post closes at 6pm so it's advisable to get the earliest, leaving at around 6am, to allow for any hold-ups. Buses and chapas stop en route at the little town of Nhamatanda, just under half-way to Zimbabwe, where you can buy bottled drinks and fruit. From Machipanda you can easily hitch the last 5km to Mutare. If for any reason you're dropped in Chimoio you can also hitch from there. Hitching from Beira is more difficult as you need to go quite far out of the city before you pick up the Zimbabwe road. Note that landmines were planted along the Zimbabwe-Mozambique border during the war, so it would be unwise to go tramping off into the bush.

If you are coming in the other direction from Zimbabwe to Beira it is easy to hitch a lift from the border post at Machipanda, and there are also regular chapas which pick people up at the roadside. In Beira you will either be dropped off at the main market, or the bus station. Again, the earlier you set off from Machipanda the better as Beira is not the most pleasant place to arrive in after dark.

Beira to the Zambesi river

From Beira, take a chapa to Dondo (30km west of Beira) and get a lift – you'll see a large crowd of people waiting on the road to the north. Once at Caia you can either cross the river in a bark dugout or on the one remaining 'ferry', (see section on *Private Cars* above for options). You will almost certainly have to spend the night at the river, in which case you can either follow the other passengers' example and sleep in the truck yard, or get a room in the large reed hotel on the north bank. Once you have crossed the river it's easy enough to pick up a lift going north to Quelimane or Nampula.

TRAIN

Beira station may be big and modern, but it sees few trains. There is a very slow, mainly freight service connecting to Mutare on the Zimbabwean border, stopping at Dondo, Tico, Nhamatanda, Chimoio and a few other towns along the way. In theory the train goes as far as Mutare, but at the time of writing there is some doubt as to whether this will continue. At present you can certainly get as far as Nhamatanda. Trains leave on Tuesdays, Thursdays, Saturdays and Sundays at 7.30am, for Nhamatanda, and another leaves between 5pm and 6pm going only as far as Dondo. Second class costs $1.70, third class 80c.

BOAT

Beira is a major port for international and coastal shipping, and it is quite possible to hitch a lift up and down the coast, and further afield to Durban, Mombasa and Dar es Salaam. You may have to wait several days or longer for a ship, but it should be a dramatic and interesting way of travelling. For larger and international ships contact the shipping agents in the port and in the Avenida de Poder Popular, near the railway station. The major agents are King and Sons (Ave de Poder Popular), Marbeira (in the port, running fishing trawlers), AMI (Ave de Poder Popular), and Mocargo (near AMI). A passage to Quelimane should cost around $20.

Accommodation

Hotels

The most expensive hotel in Beira is the slightly run-down *Hotel Mozambique* (Rua Artur Do Canto Resende; tel 03-329352; fax 03-325060). With air-conditioning and hot water, singles are $50, doubles $65 and suites $80-$90, breakfast extra. There is a public swimming pool opposite.
Hotel Embaixador (Rua Major Serpa Pinto 203; tel 03-323121; fax 03-323788) is shabbier but cheaper and more central with singles without air-conditioning for $30, and air-conditioned doubles for $50-$60.
Hotel Miramar (Rua Vila Boas True 157; tel 03-322283/323471) is very close to the nearest beach to the centre of town, near the Praça da Independencia. Doubles with and without air-conditioning are $15-20.
Infante Residencial (Rua Jaime Ferreira 218; tel 03-323042). One of the best-value hotels in Beira. One block east of Praça da Municipalia, it is very central, the rooms are clean, and there is a lively bar and restaurant on the top floor. Doubles with fan are $20-$25, hot water buckets supplied.

Any other accommodation in town is pretty basic: the rather smelly *Monaco Restaurant* (Rua Madeira; tel 03-323232) has rooms for $9 per person, and the *Messe de la Policia* (Daniel Napatima, in the enormous block from which buses and taxis leave) will put you up for around $15.

Camping

As is so often the case in Mozambican towns, by far the best option is to camp. *Biques* campsite (tel 03-312853, pronounced 'bee-kees', on Ave das FPLM halfway between Clube Nautico and the Estoril lighthouse,) has an excellent reputation and – short of the biggest hotels – is the only place in Beira where you'll get a hot shower. It is clean, has a 24-hour guard, pitches cost $5 per person, it's on one of Beira's best beaches, and there is a good restaurant and bar. It is 45 minutes' walk from the centre of town so it's best to take a chapa going to Estoril, and ask for Biques. Clube Nautico (see *Eating and Drinking*, below) also has camping spots, but they are sandy and windswept and decidedly inferior to Biques.

Eating and Drinking

Beira has a couple of excellent restaurants and some lively and interesting bars and cafés; and you can eat out several times without having to go to the same place twice. Remember you're in a port and be careful of badly-lit areas at night – the station forecourt and the dark streets around it have a nasty reputation for hold-ups.

Restaurants

Locals recommend the *Restaurante dos CFMC* (inside the station; tel 03-328280) as the best eating to be had in Beira. Prices range from $4 for basic chicken dishes to $25 and up for seafood, the chairs are padded, tablecloths starched, and the waiters wear spotless napkins on their forearms. If you want something slightly less old-fashioned, one of Beira's most popular restaurants is the Portuguese-run *Pic-Nic* (Rua Costa Serrão 115; tel 03-326518). Main courses are $5-$16, the service and food is excellent and the waiters speak English. Less formal but with an equally good reputation is *Arcádia*, best-known as *Johnny's Place* (Rua Poder Popular 200, near the station; tel 03-322266). You can eat at tables with pink tablecloths on a covered terrace on the street – the piri-piri chicken for around $8 is delicious. Opposite the Pic-Nic in the disused *Cinema Nacional* (Rua Costa Serrão; tel 03-322463), a Portuguese family has opened a restaurant and bar. It's a friendly place and well worth a visit, with seafood on the menu starting at $5. If you're tired of chicken and seafood the smart *Clube Tropicana*, also known as *Cutty Sark* (Ave das FPLM 296; tel 03-313036) does very good pizzas. It looks onto a private beach and has a swimming pool, barbecue, saunas and disco. If you really like it, a year's membership costs $180.

Other good options are the *Take Away 2+1* (Rua 7 in Maquinio; tel 03-322206, parallel to Daniel Napatima, near the bus station), which specialises in seafood and Mozambican dishes and is considered one of the best fast-food places in Beira. Locals speak very highly of the seafood at *Palmeiras* (Ave de Nampula, in the Palmeiras district between Macúti and Pontageia); the *Miramar* (Ave Mateus Sansão Muthemba, east of Praça da Independencia; tel 03-323471) has a breathtaking sea-view and is well-known locally for its seafood and especially prawns, but its quality fluctuates. Just along from the Miramar is the *Bote Oceana* (Ave 27 de Abril, near the Hotel Miramar), which has a chinese restaurant and a nightclub, with the occasional stripper. It is newly opened and thus the centre of attention, although the food isn't anything special. *Restaurante Clube do Golfe* (at the golf course; tel 03-329533), open Thursday to Sunday, has a disco at the weekends for well-heeled Beira youth.

Cafés

The best café (or *saloa de chá*) in Beira is undoubtedly the *Capri* in Praça da Municipalia. It serves good coffee and cakes, and its tables on the attractive square are enticing. Further round the square is the *Riviera*, which at lunchtime is packed with locals watching the latest imported TV film. Just off the square is the *Scala*, also a good place to sit and watch African city life.

Exploring

You are unlikely to be staying long in a city that does not offer much for the tourist, but a couple of days can pass very enjoyably. The two main squares, **Praça da Municipalia** and **Praça do Metical**, are more or less next door to one another. You will find it's best to orient yourself from the former, a fine space with a couple of lively cafés and some **beautiful colonial buildings** around a pleasant central precinct. The square's most impressive building is the marble **municipal hall** on the south-east side, which has a tile mural of the old fort at Sofala in the entrance hall. In the north corner of the square is the **Beira Jail**, a Victorian edifice where you can see grimy clothes hanging from the barred windows, and the unfortunate prisoners peering out as the everyday business of the town carries on around them.

In the Praça do Metical there are also some fine old colonial buildings, notably the red-brick **Casa Portugal**, one of the Beira's best examples of a turn-of-the-century Portuguese dwelling. The square – appropriately named after Mozambique's currency – is ringed by banks: Banco Standard Totta, Banco Comercial and others. At the northern corner of the square is the Avenida de Poder Popular, at the end of which is the **Casa Infante Sagres**, a beautiful, mosaic-tiled colonial building renovated in 1992. Ten minutes to the north, along an unmade road, is one of the most impressive sights in Beira: the immense modern **railway station**, which was completed in 1966. Whether you consider it an ugly example of Sixties' brutalism, or an elegant tribute to the romance of the railways, it's worth seeing for its great frontal arch and echoing main hall. It also has what is supposed to be the best restaurant in Beira. The tourist literature advises you to take the time to look at the ornamental fish pond inside – a couple of depressed-looking goldfish huddled in the corner of a tiled pool. It would be difficult to make a case for it as one of the main attractions of this extraordinary building.

Beira Cathedral on Ave Correira de Brito should not be missed. Completed in 1925 partly out of stones taken from the ancient fort at Sofala, it's a fairly conventional example of early 20th century ecclesiastical architecture. It has a cool and calm interior which is pleasant after the noise of the city. It is not clear whether – like the cathedral of Nossa Senhora de Conceição in Maputo – it was built with forced labour.

On the other side of town, at the end of Avenida das FPLM (called Oliveira Salazar on older maps) and towards Biques campsite, is the **lighthouse**. It's well worth a walk out there, if only for the excellent beaches. Mines have been found around here, so be careful about any areas that do not seem to be frequented.

One of the most astonishing sights of central Beira is the **ships graveyard**. When the Portuguese pulled out in 1976 they scuttled what ships they had in harbour – about 20 of varying tonnage, from grain transporters to ocean-going container ships. These rusting hulks sit on the beach to the south of the main port as if they had been thrown out of the sea by a tidal wave. You get a glimpse of a rusty prow as you walk south from the Praça da Municipalia – it's so close it makes you do a double take. Close up, it's an incredible sight, a mass of metal stretching far into the distance, silent except for echoes and the sound of blow-torches and ripping metal, as teams of workmen break up the wrecks for scrap. Street children live in some of the ships – you see them clambering along ancient walkways that look as if they wouldn't take the weight of a monkey.

If you fancy an excursion and a barbecue, the **Complexo Turístico Six Miles** is a pleasant picnic spot with excellent bird life, 3km out of town on the Dondo road. You can get there easily by chapa (see *Arrival and Departure* for details). If you have your own transport note that the road is only passable in 4WD. The restaurant at the Complex has reportedly gone downhill, although it has recently been bought up and is being renovated.

Nightlife

Beira's bars are concentrated around the railway station, between Ave Armando Tivane, Ave Poder Popular and Ave Artur Do Canto Resende. Be careful in the darker streets at night. Places like *Johnny's* (see above) are always good for a drink or two, and you just have to sample the other establishments, some of which are decidedly unsavoury and fly-blown. You might not want to go there at night but down in the port there is a boisterous bar in one of the warehouses, where you'll get the coldest beer served anywhere in Beira.

There's also a good choice of discos, churning out the usual mix of imported rock and roll, with a couple of clubs offering more Latin-American beats. The *Tropicana* (see above) is very popular on Friday and Saturday nights, though with a definitely teenage clientele, and the *Clube de Golfe* not far behind. Other discos include the *Boite Gruta* (Ave Armando Tivane 517; tel 03-325976) and the *Complexo Viveiros* (at the airport; tel 03-301418) which have a local following. One of the most sophisticated clubs is the *Oceana* (see above) which plays mainly Latin-American music.

Cinema

There are two main cinemas in Beira, the Novocine and the Olimpia.

SHOPPING

Beira has its share of enjoyably chaotic markets. On Ave Armando Tivane is the *Mercado do Goto* (also locally known as Chungamoio), which sells second-hand and new clothing, capulanas, electrical goods, shoes, furniture and just about anything else you might need. For fruit and vegetables, fresh seafood and local arts and crafts, check out the *Mercado Centrale*, just off the north-eastern corner of Praça da Municipalia, between Rua Correia de Brito and Jaime Ferreira. One of the most interesting markets is the *Mercado do Maquinio*, north of the golf course in the Maquinio district, where you will find traditional medicines and herbal potions, as well as vegetables and livestock – goats, chickens and ducks.

HELP AND INFORMATION

Tourist Information

There is no tourist office in Beira. The Hotel Mozambique has fairly informative staff, and staff at the LAM office (see below) speak good English and will help you as much as they can.

Travel Agencies

Most of these can be found in the Praça do Metical.

Car Hire

There are three main companies operating in Beira: *Avis* (Beira Airport; tel 03-301263; fax 03-301265), *Hertz* (Ave Armando Tivane; tel 03-322315; fax 03-322415), and *Interfranca* (tel 03-322480).

Post Office and Telecommunications

The main post office is a massive, gloomy edifice off Praça da Municipalia. It is open from 10am to 7pm weekdays, and until midday on Saturdays. It's worth a look even if you haven't got anything to post. For local phone calls there is an efficient call centre attached to the Café Capri in Praça Municipalia; international and trunk calls can be made from the Telecom office in Rua Major Serpa Pinta, which is open from 8am to 9pm every day.

Changing Money

Banco Comercial in Praça do Metical is the only bank that will change travellers cheques, and then only with a receipt. Banco Standard Totta changes only Thomas Cook travellers cheques (again you must have a receipt). If you are desperate, most of the banks will charge a 25 per cent commission for changing travellers cheques without a receipt.

Medical Treatment

For emergencies call Dr Mirander on 03-311500; the Central Hospital (tel 03-312071) in Macúti near Clube Nautico is not the sort of place you would choose to linger, but there are always doctors there who speak English and will be able to help you. Otherwise in the Macúti Housing Complex (Ave Martires da Revolucão; tel 03-311925) there is a clinic run by an English nurse, where you can be treated for most ailments. Ask for Samantha.

Libraries and Information Centres

The Biblioteca Municipal, on Rua Correia de Brito just behind the cathedral, has the daily papers and other useful publications. Better stocked with books, magazines and papers from Portugal (though with practically nothing in English) is the Centro Cultural Portugues on the corner of Rua da Cruz and Rua António Enes. The Portuguese Embassy is in the same building.

FURTHER AFIELD

DONDO, TICA, NHAMATANDA, INCHOPE

There's no reason to stop in these towns, beyond filling up with gas or buying provisions. At Tica the *Complexo Turíistico Beira Safari* serves basic meals. Inchope is a major intersection and truck stop, and the turning for Gorongosa National Park.

SOFALA

President Chissano likes to come to Nova Sofala (as it is called on some maps), regarding it in some ways as the spiritual heart of Mozambique. It is certainly the very oldest Portuguese settlement, although the old town has long been submerged by the encroaching sea, which has eroded the shoreline over the years. There are buses and chapas to Sofala from Buzi, which is accessible by boat from Beira. The beach is beautiful, and you should be able to camp there: take all provisions.

MANICA PROVINCE

GORONGOSA NATIONAL PARK

Once home to more game than South Africa's Kruger National Park, Gorongosa was Mozambique's showpiece reserve. It had two major tourist camps, Chitenga and Boa Vista, and at its height in the 1970s was receiving 11,000 visitors a year.

The civil war changed all that. Renamo had their base in the park, which was the scene of several battles between the rebels and the Frelimo government. It was in Gorongosa, in a Renamo stronghold called Casa Banana captured by government troops in 1985, that papers were found proving that South Africa was still supporting the movement.

During the conflict most of Gorongosa's animals were either killed for meat or by mines, or simply fled. The park was officially closed to tourists in 1983. Recent plans by a Zimbabwean group to restock with 300 elephants have yet to be realised so it's unlikely you'll see any game. At present birdwatchers have taken the park to their hearts and regard it as excellent birding territory. The South African birders' website (www.sabirding.co.za) says locals believe Gorongosa is holy ground, and adds that most birdwatchers feel the same, it being one of the few places in Mozambique where you have a chance of seeing the elusive Greenheaded Oriole.

At the time of writing there is no formal accommodation in the park, but it is still possible to visit, or to climb Mount Gorongosa (which has some of

Mozambique's only true rainforest). Chitenga camp has been partially repaired and a provisional HQ has been established there to coordinate anti-poaching operations. If you have your own transport, take the Gorongosa road from Inchope and turn off after 40km, at Nota. From there it is 11km to the gate, and another 17km to Chitenga, where you should be able to camp. Take all your provisions, and at all times be careful of mines.

If you want to climb Gorongosa, one option is to go through Gorongosa town on the western border of the park, and take the road to Vinduzi (30km north). When the road forks, one kilometre out of town, keep right. When you get to Vinduzi there is accommodation in the form of a lodge with thatch shelters, where food is available. There you can arrange a guide to take you up the mountain; you should not attempt to go up without a local guide: apart from the danger of mines you will come across officials who you will find difficult to deal with. The summit can be reached in three hours. Veterans advise it is a hard slog, and doubly so if you are unfit, but well worth it.

CHIMOIO

The capital of Manica province is Mozambique's fifth largest city, a marketing hub, as the tourist literature describes it, 'for all the wonderful produce' coming in from 'the garden-land province'. It is true Manica is a great exporter of oranges, lemons, grapefruit and other fruits: the road to Chimoio takes you through acres of citrus groves. There's not a lot to do here, but it's a pleasant enough place to stop for a night or two and stock up with provisions. Like Nampula, Chimoio boasts a **Cabeça do Velho** (Old Man's Head), a stone outcrop remarkably like the face of an old man. You can get a good view of it from the **Mercado Magarafa** in the centre of town, or you can walk or drive the 3km to the base of the hill and climb up to the 'eye' for an excellent view.

The town has a Banco Comercial and a Banco Standard Totta, as well as a casa de câmbios called Rechi's (Ave 24 de Setembro - the main street). There is a telecom office for international calls (Rua Patrice Lumumba), and a library which is currently being stocked with English books (Ave 25 de Setembro). Chimoio also has a good selection of shops, markets and supermarkets.

ARRIVAL AND DEPARTURE

Private Car

The Beira-Mutare road is well-surfaced and should present no problems. If you are going on to Tete, the turn-off is on the right, 22km along the Mutare road

Public Transport

Chimoio is a transport hub and so is well-served by bus and chapa. The journey to Beira takes about three hours, and to the border about two hours (an hour in a private car). Buses and chapas stop outside the railway station. If you are going on to Tete you can catch the Maputo-Tete Virginia bus which stops overnight at Chimoio, or there are several buses and chapas that start from Chimoio very early in the morning.

Train

The Beira-Mutare train stops at Chimoio (see *Beira* above for details). Unless you are a rail enthusiast there are many better ways of getting around this part of the country.

Air

There are no scheduled flights to Chimoio, although it is possible to charter a small plane. The LAM office (Rua dos Operarios; tel 051-22580) or the airport (tel 051-22242) have details.

ACCOMMODATION

The very best hotel in Chimoio is the plush *Executive Manica Hotel* (about 200m out of town on the Beira road; tel 051-23135). It has a swimming pool as well as a restaurant and bar, and safe parking. Rooms are between $50 and $60, all with air-conditioning and bathroom. Also off the Beira road, about 2km further out, is the delightful *Moinho* (tel 051-231300). Moinho means windmill, which is what the building is, complete with little sails on the roof. Several of the rooms have private balconies over looking the forecourt, and are good value at $18-$20 for singles and doubles. The restaurant attached is excellent and well worth a visit. In town there is very little choice: the *Flor de Volga* (above the Banco Popular de Desenvolvimento) has decent-sized rooms and shared bathrooms for $10-$20. Lastly there is the *Complexo Nhamite* on the Mutare road, also on the outskirts of town, which has a few rooms with bathrooms for $15-$18.

EATING AND DRINKING

The *Moinho* restaurant is one of the best in town, but there are a couple of other decent places. In the *Feira Popular* (a nondescript collection of bars and discos in the centre of town) *Maúa* has a good reputation for Mozambican and seafood dishes. *Restaurante Concorde* (Araújo de Lacerda) is also worth a visit, as is the *Restaurante Piscina* (Bairro Textafrica Soalpo) for reasonably-priced meat and seafood dishes.

CHICAMBA DAM

If you don't need to stop in Chimoio on your way to Mutare, or fancy a break coming from Zimbabwe, the Chicamba dam makes an excellent overnight stop. The dam and reservoir lie almost equidistant between Chimoio and the border. If you're on public transport, ask to be put down at the Chicamba turn-off (signposted Casa Msika Hotel) from where you won't find it too difficult to hitch a lift down to the lake shore. *Casa Msika* has one- and two-bedroom chalets for $25-$40, a campsite on the lakeshore, a restaurant and swimming pool. The wooded slopes are relaxing to look at and stroll in; Zimbabwean birdwatchers stop off here for a bit of practice before heading into the serious birding country of Gorongosa. The miombo rockthrush and red-faced crombec can be seen here. Nearby is a crocodile farm which the owners of Casa Msika can arrange visits to.

MANICA

Manica is a picturesque little town, known for its coffee, the Aqua Vumba mineral water factory, open-cast gold mines, and its entrance gates dedicated to the memory of Samora Machel. Gold is one of the chief products of the area, and it may be possible to visit the mines. Otherwise, you'd have no reason to stay here for long. There is no formal accommodation, but the *Piscina de Manica* restaurant, at the swimming pool, is reasonable.

EXCURSIONS INTO ZIMBABWE

The Machipanda border is open from 6am to 6pm. If you need a visa you can get one at the border. As you leave Mozambique you will need to get your passport stamped and register your vehicle if you are driving. Immigration fees for vehicles are $4.50 for a car, $10 for a truck, and $2.50 per person.

MUTARE

If you're not intending to push on into Zimbabwe but are interested in hiking, the Zimbabwean town of Mutare and its surrounds – the Bvumba and Chimanimani Mountains – have some wonderful opportunities for walking. You can also reach Mozambique's highest mountain, **Mount Binga** (2,436m), more easily from Zimbabwe, by going 150km south from Mutare to

Chimanimani. Mutare, nestling in the foothills of the Bvumba Mountains, is quite a contrast to many Mozambican towns, with well-stocked food stores, chemists, dentists and doctors. The main street, Herbert Chitepo, has a supermarket, clothes shops and tourist shops. Everything is much cheaper and more readily available here than in Mozambique so if you are going into Mozambique from Zimbabwe it's a good idea to stock up on anything you need. For accommodation the backpackers' favourite is *Ann Bruces' Guest House* (99 Fourth Street/Sixth Avenue), which serves home-made meals and has laundry facilities. For hiking, try the *Inn on the Vumba*, the *White Horse Inn* or *Eden Lodge*, all within 40 minutes of Mutare.

Tete Province

Cahora Bassa Dam

When the European powers partitioned Africa at the end of the 19th Century they considered political expedience more than geographical convenience. As a colonial power Portugal was little more than a satellite of Britain, which is why Mozambique found itself in the uncomfortable embrace of a huge swathe of British territory – and why Tete province looks as if it would rather belong anywhere but behind Mozambican borders. Surrounded as it is by Malawi, Zambia and Zimbabwe, Tete can often seem anything but Mozambican. The hundreds of travellers who make the long and difficult journey overland from Blantyre to Harare, along the Tete Corridor that directly links the two cities, have no need to spend any more than one night in Mozambique. Indeed, if it were not for the border posts at either end of the road necessitating entry and exit taxes, some might not realise they had been in Mozambique at all.

The eponymous capital of the province is a convenient stopping-off point for Malawi, and it's a pleasant if not particularly riveting place. Until you get up into the highlands the landscape around is dry, dusty and hot, with little to inspire you as you trundle through. Probably the best reason for visiting Tete province is to take a look at the Cahora Bassa Dam across the Zambesi, the fifth largest dam in the world.

TETE

By virtue of the fact that it is custodian to Mozambique's only bridge over the Zambesi, Tete is a significant place. It is also one of the most unusual and isolated big towns in the country, 500km from Beira, 600km from Quelimane, and cut off from the north by Malawi, and the geographical barrier of the Zambesi. Tete is set on the broad floodplain of the Zambesi, only 175m above sea-level, which accounts for its reputation as one of the hottest places in Mozambique. It is a prosperous place, its position just downstream of one of the five biggest dams in the world ensuring it has a regular electricity supply. Tete expanded massively during the construction of the Cahora Bassa dam (today's population is about 50,000, compared to 2,500 in 1928) and the bulk of the town is modern, with a dilapidated old town much in need of restoration. For many tourists the only reason for going to Tete will be to visit the dam, but you'll find some decent restaurants and an agreeable atmosphere, notwithstanding the inhospitable climate. The Zambesi gives the town a very different character to the coastal settlements; one of the nicest things about it is the row of bars and restaurants overlooking the riverfront – Tete is also one of the only places in Mozambique where the river is easily accessible to tourists.

Tete came to prominence at the end of the 18th century when the seat of government of the Shire and Zambesi rivers region was transferred there. The then capital, Sena, a once-booming town some 200km downstream, was facing a crisis due to disease. Tete was certainly an Islamic centre long before the arrival of the Portuguese, having been a focal point for the gold and ivory trade fairs held regularly in the region. During the 17th century the Portuguese become interested in the area when they began to acquire most of what is now Zimbabwe. Land rights were granted to settlers and by the 1630s there were some 20 hardy Portuguese families there, living in thatched stone houses surrounded by a wall (parts of which were still visible in the 1880s).

The town wasn't exactly booming – it seems the Portuguese even considered abandoning it altogether at one stage – but it remained standing,

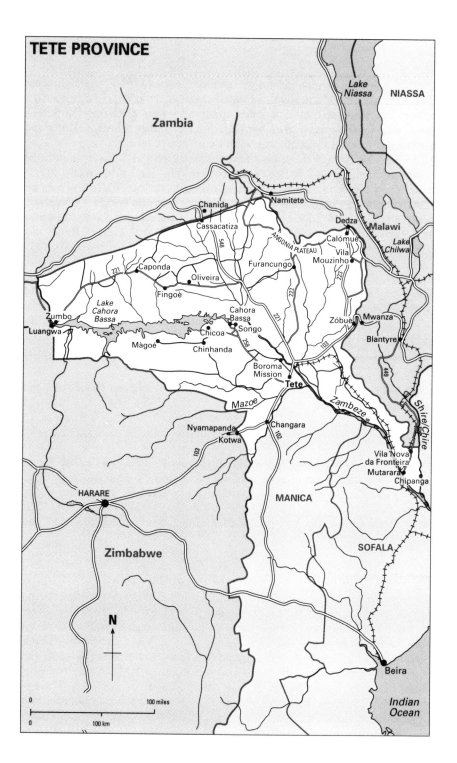

and when the seat of government was moved there in 1767 things looked up. Two forts were built, a hospital, a council chamber, an arsenal, a prison, and a governor's mansion. Two companies of soldiers were posted to the forts – most of them *degredados*, men banished from their battalions for crimes and misdemeanours. Tete was obviously not a cushy post.

In the 19th century the town's fortunes fluctuated, and it wasn't until the following century that it began to prosper. The region became a major recruitment centre for the booming sugar industry in the 1920s, and railway construction and the building of the Zambesi suspension bridge – which was completed in 1935 and took 20,000 men – further brought the town to prominence. The population increased, and by the time Cahora Bassa was built in 1974, Tete's status as one of Mozambique's major cities was assured.

Nowadays the city remains an important transit point for trucks and travellers, and is really a very nice place despite the ferocious temperatures. There may not be much to do for entertainment and excursions, but it's well worth the stop just to see the great Zambesi.

ARRIVAL AND DEPARTURE
Air
LAM has one direct flight a week from Tete to Lichinga and Quelimane, and two a week to Maputo.

Private Car
The main roads connecting Tete to Harare, Blantyre, Beira and Cassacatiza on the Zambian border are in good condition and passable in a saloon car. The road to Zambia is very little used, and is not covered by any formal public transport, so the only way along it is in your own vehicle or hitching. The latter option would take you several days. The 225km from Blantyre to Tete should take about three hours.

Public Transport
There are frequent chapas to and from Zóbuè on the Malawian border, costing around $5 and leaving from the market in front of the fort by the bridge. Other chapas go to Beira and Chimoio, Songo and Chitima (from in front of Hotel Kassuende). Transportes Oliveiras have a daily bus to Chimoio and Beira, leaving from the Pensão Alves at around 6am (check times at the pensão). The terminal for Transportes Virginia is near the Mercado 1 Maio; they run local routes like Songo and Chimoio but are not considered very reliable. There is also a daily bus from Zóbuè to Maputo, which stops in Tete at the Mercado Organizacao Unidade Africana (OUA) in the centre of town at about 8.00am.

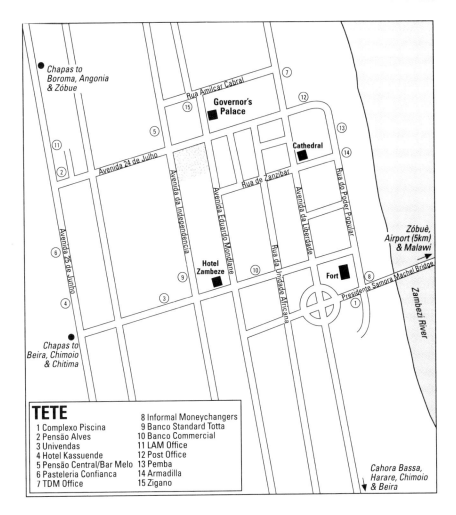

TETE

1 Complexo Piscina
2 Pensão Alves
3 Univendas
4 Hotel Kassuende
5 Pensão Central/Bar Melo
6 Pasteleria Confianca
7 TDM Office
8 Informal Moneychangers
9 Banco Standard Totta
10 Banco Commercial
11 LAM Office
12 Post Office
13 Pemba
14 Armadilla
15 Zigano

Hitching

A good place to get lifts is on the Zambesi bridge.

ACCOMMODATION

One of the most popular places with ex-pats and tourists is the Portuguese-owned *Complexo Piscina*, almost under the Zambesi bridge (tel 052-24021), which has air-conditioned doubles with bath for $18-20. The Complexo has a reasonable restaurant, and a camping ground with clean communal bathrooms for $1.50 per night. The *Hotel Zambesi* (tel 052-23003, at the main crossroads on Ave Eduardo Mondlane) needs refurbishment but all the rooms have private bathrooms (doubles from $12-25 with and without air-conditioning, breakfast included). Another good bet is the *Pensão Alves* (tel 052-22523), a recently refurbished, family-run hotel near the mosque. Doubles with bathroom cost $15-20 with and without air-conditioning. If you are heading for Beira it is convenient because Oliveiras buses leave from in front of the hotel. Well worth a look are private rooms above a furniture shop called *Univendas* (tel 052-23199), next door to the Banco Standard Totta. The owner, Sr Isaias Marrao, lets out very clean rooms without bathroom for $15. Lastly, the *Hotel Kassuende* (tel 052-22531) is noisy and the rooms aren't up to much. Doubles with bathroom are $12-27 with and without air-conditioning.

EATING AND DRINKING

Tete has a very good selection of restaurants. One of the most popular places with locals is the *Bar Melo* or *Pensão Central*, owned by Maria and Jesse Hickman. The food is probably the best you'll get in Tete (the average price for chicken or steak is $6), although the drinks are expensive. Jesse Hickman ran convoys during the days of the Tete corridor, and is a veritable quarry of information on everything to do with the town and its surrounds. The bar also has satellite TV, and a disco at weekends. Otherwise there is the Complexo Piscina (see above) which has a nice atmosphere, with an air-conditioned dining room and satellite TV. One of the best places in Tete, the *Restaurant Freitas*, has recently been closed due to a legal dispute. Another very popular place for obvious reasons is the *Pasteleria Confianca* (in the same road as Hotel Kassuende) the only café that sells freshly-baked cakes, biscuits and bread as well as snacks and ice-cream.

NIGHTLIFE

You shouldn't leave Tete without sampling one of the riverside bars, such as the *Pemba* near the Alfandega (Customs) or the *Armadilla*, which is at its liveliest on Sundays. There are also a couple of discos – notably the *Zigano* near the Catholic church, which is very jolly, with a mainly teenage clientele.

SHOPPING

There are plenty of shops with reasonable choice, but expensive groceries. Drivers looking for **petrol stations** will find that there are several in Tete itself, including a 24hr BP station on the Malawi side of the Zambesi.

Garages You shouldn't have any trouble finding garages and spares shops in Tete. Most are open every day except Saturday afternoons and Sundays.

HELP AND INFORMATION

Tourist Information

There is no tourist office in Tete. Make friends with Jesse Hickman (see *Eating and drinking*, above) and he will tell you all you need to know. The local LAM Office is next door to the mosque and Pensão Alves.

Post Office and Telecommunications

On the main road fronting the river, near the Governor's palace. The post office has poste restante facilities and EMS courier service. The Telecommuniçacões de Moçambique (TDM) building for international and national calls, is just past the post office.

Changing Money

There are four banks in Tete. Travellers cheques can be changed at Banco Internacional de Moçambique. You will get a better rate for dollars and Malawi kwacha from the black market money changers under the Zambesi bridge.

Medical treatment

Tete has a basic and very cheap hospital, which is equipped for medical emergencies with X-ray facilities and a laboratory for Malaria tests (which locals say are not always reliable). If you can wait it would be better to get to Harare or the Adventist Clinic in Blantyre, where the facilities are much better. There are three pharmacies which sell a good range of medicaments: the privately-owned Farmacia Linda (ask directions) is the best. There is also a good pharmacy in Moatize, 10km from Tete.

EXCURSIONS AROUND TETE

Boroma Mission

A beautiful nineteenth-century church on a hill overlooking the Zambesi, the Boroma Mission is difficult to get to, but well worth the trouble. It is about 30km from Tete – you can pick up a chapa from beyond the market a couple of blocks north of Pensão Alves. The Mission was abandoned shortly after independence, and at present is being used as a school.

Angonia Plateau

Another interesting day trip is to the Angonia Plateau. It is the main agricultural area of the state, and although there are no facilities it is cool and pretty and very relaxing. The plateau would perhaps be best appreciated if you are travelling en route from Tete to Lilongwe via the Dedza border. There are two nondescript towns, Ulongwe (which has a hotel, three or four restaurants and some shops) and Tsangano. Take the turnoff about 110km from Tete, just before Zóbuè, and choose your own picnic spot. You should be able to camp in any of the towns for a small fee.

Furancungo

This small town is located in a very beautiful hilly area, 200km north of Tete. It's accessible by public transport – pick up a chapa from the same place as for Boroma Mission (see above), or just outside Tete where the main road forks left to Cassacatiza and Zambia, just past the BP service station, 3km after the bridge. A Dane called Kim is building a camp there, which is unfinished at the time of writing but is catering for tourists. The Mozambique Leaf Tobacco office at Bar Melo (see *Tete* above) will contact Kim on their radio for you.

THE CAHORA BASSA DAM

Completed in 1974, the Cahora Bassa Dam is the fifth largest in the world, its five giant turbines designed to produce 3.6 million kilowatts of power. That one of the world's greatest civil engineering projects should be completed in an impoverished and backward part of Africa, after a 10-year war of independence, is one of the modern marvels of Mozambique.

In the local Matheema dialect Cahora Bassa means 'the place where the work ends', a reference to the impassability of the now submerged Zambesi rapids, which cascaded 80km down the valley, with two vertiginous 200m drops. Livingstone never managed to overcome them. On his first trans-African expedition he skirted round them, and his boat the *Ma Robert* was wholly unable to negotiate them during the Zambesi Expedition of 1858.

The idea to harness the power of the Zambesi was first conceived in 1961 by Portuguese president Salazar, but work on the dam did not begin until 1969. Cahora Bassa was both politically and economically motivated. South Africa was to be the biggest client (the electricity generated at full capacity would be ten times the requirement of Mozambique); it was also thought that the vast lake created by the dam would be an effective barrier against Frelimo, operating from strongholds to the north of the Zambesi. Frelimo tried constantly to put a stop to the building, attacking fortified construction sites and mounting a propaganda war in Africa and the west, under the slogan 'Cahora Bassa must be destroyed.' Taking on the dam was too ambitious, however, and beyond destroying power lines and harrassing the garrisons, they were unsuccessful.

Today Mozambique owns 18 per cent of Cahora Bassa, with the other 82 per cent owned by a Poruguese-led consortium. At the end of the civil war the dam was running at a fraction of its capacity, with only two of the five turbines working. Over 2,000 pylons had been destroyed, and it was not until 1997 that the dam started supplying South Africa, which buys three-quarters of Cahora Bassa's capacity. Mozambique itself, whose entire electricity needs could be supplied by a tenth of the giant turbines' power, is still subject to power cuts. 'When we get electricity direct from Cahora Bassa' is a frequently-repeated mantra all over the country.

The dam is a wonderfully impressive sight, set deep in the Cahora Bassa gorge. Visits can be arranged either from Songo (contact the Hidroeléctrica de Cahora Bassa head office, tel 052-82221/2/3/4) or more reliably from Tete, where you should contact Sr Ribeiras, the HCB rep (tel 052-22788; fax 052-23982). You should give three days' notice for any visit, so if you are only intending to be in Tete a couple of days, ring before you arrive.

SONGO

Songo was purpose-built in the late 1960s for the crews working on the dam; most of the population still works on the dam in some capacity. With a population of over 15,000 it's a fair-sized town, and, with its clean, well-lit streets and attractive gardens it is quite unlike any other in Mozambique. Sitting high above sea-level, the climate is cool and fresh – the evenings especially are a delight, the air full of the scents of eucalyptus and tropical blooms. The drive up to Songo – which lies 150km from Tete – is spectacular, winding through wooded hills. There is only one place to stay in the town, the *Pousada Sete Mentes*, which has reasonably-priced rooms and a good restaurant. You can also get permission from HCB to camp near the walls of the dam, for which you will have to take all necessary food and water. Chapas leave for Songo from in front of the Hotel Kassuende in Tete, and Transportes Virginia run two buses a day, in the morning and the afternoon. Their timetables are unreliable, so make sure you check the exact time of departure and be at the terminal at least half an hour before that.

Zambésia

Colonial Architecture Quelimane

Many travellers en route for Nampula or Beira barely register Zambésia as they rattle around on the metal floor of a four-ton truck, or fly over the province in one of LAM's comfortable Boeings. The EN1 – at this stage not in the best condition – toys with the idea of visiting the coast, but changes its mind 50km short, and swoops back 200km inland. As a result the beaches are difficult to get to and remain undeveloped, though as with the rest of Mozambique's coastline, they are beautiful and unspoiled. The only one that you can get to easily is Zalala, 27km from the provincial capital Quelimane.

It is a shame that Zambésia is so difficult to travel in; in many ways it's one of Mozambique's most interesting provinces. It has varied landscape, with impressive mountains to the north – including the country's highest peak, the 2,419m Mount Namuli. The highland region to the north gets a very high rainfall, which makes it ideal for growing tea, while on the coast just outside Quelimane is the country's biggest coconut plantation.

If you are interested in what Mozambique has to offer apart from beaches, Zambésia is worth exploring. Some of the highland areas – in particular Gurúe – make a refreshing change from the humid air of the coast. If you have no other reason for going there you may find Quelimane a useful break in your journey north or south. It has good facilities, a decent beach and, although a little bland, is generally one of Mozambique's pleasanter towns.

QUELIMANE

Mozambique's fourth-largest city, situated at the mouth of the Qua-Qua river, is a low-key place with an agreeably relaxed air and a thriving business community. Along with Sena and Tete, Quelimane was an important Muslim settlement carrying on trade along the Zambesi long before the arrival of the Portuguese. Throughout the 17th century ships would trans-ship their cargoes there, ready for them to be taken up the river. There was a wooden fort there in 1634, which gave protection to local chiefs when the Maravi tried to take control of the town. At this time there were four Portuguese living in Quelimane, along with a captain who reported to the Captain of Mozambique. For the next hundred years the settlement changed little. It was controlled by one or two powerful *prazo* holders, who protected it with their private armies and traded with passing ships. It wasn't until the middle of the 18th century that prosperity came, in the form of the slave trade and all its attendant economic activity. By 1788 Quelimane had a couple of stone houses, a prison – and a flogging post.

As the slave trade took off (see page 20) the town came into its own. By the end of the 18th century the coast of Mozambique was thriving on the export of slaves and ivory. During the 19th century the trade became more and more lucrative. In the years up to 1836 (when Portugal officially abolished slavery), about a thousand human beings a year were exported from Quelimane. In 1839, that number had increased to 4,900 a year, all of them shipped at night in converted barges and whalers. Only the most observant visitors realised anything was going on – on the surface there was no sign that Quelimane was anything but a busy merchant town.

As the slave trade gradually came to an end, Quelimane continued to prosper, mainly from the export of food to places like Ilha de Moçambique. David Livingstone was appointed Honorary Consul to the town in 1858 (he used it as a base for exploring the Zambesi). By 1928 it had a population of nearly 10,000.

Today around 140,000 people live in Quelimane, and it still keeps its air of prosperity, even though the port is badly silted and the docks need renovation. Nowadays there are only a few rusty boats loading cargo and the waterfront doesn't give the impression of great activity. The main industry now seems to be development. Aid agencies from all over the world are spending a lot of money in Zambésia province, and Quelimane is their base. Four-wheel drive trucks with the logos of Unicef, WHO, World Vision and Concern are ubiquitous.

If you've got a few days to spare, Quelimane is a good place to stop on your way north. If you stay much longer than three days, you might find the

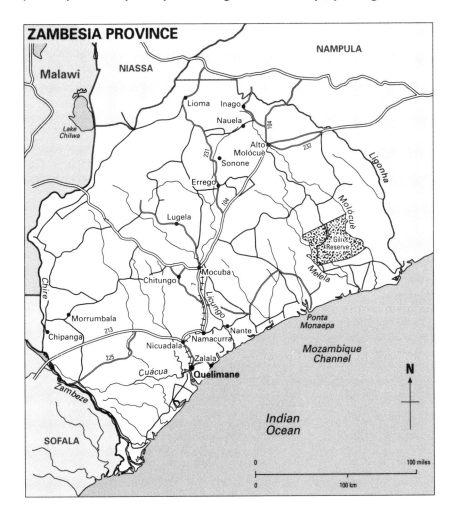

atmosphere gets a little claustrophobic. But the town has many facilities, and there are some well-stocked food shops selling imported South African and Portuguese goods: fresh fruit juice, mineral water and the creamiest of yoghurts.

In the centre of town the architecture is resonant of the Portuguese colonial era, with beautiful buildings, some now sadly dilapidated, lining the streets. There is also some interesting modern architecture. The cube-like 1960s **library** (near the main market and bus station) is worth seeing, as is the modern interior of the **Chuabo Hotel**. Another attractive building is the **Provincial Governor's house** near the waterfront, which is covered with blue mosaic tiles. You should also have a look at the dilapidated **18th century church** on the waterfront. It will seem closed (the interior is rapidly falling into disrepair through lack of use) but ask around until you find someone who will let you in. It is interesting to stand in the nave and imagine the good Portuguese colonials worshipping here, even as they grew fat and prosperous on the proceeds of slavery.

ARRIVAL AND DEPARTURE
Air

LAM has several flights a week between Quelimane and Beira (four a week direct), Maputo (one a week direct, several connecting), Nampula (two a week direct) and Tete (one a week direct).

Private Car

The 264 km from Beira to the Zambesi is very bad, and the drive can take ten or more hours. To cross the Zambesi you need to get to Caia where there is a sporadic vehicle ferry (you can stay the night there if necessary – see *Public Transport* below). At present the only other way across the Zambesi is the three-kilometre road bridge at Vila de Sena (60km upstream from Caia). It was sabotaged during the war, and has just been reopened. You should bear in mind the Sena route is difficult to follow and is only passable with 4WD. See p.167 *Beira* for more details on this route.

From Caia to Quelimane is straightforward: the main road is in good condition apart from the last 40km, which is badly rutted and takes about an hour to cover. If you are driving on to Nampula, you will definitely have to stay the night in Quelimane. There are a number of difficult sections, especially around Alto Molócuè, and you shouldn't attempt this road in a saloon. If you have the time, you might take a detour to Gurúe (see below). Another interesting spot is the town of Chupanga, 30km downstream, where in 1862 David Livingstone buried his wife Mary, dead from fever at the age of 41, in the shade of a massive baobab in the grounds of the mission.

Public Transport

From Beira, take a chapa to Dondo (30km west of Beira) and get a lift to Caia, 230km to the north, where you can cross the Zambesi. Once at Caia you can either cross the river in a bark dugout or on the one remaining 'ferry', (see section on private cars above for options). You will almost certainly have to spend the night at the river, in which case you can either sleep in the truck yard, or get a room in the large reed hotel on the north bank. There is no difficulty in picking up a chapa on the north bank of the river – expect the 200km to Quelimane to take the best part of the day. Chapas deposit their passengers at the main bus station in Quelimane. Chapas for Nampula leave from here at 5 or 6am; if you can't get one direct to Nampula, get a lift to the junction 40km out of Quelimane (marked with a petrol pump and a derelict building) and get another lift going north. If you leave early enough you can make Nampula in a day. If you are coming in from Malawi, there are several chapas a day from Milange on the border, which will drop you at Mocuba, from where it is easy to pick up a lift to Quelimane or Nampula.

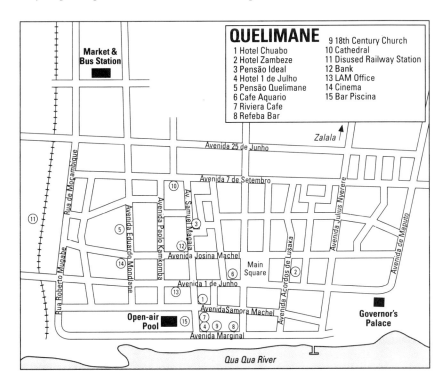

ACCOMMODATION

Quelimane is not the sort of town you'd expect to find the *Hotel Chuabo* (Ave Samora Machel). This is a four-star establishment (named after the 17th century inhabitants of the *prazos* in the area), with rooms ranging from $85 for the cheapest single to $330 for a suite. Who they are catering for with prices like that is anybody's guess (though the UN agencies and foreign aid delegations provide a regular stream of customers). The comfortable, wood-panelled rooms have TV and fridge and gleaming bathrooms. There's an amazing spiral staircase, marble floors and pantiles on the walls. On the eighth floor is a good though expensive restaurant, complete with smart waiters and a terrace with a wonderful view over the old cathedral on the waterfront. If you can't afford the rooms there's nothing to stop you having a look at one – and make sure you have a drink in the restaurant. Otherwise, there's not a huge choice of places to stay. The *Hotel Zambeze* (Ave Acordos de Lusaka), $13 for a single room, is basic and clean but rather depressing and comfortless. It serves food but the restaurant is unfinished and permanently empty. The *Pensão Ideal* (Ave Samuel Magaia), has a very good reputation and is excellent value doubles cost $8-10 with and without air-conditioning. Right on the river is the *Hotel 1 de Julho* (Ave Samuel Magaia), which has doubles for around $15, and a couple of blocks to the northwest the *Pensão Quelimane* (Ave Eduardo Mondlane), which charges between $20 and $30 for rooms with and without bathrooms.

EATING AND DRINKING

One of the nicest places to sit and enjoy a coffee is the *Café Aquario* (Ave Heroes da Liberdade). It overlooks the very unstructured main square, beside a newly-renovated fish pond. You can sit outside under the shade of the trees and drink a good strong cup of coffee made with hot milk. Snacks are available all day and a slightly more extensive menu at night, when service can be painfully slow. Just round the corner, opposite the open-air public swimming pool, is the *Riviera Café* (Ave Samora Machel and Samuel Magaia). The Riviera's fame has spread well beyond the confines of the city. It has mirrored windows and air-conditioning (and a slight problem with flies, although one waiter is permanently employed to swat them). The menu includes milk shakes, delicious pastries and huge ornate cakes. Excellent espresso coffee is served in tiny cups. The usual lunches are available: fish and chips, burgers and chips, chicken and rice, as well as sandwiches. There are tables outside, but unfortunately you're then a sitting target for the numerous urchins hanging around. The *Refeba* bar (Ave Marginal) looks like a disused petrol station, but being off the main street and just over the road from the waterfront it's a nice place to sit. The menu is standard and the food is rather greasy. On Fridays and Saturdays it transforms itself into a 'wild' party spot with disco and mirrored globe. Entrance after a certain time is by ticket only, but it's never particularly busy. There are several other small places serving coffee and drinks: the *Piscina* opposite the Hotel 1 de Junho has tables on the roof, and serves good cold beer.

FURTHER AFIELD

ZALALA

Easy to get to from Quelimane, and one of the only really accessible beaches in Zambésia, Zalala is almost completely undeveloped. It lies 27km from the centre, through a vast coconut plantation. To get there, take Ave Julius Nyerere north out of town. The road is fairly busy so you will have no problem getting a lift if you walk a little way along. At the beach there is a café and bar (which gets quite lively in the evening), and cabins at *Complexo Turistico Kass-Kass* for $15-20 each. You can also camp there, and buy fish from local fishermen.

NORTH FROM QUELIMANE - THE ROAD TO NAMPULA

The EN1 north from Quelimane is in poor condition and should only be attempted in a 4WD or a saloon with good clearance. However, extensive road-improvement programmes mean the highway may soon be upgraded. The journey at present takes a good 10 hours.

MOCUBA

A pleasant, busy town some 150km north of Quelimane, Mocuba is at the junction of the EN1 and the main road to Milange on the Malawian border. You can pick up transport to Malawi here, although there are no regular buses and you might have to wait a day or two: ask around in town for the next truck to leave. The Milange road is a right-hand fork off the Quelimane road, a few kilometres out of town.

There are a couple of places to stay in Mocuba, both of them rather run-down: the *Pensão Cruzeiro* on the main street, and *Pensão São Christorao* down the hill.

ALTO MOLÓCUÈ

This is a dusty, run-down little place which you would have very little reason to want to stay in. If you find yourself obliged to spend the night, the *Pensão São Antonio* and restaurant on the main road at the top of the square will accommodate you; there is also a government hostel at the bottom end of the square. Up the hill on the north bank of the river the town becomes much nicer – there is an attractive church and a couple of interesting turn-of-the-century buildings. All public transport vehicles and most trucks stop at Molócuè.

NAUELA

An interesting little town, with a fort and a church and a few dilapidated turn-of-the-century buildings. There is no formal accommodation but you should be able to camp if you ask around for a suitable spot.

GURÚE

Gurúe is an unusual town, high in the Planalto Moçambicano, at the foot of Mozambique's second-highest peak, the 2,419m **Monte Namuli**. The town is surrounded by tea plantations and has the highest rainfall of any town in Mozambique. After the heat of the coast the cooler air makes a welcome change – and at night the temperature falls appreciably. Gurúe is a fairly prosperous place, with a couple of good restaurants along a main street dotted with well-stocked shops. The winding mountain road to Gurúe takes you through some of the most impressive scenery in Mozambique – scrubland on the lower slopes gives way to miombo-wooded hills, passing through tiny villages with the straw houses characteristic of the area. If you come from Nampula you will clearly see the magnificent basalt outcrop known as *El Velho*, the Old Man, an extraordinarily lifelike silhouette of an old man in repose.

There are some good walks around the town, into and around the tea plantations, but you should be careful before heading anywhere that does not look well-trodden. Ask in the Pensão Gurúe or at the aid workers' residence next door for advice on the best walks. One route to take is at the top of the hill leading out of town on the Alto Molócuè road, which leads up to an abandoned church after about 5km.

Just by the roundabout is a bank where you can change money – but don't count on their taking travellers cheques.

Private Car

4WD is essential to complete the journey if you are going via Alto Molócuè and Nauela, as you will need to ford a couple of difficult streams. Buses disgorge their passengers at these points and pick them up the other side. The road between Nampula and Alto Molócuè is in good condition and is the best option; if you are coming from Quelimane and Mocuba take the Nampevo/Errego route. The road between Gurúe, Lioma and Mutuali is in good condition, apart from a couple of unstable bridges. In the rainy season it turns to mud and you should count on journeys taking double the normal time.

Public Transport

From Quelimane take the Nampula bus and change at Alto Molócuè, or at Nampevo and continue north through Errego. This latter road is in better condition and sees more traffic, though you will be missing some fine mountain scenery. The bus from Nampula leaves between 4 and 5am from the Transnorte bus terminal. It generally takes 8 hours but you should allow far more time – the mountain roads are pitted and take their toll of any vehicle. Take plenty of water as the roads are extremely dusty.

In this part of the country vehicles are rare. In each town or village there will be only two or three cars or trucks passing every day, so make sure you are at a junction very early in the morning or you may have to wait several hours – or a day – for a lift.

Another option if you are using public transport is to take the Nampula-Cuamba train (see *Nampula* for details) and get off at Mutuáli (7.30am coming from Cuamba, 1.30pm coming from Nampula). From Mutuáli you should be able to get a lift going the 100km to Gurúe via Lioma. Again, be warned that passing vehicles are extremely rare. Lioma is a tiny village with a large maize processing plant, and should you be stranded there the foreman will look after you and give you a lift, and somewhere to sleep if need be.

There is one bus that leaves Gurúe for Cuamba at 5am from the market at the bottom end of the main street. If you miss this bus wait there for a lift. Transport for Alto Molócuè and Mocuba passes by the petrol station at the top of the town, north and to the right of the main roundabout.

ACCOMMODATION

The *Pensão Gurúe* is halfway down the main street. It has good-sized double rooms for $13-15 and an excellent restaurant. As it is the only reasonably decent hotel in town it is often fully booked; next door there is the *Olivera*, a hostel used by aid workers which will put you up for $10 for a small room, with shared bathroom and shared cooking facilities. There is also the *Complexo Turistico Sanzala* on the road parallel to the hostel, which has small doubles for around $10.

EATING AND DRINKING

You can either eat at the *Pensão Gurúe*, or at the *Namuli* restaurant on the roundabout at the top of the main street. They will do you a good chicken dish for a reasonable price. There are other bars and restaurants in town, and a lively disco and cinema next to Namuli.

Nampula
Province

Cannon at
São Sebastião fort
Ilha de Moçambique

Nampula province has some of the most interesting scenery in Mozambique, miombo forest giving way to open savannah, interspersed with fantastically-shaped granite outcrops and moutains. Tourist information frequently claims that the province is a rock-climber's paradise; although at present there is absolutely no infrastructure for climbing, some of the peaks and faces would certainly present a challenge to professionals.

The provincial capital – Nampula – is the biggest city in northern Mozambique. It is a prosperous, friendly place, and very pleasant to visit for a couple of days. Indeed, as the regional transport hub it is impossible to travel anywhere in the area without stopping there at least for one night.

The overwhelming reason to come to the province is to visit Ilha de Moçambique, the seat of Portuguese power for 400 years. The island – four hours from Nampula – has one of the best-preserved and biggest forts in the country, as well as elegant colonial houses, the absorbing Palace Museum and a teeming reed village. It is a working town that nevertheless manages to present a perfect snapshot of four centuries of history. It should not be missed under any circumstances.

From Nampula a crowded and enjoyable train runs to Cuamba in Niassa province, a good jumping-off point for Malawi. Whether you intend to go onto Malawi or not, it makes a fascinating two- or three-day trip through the middle of the province.

NAMPULA CITY

A Mozambican saying has it that Nampula is the best place get married because the women of the town are so obedient. It's difficult to gauge the truth of this assertion, but another good reason for marrying and settling down there would be that it is a very agreeable town. The provincial capital is a prosperous, energetic, middle class town. It is a vibrant commercial centre, as evidenced by the well-dressed townspeople, well-stocked shops, sophisticated bars and restaurants, and the local bourgeoisie's penchant for driving up and down the main street very fast in gleaming Toyota Landcruisers. There may not be that much to do in Nampula, but it has a completely different atmosphere to the tourist centres of the south, and its wide quiet streets are a delight after the hurly-burly of Beira. When you've been through the rigours of windy chapas and dusty, bone-shaking buses it is a pleasure to be able to sit in one of the town's smart restaurants, drinking cold beer and planning your onward journey.

Nampula did not assume any sort of prominence in mainstream Mozambican affairs until after 1945, when it began to emerge as an important administrative centre and railway junction. By the 1960s it was one of Mozambique's most significant provincial towns. Much of the architecture is turn-of-the-century Portuguese, although there are few buildings of any real note. The **early 20th century cathedral**, a rather lovely white edifice set in a dusty square, is quiet, open and airy inside, with a magnificent half-hemispherical altar. Nampula also has an excellent **museum**, of which Makonde masks and old musical instruments make up the main collection. Just behind the museum is a **Makonde carving cooperative** where you can watch the craftsmen creating the beautiful wooden masks and carvings that will eventually find their way down to Maputo and to suburban sitting rooms all over the world.

ARRIVAL AND DEPARTURE

Air

The airport is 4km east of Nampula on the Pemba road. There are regular chapas to and from the centre of town, for which you shouldn't pay more than $2.50. LAM has regular direct and connnecting flights to Beira (six times a week), Lichinga (three times a week), Maputo (daily), Pemba (once a week), Quelimane and Tete (twice a week). Beira-Nampula costs $155. Should you need to you will also be able to charter planes from Nampula airport.

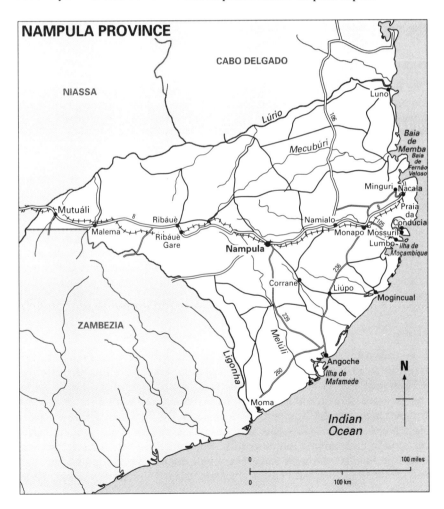

Private Car

Resurfacing continues apace all over northern Mozambique, and seasoned drivers are frequently delighted to find what was once a gullied obstacle course has become gleaming blacktop. Get updated by locals before you set off anywhere, and if in doubt assume the worst. The roads connecting Nampula with Pemba, Nacala and Ilha de Moçambique are in good condition and passable in a good saloon car. Note that Ilha is connected to the mainland by a bridge. The road to Cuamba is not so good, and requires 4WD. You could take the scenic route via Gurúe – it is dusty and slow, definitely requires 4WD, but is some of the most impressive scenery you'll pass through (see the section on Gurúe for details). Allow 12-14 hours for the journey. The route to Quelimane also requires 4WD at present.

Bus

The main bus station in Nampula is the Transnorte terminal which is past the Universidad Católica on Ave Filipe Samuel Magaia. From there you can catch buses going to Pemba (on Mondays, Wednesdays and Fridays), Ilha de Moçambique (daily), Nacala, Ribaué, Angoche, Gurúe and several other destinations. For Quelimane you can take the Gurúe bus and change at Molócuè. Buses are advertised to leave at 4am sharp but in practice rarely get going until after 5am. Another place from which to catch the Quelimane bus is along the Quelimane road (Ave de Trabalho) to the west of the railway station. Be sure to get there early. Buses going to Quelimane usually stay overnight in Mocuba; coming into Nampula from Quelimane they spend the night in Molóue.

You can get a chapa to connect you to most destinations from in front of the station. If you're headed to Ilha de Moçambique and can't face the early start necessary for a Transnorte bus, take a chapa to Monapo ($1.80), and change there for Ilha. The whole journey takes about four hours and is quite simple, as it is a very popular route.

Train

If you are coming from Niassa province or Malawi there is an excellent daily train between Cuamba and Nampula. Trains leave in either direction at 6.20am (and tend to be absolutely punctual). Wooden third class seats are $4 (make sure you get there early in order to get a place); 2nd class compartments are $8. It's best to go in second – the journey takes at least eight hours and third class gets very full indeed. There is an excellent buffet car serving meat *pregos* and other rolls, tea, coffee and beer. In any case, you won't go hungry: the train stops every half hour or so and is overrun with hawkers selling live and cooked chickens, canned drinks, flapjacks, toffee, potatoes, sugar cane, boiled eggs, spitted mongoose and river fish, batteries,

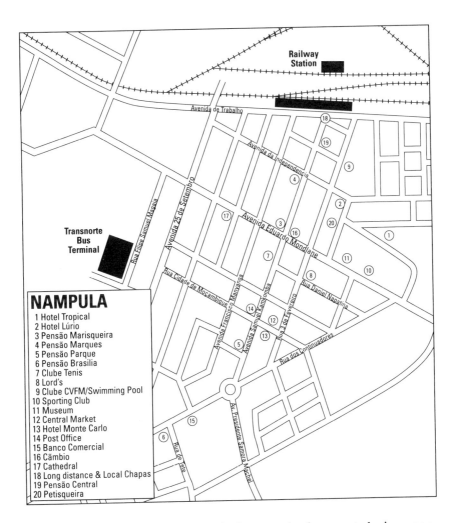

NAMPULA

1 Hotel Tropical
2 Hotel Lúrio
3 Pensão Marisqueira
4 Pensão Marques
5 Pensão Parque
6 Pensão Brasilia
7 Clube Tenis
8 Lord's
9 Clube CVFM/Swimming Pool
10 Sporting Club
11 Museum
12 Central Market
13 Hotel Monte Carlo
14 Post Office
15 Banco Comercial
16 Cãmbio
17 Cathedral
18 Long distance & Local Chapas
19 Pensão Central
20 Petisqueira

hats, and any fruit and vegetable, cooked or raw, that happens to be in season. The wheels squeal to a halt in what looks like the middle of unpopulated grassland and in an instant the train is surrounded by hundreds of people, from babies to old men, all yelling at the tops of their voices and forcing their way up the steps, thrusting anything remotely saleable in your face.

You can pick up the train at any one of its numerous stops: basically any settlement along the line. As a rough guide, the main places the Cuamba-Nampula train stops at are Lúrio at 6.40am, Mutuáli at 7.30am (1.30pm going the other way), Nacata, Malema between 8.30 and 9am, Mussa, Poiane, Iapala, Ribáuè at midday.

ACCOMMODATION

There are plenty of reasonably-priced hotels in Nampula. The most upmarket is the *Hotel Tropical* one block away from the museum in Ave Eduardo Mondlane (tel 06-212232, or contact the Maputo office tel 01-427466; fax 01-427464), which is used by UN staff and has air-conditioned rooms for $30-40. Nearby in the Ave Independência is the *Hotel Lúrio* (tel 06-212520), which has rooms for $15-20 and is clean and friendly.

Many of the best budget hotels are often fully-booked with commercial travellers and businessmen, but you shouldn't have any difficulty finding a bed. One of the best is the *Pensão Marisqueira* (Ave Paolo Samuel Kamkomba and Eduardo Mondlane, tel 06-213611) which has clean and neat doubles for around $18. Further up Ave Samuel Kamkomba is the *Pensão Marques*, which is very popular with backpackers and has clean doubles for $18 and dormitory beds for $6-7. Further up the street the *Central* is similar in price and quality; the *Nampula*, just off Ave de Independencia, should be your last resort.

At the lower end of Ave Samuel Kamkomba, towards the roundabout, the *Pensão Parque* is also very good value with double rooms for $13-15 and dormitory beds for $6-7. Turning right off the roundabout is the *Pensão Brasilia* which has decent, clean rooms for $13-15, or $20 with air-conditioning.

EATING AND DRINKING

There are lots of places to eat and drink in Nampula, from high-class restaurants to smart little cocktail bars. One of the nicest places is the *Clube Tenis* (Ave Samuel Kamkomba and Daniel Napatina), which has outside tables under reed canopies round a central courtyard, and a pool table in a state of hopeless disrepair. Frequented by the beau-monde of Nampula, the food is excellent, especially the reasonably-priced prawns. *Restaurant Lord's* (Daniel Napatina) is a slightly seedy but friendly 'cocktail bar' that serves good meals at reasonable prices, as does the restaurant in the *Hotel Tropical*.

A nice place to escape the heat is the air-conditioned *Clube CVFM*, which has a swimming pool set in bougainvillea gardens, a surprising oasis in the middle of this dusty town. Looking down on the gardens across the road is a cheerful bar where you can get cold beers and good cheap goat stew. Another outside restaurant is the *Sporting Club* (Ave Eduardo Mondlane) next door to the museum, which does decent coffee as well as cold beer and good food. Near that is the *Petisqueira*, which does seafood snacks and cold beers.

There are also some fine cafés selling cakes, imported chocolate and excellent coffee. One of the best places for a late-night drink is the (somewhat empty) café next door to the *Pensão Marisqueira*. Also check out the disco on the roof at *Hotel Monte Carlo* (in front of the market in Ave Samuel Kamkomba).

SHOPPING

There is a craft market on Sundays selling furniture, fabrics, reed mats and baskets as well as livestock, fresh fruits and vegetables, and a daily market on Rua Cidade de Moçambique.

HELP AND INFORMATION

Post Office and Telecommunications

The Post Office is on Ave Samuel Kamkomba and Cidade de Mozambique. There are numerous public telephones on Samuel Kamkomba near the post office.

Changing Money

The best place to change money is the *câmbio* opposite the Pensão Marisqueira on Ave Samuel Kamkomba. Banco Comercial (Rua dos Continuadores) changes travellers cheques with a receipt.

Medical Treatment

If you are in desperate need of medical treatment your best bet is to ask at the cathedral for help. There is a a medical centre at the Monasterio Mater Vei, about 7km out of town. It is a closed order of nuns and you would be unlikely to find it without help.

LAM Office

At the top end of Ave Francisco Manyanga. Tel 06-213311.

THE COASTAL TOWNS

ANGOCHE

The historic Muslim town of Angoche lies on the coast 198km from Nampula (from where it is most accessible by road) and a similar distance south of Ilha de Moçambique. The town enjoyed considerable prosperity in the early years of the 16th century, when its population rose to about 10,000. It was later superseded as a coastal trading centre by Quelimane, though ivory continued to be traded from there until the 18th century. In the 19th century it also enjoyed a good deal of importance as a slaving centre, as its shallow bay made it easy for the Muslim traders to avoid the British gunboats that policed the coast in the 1840s. Until the civil war Angoche was a popular resort for the Portuguese, who took advantage of its attractive beach and the archipelago of islands, of which Mafamede is the largest. It is very rarely visited now, but if you have the time, or your own 4WD transport, a few days spent round here would be well worth it. At Angoche the *Pensão Oceana* has basic rooms, and you can organise dhow trips to the islands. There are a couple of restaurants and a market where you can buy fresh fish. It is not difficult to hitch a ride north via Liúpo to Quinga beach, which is untouched and delightful. Note that this part of the coast is completely undeveloped and you are highly unlikely to find any formal accommodation, and little food or drinking water.

Buses from Nampula to Angoche leave at 5am from the Transnorte terminal on Tuesdays, Thursdays and Fridays (see Nampula section for details). It is also possible to pick up chapas starting from outside Nampula station.

MOGINCUAL

About 80km south of Ilha de Moçambique is the town of Mogincual, an important settlement in the 17th and 18th centuries, when it was ruled by an Arab sheikh. There is a beach camp here called *Fim do Mundo* (e-mail: fimdomundo@teledata.mz), with two-bedroomed chalets with toilet and shower for $20 per person, camping for $5, restaurant and bar. The owner runs diving and fishing trips, bush trails, and dhow trips up and down the coast. You can get to Mogincual from Nampula via Corrane and Liúpo, or via Monapo, where you should take a chapa going to Angoche and ask to be set down at Liúpo. At Monapo you could also try asking for Ussufu's chapa – he goes to Mogincual and back daily and charges $2.50 for the ride.

NACALA

North of Ilha de Moçambique is Nacala, a bustling little port on the eastern side of the beautiful bay of Fernão Veloso. There's nothing there to interest tourists, although it has an excellent supermarket at which you could stock up on essentials. At the entrance of the bay, about 15km north of Nacala, the diving and snorkelling is reputedly very good. There is no accommodation up there but there is a small restaurant where you can camp.

There are only two places to stay in Nacala: the seedy *pensão* at the main crossroads in the middle of town – ask for directions at the Carioca Pasteleria (see below) – or the much nicer and cleaner *Hotel Nacala*, where rooms are $15-30 with and without air-conditioning. The best place to eat is the *Restaurant Boite*, an upmarket establishment which has an excellent and varied menu. Other eateries worth trying are the *Restaurante O Casarão*, the

Asterix Snack Bar and, if you want to satisfy a craving for cakes, pastries and ice-cream, the *Carioca Pasteleria*.

Nacala is well-connected by bus and chapa; if you are driving, the road from Nampula is in very good condition. Transnorte buses run between Nampula and Nacala, leaving at 5am both ways. The journey takes about four hours. This route is also well-served by frequent chapas, although you may have to change at Monapo or Namiálo. To get to Pemba it's best to catch the Nampula-Pemba bus as it passes through Namiálo at about 8am. If you get a very early chapa from Nacala (say at 4.30am) you should be able to get to there in time for the bus. If you miss the bus, a fair amount of traffic passes through Namiálo on the way to Pemba. All transport in Nacala leaves from in front of the Hotel Nacala.

ILHA DE MOÇAMBIQUE

Ilha de Moçambique (Mozambique Island) is a fascinating and evocative place. Mozambique, as the town that occupies the whole island is called, is one of the most ancient European settlements in the southern hemisphere, and the capital of the Portuguese East African empire for four centuries. The name Mozambique (which only in the 19th century came to be used for the whole of Portuguese East Africa) probably derives from Moussa ben Mbiki, the incumbent sheikh when Vasco da Gama first landed on the island in 1498.

The island, connected to the mainland by a 3.5km bridge, is only two and a half kilometres long and 'so narrow in the middle that a stone may be thrown from one side to the other' as one 16th century priest described it. Despite its small size it has had more impact on Southern African history than almost any other colonial centre. Arriving on Ilha (as it is now popularly known), you enter a world where over four hundred years of history seem to be gloriously current. From the reed village at the southern end, which is hardly different to the way it was described by the British captain James Prior, visiting in 1812, to the gubernatorial palace and the mighty fort of São Sebastião, started in 1546 and last used for military purposes in 1976, Ilha gives you a marvellous glimpse into the workings of history.

Ilha de Moçambique has been declared by UNESCO to be part of the 'Cultural Heritage of Mankind'. But it is not a museum, nor a sterile heritage site. It supports a population of around 7,000 people who lead their lives as they would in any Mozambican town. Children in smart white shirts go to school, fishermen mend nets, the markets thrive, dogs bark all night, houses are built and barmen hand out cold beers. The only real difference is the fact that, due to the island's size, everyone lives cheek by jowl. It is a thriving and exciting town, and like all of Mozambique, so rarely visited by tourists that you feel privileged to be there. To miss it would be unthinkable.

Vasco da Gama was the first European to record his landing on the island, late in 1498, but he was by no means the first important visitor. For centuries the island and its harbour had been used by Muslim, Indian and African traders selling ivory, gold and ambergris up and down the coast. It was a well-known boat-building centre and a natural stopping place for shipping going between Kilwa to the north and Sofala and the southern trading posts. Da Gama came again in 1502, and in the same year the Portuguese, who already had a fortified trading centre at Sofala (just south of Beira), established a factory. Over the next few years they built a small fort to house an *alcaide*, a colonial officer, and built a chapel, Nossa Senhora do Baluarte, which still stands today. In 1546 the King instructed the Viceroy Dom João de Castro to build a major fortification: the fort of São Sebastião, which by the time it was completed towards the end of the century was the largest single structure in southern and central Africa.

By the end of the 16th century, Ilha de Moçambique supported a sophisticated and sizeable town; it was a thriving trading settlement, a naval base and an ecclesiatical centre, the island being the local headquarters of the Dominicans and the Jesuits. There were chapels like Nossa Senhora de Baluarte, a favourite place of pilgrimage for residents and homesick sailors, hermitages, garrison churches and parish churches.

In 1607 the Dutch, in an attempt to make Ilha de Moçambique the westernmost stronghold of their African empire, besieged the fort for over a month. But their soldiers were decimated by disease, confounded by the tenacity of the defenders and the impregnability of the fort itself. In 1608 they tried again, and in 1628 the English blockaded the island. The fort stood firm against all attackers. Between 1635 and 1640 the Portuguese signed peace treaties with both the Dutch and the English and good commercial relations ensued.

While it proved impossible to capture the fort, during these protracted sieges the town of Mozambique suffered. The Dutch destroyed it in 1607 and the Arabs plundered and sacked it in 1671. But it emerged at the end of the century richer and more splendid than ever, exporting huge amounts of ivory, ambergris, gold – and slaves.

The island's prosperity reached its peak in the 18th century. Important buildings, including a customs house, were added, and the Jesuit College (the Jesuits having been expelled in 1759) became the governor's palace. In the reed village at the southern end lived the native population of the island, while at the northern end the Portuguese had built the elegant royal hospital, the customs house, and 'noble houses, some of them so vast and well-constructed that they could rival the fine palaces of large cities,' as Bishop Bartolomeu dos Martires described it in 1822.

During the 19th century the town seems to have changed little. It began to decline in importance when the colonial economy shifted southwards and

Lourenço Marques assumed greater importance as an economic centre. Another factor in Ilha's decline was the discovery that Nacala had a far superior harbour (the fact that it wasn't exploited until the 19th century is more to do with Ilha's better natural defences, than any lack of initiative on the part of the Portuguese). When Lourenço Marques was made capital at the beginning of the 20th century, Ilha began to sink into graceful decay. In 1935 the provincial government was shifted to Nampula, and Ilha's eclipse, after four centuries, was complete.

The island is uniquely preserved. One feels practically nothing has changed in the last hundred years – and little before that. The ancient fort, with its cannons pointing seawards as if a Dutch man o' war might still be sighted on the horizon, the church of Senhora Baluarte – the oldest European building in the southern hemisphere – the reed town which has been there since before da Gama, all give a remarkable sense of continuity. Even the people add to this telescoped perspective – there have probably been fishermen mending nets in front of the cathedral on the southeastern promontary for five or six centuries, and they are still there now.

The romance of history aside, the government of Nampula is fully aware of the potential of Ilha. Zimbabweans (and Rhodesians before them), have been coming here for decades. It's not uncommon to see groups of grizzled 'Rhodies' sitting around in Ilha bars reminiscing about the old days. 'Haven't been here for 25 years,' they will say, 'and my God how it's changed.' The island is much-visited now, and although at the time of writing there is still no formal accommodation, the Pousada Hotel in the north of the island is being renovated to five-star standards by the Polana Group of Maputo.

A glance at some of the old photographs show the town as it was in the days of the Portuguese, with the Palace lit up, its gardens impeccable, smart cars outside and men in suits strutting about. There's little electric light now; sitting in front of the palace as the sun goes down over the Indian Ocean and darkness falls over this remarkable little island, will surely be one of the high points of your trip.

ARRIVAL AND DEPARTURE

Air

There is an airstrip at Lumbo, 5km away on the mainland, to which it is possible to charter planes from most major airports.

Private Car

The roads between Pemba, Nacala, Namialo and Nampula are in good condition apart from a few potholed sections, and easily passable in 4WD. A saloon would get you there, but it's not advisable.

Public Transport

Ilha is easily accessible. A single-lane, 3.5km causeway, passable in any vehicle, was built from the mainland in 1967. From Nampula take a chapa to Monapo and change there. From Pemba change at Namialo. All transport from the island leaves from just by the causeway. Chapas are frequent throughout the day. If you are heading for Pemba you must catch the 8am bus at Namialo, so make sure you leave the island by 5am at the latest to allow for breakdowns and other delays.

Boat

Dhows sail to Ilha from Nacala, Angoche and Mossuril, but it's so easy to drive to the island it probably isn't worth looking for a boat to take you there.

ACCOMMODATION

The Hotel Pousada is due to be finished at the end of 1999, in which case expect a 5-star establishment with prices to match. Eighteen rooms are planned with restaurant and swimming pool. No telephone number is available, but the Polana group in Maputo (tel 01-491001/7; fax 01-491480) should be able to help you. At the time of writing the only formal accommodation on Ilha is the pensão attached to the *Copacabana* restaurant on the right of the main road, just past the reed village. It is cheap ($8 for a room) and friendly but very basic, with no washing or toilet facilities beyond a bucket and a concrete hole. A far better bet is to use the informal network of guest houses that usually operates in this part of the country. There are several private householders who are happy to put up tourists for a reasonable price; the accommodation is almost always clean and comfortable. The owners of the *Reliquiés* restaurant (see below) will put you in touch with a number of places – rooms are $15-20 depending on conditions. Another option is Himo, the owner of the cinema at the northern end of the island. He has around 10 beds in three or four rooms and charges $18 per person. Camping is not an option on the island due to lack of space.

EATING AND DRINKING

One of the best restaurants on Ilha is the *Reliquiés* in the Rua da Republica, about a block south of the Palace. Housed in a building that used to be a warehouse and fish shop, with tables on a terrace over the sea and photos of old Ilha on the walls, it is a friendly, family-run place, serving good seafood at reasonable prices. One the other side of the island is *Complexo Indico*, a large open-air restaurant overlooking the sea; good food, cold beer – also worth a visit. At the time of writing there are few other places to eat, until the Pousada hotel restaurant opens. The dismal *Ancore d'Oura* (near Reliquiés, a block

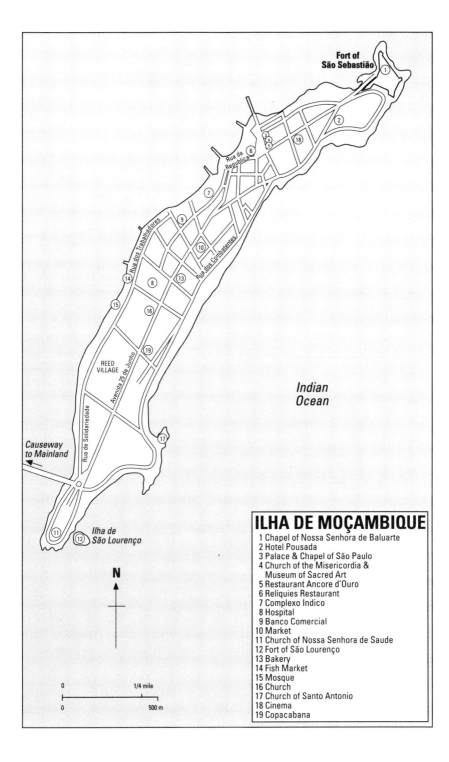

Fort of São Sebastião

Rua da República

Rua dos Trabalhadores

Rua dos Combatentes

REED VILLAGE

Avenida 25 de Junho

Rua de Solidariedade

Indian Ocean

Causeway to Mainland

Ilha de São Lourenço

N

0   1/4 mile

0   500 m

ILHA DE MOÇAMBIQUE

1 Chapel of Nossa Senhora de Baluarte
2 Hotel Pousada
3 Palace & Chapel of São Paulo
4 Church of the Misericordia &
   Museum of Sacred Art
5 Restaurant Ancore d'Ouro
6 Relíquies Restaurant
7 Complexo Indico
8 Hospital
9 Banco Comercial
10 Market
11 Church of Nossa Senhora de Saude
12 Fort of São Lourenço
13 Bakery
14 Fish Market
15 Mosque
16 Church
17 Church of Santo Antonio
18 Cinema
19 Copacabana

south of the Palace) will serve you up a prego if you are desperate, but it's a fly-blown place and best avoided.

EXPLORING

Ilha can be explored in a day, but two days – or longer – will serve you better. Being only a couple of kilometres long you can walk around the island in a few hours.

Fort of São Sebastião when it was finally completed in the 16th century this was the largest single structure in southern or central Africa. The main body was not finished until 1583, and bits were added on over the next hundred years. The cistern (which is still the island's only supply of fresh water) was not installed until the 17th century. A second fort, **São Lourenço**, was built at the southern end of the island, and a third, **Santo Antonio**, was added in the 18th century. São Sebastião, built with dressed limestone shipped from Portugal, withstood attacks by the Dutch, English and Arabs throughout the 17th century. It has never been captured. The Dutch sieges of the early 17th century, even with formidable firepower and battle-hardened troops, were fruitless. Despite the fact that the Portuguese had made no attempt to strengthen the garrison before the Dutch attacks, it was impossible to broach the massive walls of the fort with artillery.

There is a body of opinion that suggests the Dutch failure to take the fort was instrumental in shaping the course of history in the whole of Southern Africa. Portugal at the time was a waning naval power and would never have been able to retake Ilha de Moçambique, and without that would have lost her other bases in Mozambique. It is also thought that with the island as their base, the Dutch East India Company, which came into being in 1602, would have had no need to establish the trading station at the Cape of Good Hope that later became Cape Town, and gave birth to the Afrikaaner nation.

The fort was last used for military purposes in the early 1970s, to garrison Portuguese troops. Today it is little changed. The cannons point seaward, most still mounted on their wheeled bases, and islanders still use the cistern for fresh water. The courtyards are overgrown and the once-whitewashed inner walls are dirty and crumbling, but the great limestone buttresses, seen from outside, give an impression of utter impregnability.

There is only one entrance, on the western flank, and once inside there is little to divert you apart from the extraordinary atmosphere of the place. Give yourself at least a couple of hours inside, at different times of day. You can walk around almost the entire perimeter on the battlements, which give a panoramic view of the sea.

Within the fortress, and predating it, is the 16th-century church of **Nossa Senhora do Baluarte** – built in 1522 for the island's burgeoning Portuguese community. 'Baluarte' means bastion, which was what this northern tip of the island was before the church was built. The early Portuguese inhabitants placed defensive artillery here; the church itself looks to be the sort of building that would serve as a mini-fortress. It is the oldest standing European building in the southern hemisphere.

Palace Museum. Although the fort has never been successfully besieged, during the 17th century the town was occupied, pillaged and sacked on at least two occasions. The Dutch destroyed it in 1607 and the Omanis plundered it in 1671. The former Jesuit College of São Paolo was the only building to survive the invasions, and is now the only 17th century building surviving in the old town. Built in 1619, it was a Jesuit college until that order was expelled in 1759, and it became the governor's palace. It was last used in that capacity in 1979, when President Samora Machel visited with a government delegation. Local history has it that Machel decreed the palace should be turned into a museum when one of his more portly ministers broke the seat of a 19th-century chair. It is still on display outside one of the guest bedrooms, its seat definitely broken – history doesn't relate the name of the minister.

The museum can only be visited with a guide. It is open 9am-12pm and 2pm-5pm Wednesday-Sunday, closed Mondays and Tuesdays (though if you are desperate you should be able to persuade someone to take you round), and it closes at 3pm on Sundays and holidays. The courtyard has an interesting model of one of Vasco da Gama's boats, and the original 1640 church is worth a look. The palace occupies the entire first floor of the building, and consists of about 20 rooms in slightly dilapidated condition. The guide will point out the president's bedroom and other important guest rooms – one was occupied by President Hastings Banda of Malawi – the famous broken chair, the dining rooms and sitting rooms, and an enormous modern tapestry that was allegedly found in the fort. Also interesting for the insight into the way the Portuguese lived on Ilha are the litters – palanquins – in the entrance hall. Two or four men would have carried officials around the town on these enormous wooden recliners, which look as if they weigh two hundred pounds apiece. On the walls are amazing 1970s portraits done in the classical style. As others have noted, it is disorienting to step out into the dusty and impoverished town after all this colonial splendour.

The Sacred Art Museum. Guided tours of two people or more only. Next door to the palace in the Chapel of São Paulo, which was formerly the headquarters of the Misericórdia, a voluntary charitable institution. From around 1538 the Misericórdia established and maintained one of the first royal hospitals on the island. The museum is notable mainly for its displays of statues of the saints.

Hospital. Now being renovated, the hospital is a splendid 18th century whitewashed building, on the left just at the northern end of the reed village

At the time of writing there is nothing to see inside, although it is interesting to wander through the handsome rooms.

Church of Nossa Senhora do Saude. To the south of the causeway this ancient church was used by the pilots who guided ships into port. It is the third oldest building in Mozambique, but it is in such a state of dilapidation, and has been so extensively renovated over the centuries, that little remains of the original building. It stands in a rather run-down cemetery.

Fort of São Lourenço. Built in the 17th century to defend the southern approaches to Ilha de Mozambique, the fort entirely occupies the tiny island on the eastern side of the southern tip. It's accessible on foot at low tide, but check before you go as the tide is only low enough for about an hour. There's little to see once you're there, although a couple of cannons are still in place.

Church of Santo Antonio This is an attractive 18th century building, on the small promontory off the east of the island. In front of the main doors you will see fishermen mending their nets as they have been doing for many centuries past. It's a peaceful place, away from the hubbub of the town; you may even be able to get a haircut from the barber who usually sets up his chair in front of the cathedral.

Beaches

Ilha's beaches are not suitable for swimming, due to the fact that they are used as a toilet by most of the population. There is a diving and boat club linked to the Pousada Hotel. Ask at Reliquiés for Carlos Dias (Kaku), who will arrange motor boat and dhow trips to the beaches at Goa Island, Ilha de Cobras or Chocas Mar on the mainland.

SHOPPING

Bottled water is scarce in northern Mozambique. The best place to buy it is from the shop opposite Reliquiés. There is very little fresh food available on the island (though this will change as it becomes more geared to tourism). At present the best thing to do is rely on restaurant food or buy anything you need before you arrive.

HELP AND INFORMATION
Changing Money

The best place to change money is Banco Comercial in the old town, two blocks north of the hospital on the west side of the island.

Post Office

The Post Office is just to the north of the Palace Museum. Next door is a Telecom office where you can make national and international phone calls.

FURTHER AFIELD

MOSSURIL AND CABACEIRA

Together with Cabaceira, Mossuril was one of two Portuguese parishes on the mainland, sister towns to Ilha de Moçambique. There's little to see there today; its main interest for travellers is the nearby beach of Chocas Mar. The *Complexo Chocas Mar* has rooms and a good campsite and restaurant. At Cabaceira the governor built himself a country house in the 18th century of which nothing remains today. However, the 18th-century church of **Nossa Senhora de Remedios**, and the remains of a **fort** are still there and worth a visit. At Mossuril you can also hire a dhow to take you to Angoche and other nearby coastal towns.

LUMBO

There is an airport at Lumbo (5km from the bridge to Ilha) from which charter flights can be organised. Other interesting facts about this town, which was an important transport hub, are that it has a British war cemetary, and that Ava Gardner and the Aga Khan had a romance there, in the luxury Hotel Lumbo. The hotel is now a ruin, with various families living in the once-splendid rooms.

Niassa

Lake Niassa

Niassa is the biggest, most sparsely-populated of Mozambique's ten provinces. It is also the least-explored. More easily accessed from Malawi than from Mozambique (there are only two approach roads from the east), it is bordered to the west by Lago Niassa and dense, miombo-covered mountains, and to the north by the unruly Rio Rovuma and the Tanzanian frontier. The climate of the province can be inhospitable: Niassa is one of the most mountainous regions of the country and can be bitterly cold in winter; Maniamba, 100km northwest of Lichinga, has the highest rainfall in

Mozambique.

On the shores of the great lake – still known by its colonial name of Lake Niassa in Mozambique – travellers come upon a way of life that has not changed for hundreds of years. The climate here is temperate all the year round, and although there are few places with any facilities for tourists, you should have no difficulty finding a place to pitch your tent. The very inaccessibility of the lake (almost all the access roads are passable only in 4WD, and there is very little public transport) is its greatest attraction. While the Malawian shores are developed, getting around on the Mozambican side is what many consider a truly adventurous 'African' experience.

NIASSA GAME RESERVE

Apart from the lake there is little else to attract the tourist in Niassa. The vast Niassa Game Reserve is one of the best stocked of Mozambique's sadly depleted game parks, with large herds of elephant, zebras, buffaloes, wild dogs and antelope. In 1998 the government announced plans for the development of the 22,000 sq km park, to be managed and funded by 51 per cent state ownership and 49 per cent private ownership. This plan hasn't been implemented yet, but at present the park is accessible in 4WD, and there are camping facilities. Local guides are available (and can be arranged at the Hotel Pousada in Lichinga).

LICHINGA

Lichinga, the capital of Niassa province, is a small, quiet town with very little for the tourist to do except enjoy the climate and the relaxed pace of life. The town stands at a height of over a thousand metres on the plateau to the east of Lake Niassa, and benefits from the cooler winds coming off the lake. One of the main reasons to visit Lichinga is to use it as a base to explore the eastern shores of the lake, two hours away by car, on roads that are good in parts and very rough in others.

ARRIVAL AND DEPARTURE
Air

LAM connects Lichinga directly with Maputo twice a week, Nampula three times a week, and Tete once a week.

Private Car

The roads serving Lichinga are improving, though many stretches are still unsurfaced and in the rainy season you should only attempt them in 4WD.

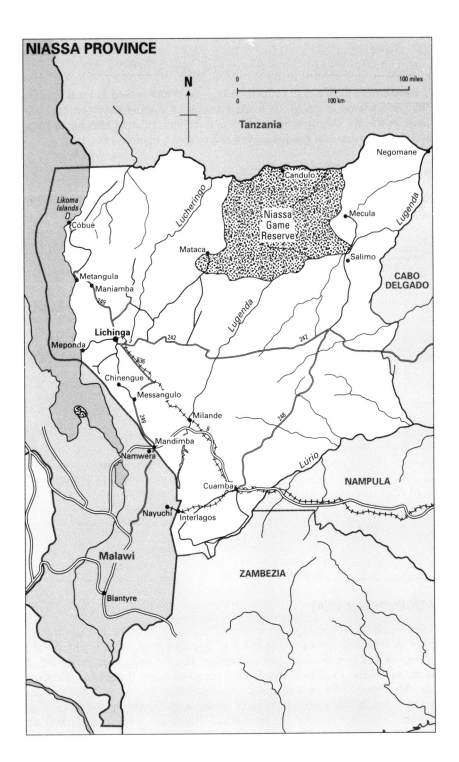

The road from Lichinga to Cuamba is in good condition and can just about be done in a saloon, although there are a couple of makeshift bridges that may cause problems. The same is true for the three-hour drive to Mandimba on the Malawian border: it is good in parts but very rough in others.

Public Transport

Buses and chapas for Cuamba and other towns leave from in front of the central market. There is a daily bus for Cuamba which leaves at 5am.

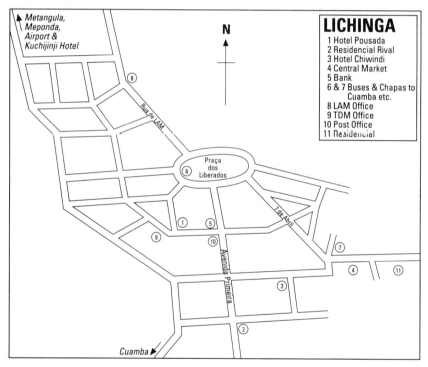

N

LICHINGA
1 Hotel Pousada
2 Residencial Rival
3 Hotel Chiwindi
4 Central Market
5 Bank
6 & 7 Buses & Chapas to Cuamba etc.
8 LAM Office
9 TDM Office
10 Post Office
11 Residencial

Metangula, Meponda, Airport & Kuchijinji Hotel

Rua de LAM

Praça dos Liberados

7 de Abril

Avenida Primeira

Cuamba

ACCOMMODATION

The main hotel in Lichinga is the *Hotel Pousada*. It has no running water but provides bucket showers and toilets. Doubles start at $20. The hotel's restaurant can best be described as average, and the drinks are expensive. A better bet is the *Kuchijinji Motel*, 3km out of town on the road to Meponda and the airport. Run by a religious organisation, it has hot and cold running water, a reasonable restaurant without a bar, single dormitory rooms ($15 per person), and 'VIP houses' for around $50. These are good value if there are two or more of you: clean, nicely decorated and fully furnished. Other options include the dismal *Hotel Chiwindi* (squalid rooms for $10-15), and the *Residencial Rival* (decent doubles with bathroom for $15). Try also the *residencial* next to the market south-east of the main square (ask for directions). The rooms are tiny, but clean and cheap at $5-6 per night.

EATING AND DRINKING

The restaurant at the Kuchijinji is worth a try, as is *Dona Argentinas* (ask directions), which is nohing more than a breezeblock shack, with about six tables and a bar. Some of the food is cooked behind the bar and the rest appears through a hole in the wall. Most of the expats in Lichinga reckon it's the best food in town. There are several other restaurants and bars, but none particularly memorable. Some of the restaurants run sweaty but enjoyable discos at the weekends.

LAKE NIASSA

Lago Niassa – known as Lake Malawi across the border – is a vast inland sea covering over 6,000 square kilometres. The World Lakes Database (www.ilec.or.ip) describes it as 'the most southerly of the great African Rift Valley lakes', 560km long and with a greatest width of 75km. It is some 700m deep at the western shore, rising to a depth of around 200m at the eastern shore. Most of the lake falls within the borders of Malawi, but Mozambique owns a 200km-long stretch on the eastern side. People have lived along the shores of the lake for centuries, and their way of life has hardly changed. The waters supply every human need from the purely physical – drinking, washing, fishing – to the spiritual – local legend has it that the water brings fertility to the land and to the wombs of women unable to bear children. The lake demands respect: every rise and fall of the water is noted and explained, and even its winds have names – the *Lichinga*, the *vuma* from the north that flattens houses and uproots trees, the *muela* from the south that brings malaria and capsizes boats.

This part of Mozambique is hardly visited by tourists. For anyone headed for Malawi, there is little you can do on the eastern shore that can't be done more easily on the western side, which is much more developed, and caters for tourists. But it is the Mozambique side's very inaccessibility that draws the more adventurous traveller. There are very few facilities; the villages that skirt the shore have few if any vehicles, and there is no public transport. Stories circulate of people who have had to walk for days before they were picked up.

The lake harbours a huge number of freshwater fish, some of which are very rare. At least 500 species have been recorded, and biologists reckon at least that many have yet to be discovered. The shores of the lake are good for birdwatching, and there have been sightings of game, although you are highly unlikely to see anything. Before the civil war hippopotamus lived on the lake and lions, antelopes and other game were not uncommon. Although the chances of seeing any wild animals in Mozambique are remote – in this sparsely-populated part of the country you may have a better chance.

There are three settlements on this side of the lake: Meponda, Metangula and Cóbuè. At the time of writing all sorts of plans are afoot for tourist developments; it remains to be seen whether any of them will come to fruition.

MEPONDA

Meponda, 600-odd kilometres from Lichinga, is a small village on a beautiful and deserted beach. There is no formal accommodation, but you could camp on the beach, where there is a café which serves cold beers, snacks and basic meals. You will need 4WD to get down to the village; if you are on public transport, take a chapa from the market in Lichinga.

METANGULA

This is the largest of the settlements on the lake, the slightly decrepit remnants of what was a large slave-trading town. There are a few shops in the centre, and a pensão if you need to stay in town for any reason. A far better bet is to make for Chwanga, 10km from Metangula, where a Mr Katawala runs a small beach resort with good-sized huts, a camping area, a bar and a restaurant. There are plans to develop Chwanga further for tourism – get there soon and you'll find it in its unspoiled state.

CÓBUÈ

This attractive little town lies on a lovely part of the lakeshore. It is perfectly placed for getting to the beautiful island of Likoma, a Malawian possession that lies in Mozambican waters. You can get a dhow from Cóbuè to Likoma – the crossing takes about an hour. On Likoma you can get a steamer to mainland Malawi. For more details on getting to Malawi see *Getting There* p.55. In Cóbuè there are various people, notably an Australian entrepreneur, setting up lodges and campsites, and it's difficult to say at what stage any of them will be ready. At the time of writing the *Hotel Santo Miguel* has rooms for about $10, and there is a basic campsite on the beach. You can get to Cóbuè either by hitching a lift on one of the (very infrequent) trucks that come up from Metangula, or see if you can get someone to take you up the shore by dhow, although that would take at least a day.

CUAMBA

Cuamba gets all its character from its position as a transport hub in the middle of barren and underpopulated country. For many travellers coming in by train from Liwonde in Malawi it is the first Mozambican town in which they stop. It is also the last stop on the railway line from Nampula – see *Nampula* p.204 for train times. Being close to the Malawian border, the town has a raffish air, its inhabitants – like frontier townspeople all over the world – are sharp and streetwise. Cuamba may be nothing much to look at but it has some good restaurants and vibrant nightlife. If you have to stay a day or two en route to Malawi or Nampula, you won't get too bored.

ARRIVAL AND DEPARTURE

Private Car

The roads connecting Cuamba to Lichinga, Malawi, Gurúe and Nampula are in good condition.

Public Transport

Cuamba is well-served by bus and chapa from Lichinga, and by train from Nampula. From Gurúe to the south there are fewer vehicles, but once you get to Mutuáli you will be able to pick up a lift for the hour's journey to Cuamba without any difficulty. You can get a bus to Lichinga from the opposite side of the railway line to the town centre, leaving at 4.30am-5am and taking about eight hours to cover the 300km. Coming from Lichinga buses leave at the same time from the main market in the town centre. There is also a fair amount of truck and chapa traffic doing the same route.

Train

One train a day goes to Nampula, leaving the station at 6am sharp. It takes around six hours; second class is $8, third class is $4. There is a buffet on the train which serves *pregos*, beer, tea and coffee; at every stop locals sell fruits in season and a variety of other delicious snacks – chicken legs, honey cakes and the like. See *Nampula* for more details. If you are going third class make sure you arrive early to get a seat; second class seats are in compartments and are much more comfortable.

From Cuamba to the Malawian border

There is a freight train from Cuamba to the small town of Interlagos on the Mozambican side of the border, which takes passengers. It is normally scheduled to connect with other passenger services going to and from the Malawian towns of Nayuchi and Balaka. Check all train times in the station at Cuamba – at present trains from Cuamba to Interlagos leave at 6am on Mondays and Thursdays, but the timetable is subject to frequent changes.

The road to Interlagos is well-served by bus and chapa, leaving from the main market in the town centre. The road journey takes about four hours, the rail journey slightly longer.

ACCOMMODATION

The most expensive hotel in Cuamba is the *Vision 2000*, at the western end of the main road that runs past the small park. Clean and quiet singles and doubles are $18-27, with hot water bucket supplied. Walking towards the park you will get to the *Pensão São Miguel*, which has clean double rooms for $13-15. A block south of the Vision 2000 is the *Pensão Formosa*, which has small singles for around $6. Further on is the *Pensão Namaacha*, probably the best choice in town, with spacious cool doubles for $6-8, and hot water bucket supplied in the shared bathroom. It is frequented by Mozambican travellers and is clean, neat and friendly. Other options are the *Pensão Namuli* and the *Pensão Nabão*, both decent enough.

EATING AND DRINKING

Cuamba doesn't have any haute cuisine on offer, but you'll find the various restaurants and bars lively and friendly. The *Restaurante São Miguel*, next door to Hotel Vision 2000, is a jolly family place with big dining room and tables outside. They will do you a leathery steak for a reasonable price. Next door in the hotel the dining room is a more sophisticated affair, with a varied menu for $5-7, although quality is not assured. One of the best places to eat is actually the *Pensão Namaacha*: warn them in advance that you will be wanting supper.

NIGHTLIFE

The *pastelaria* round the corner from the Pensão Namaacha is lively and loud and has an interesting clientele, as does the *Bar-Restaurant Floresta*, but the most upmarket night-spot in town is the Disco 2000, downstairs in the Hotel Vision 2000. There is a $4 entrance fee after about 10pm; it is here that the middle classes of Cuamba come to relax, as well as the aid workers and civil engineers you will find in every small town in Mozambique. On Saturday nights the disco hosts the Miss Cuamba competition.

HELP AND INFORMATION

Changing Money Banco Comercial, next door to Bar-Restaurant Floresta.
Post Office and Telecommunications between the park and the Hotel Vision 2000.
Hospital in front of the station.
Gasoline there is a BP garage just opposite the Hotel Vision 2000.
Market in the same road as Pensão Namaacha, three blocks south.

Cabo Delgado

Ibo Island

The low-lying hills and wild scrubland of north-east Mozambique – the modern province of Cabo Delgado – was one of the last regions to be tamed by the Portuguese. The Niassa Company nominally controlled the area north of the Lúrio river, but found it impossible to collect taxes and labour levies from the warlike Makua, Yao and Makonde chiefs who dominated the area, and constantly harassed the Portuguese garrisons. By the beginning of the 20th century most of Cabo Delgado was under control, except for the Makonde plateau in the far north-east. In fact the Portuguese never managed to dominate the region. Frelimo garnered most of its early support in Cabo Delgado, and it was in the town of Chai, 100km north of Pemba, that the young resistance movement launched the attack on a Portuguese barracks that began the war of independence on 25 September 1964.

If the people of Cabo Delgado made life difficult for the Portuguese, they also have a reputation amongst southern Mozambicans, many of whom are frightened to travel there alone. The Makonde are called 'mavia', meaning 'fierce' or 'terrible' by their Tanzanian neighbours. This may have more to do with the old practice of body decoration and adornment: scarification, tooth sharpening, and the wearing of lip plugs, than with any inherent aggression. But they can certainly be off-putting: the men appear silent and taciturn, and the women, their faces and arms covered in skin-softening paste made from the ground bark of the nciro tree, can seem unapproachable.

Cabo Delgado – the 'thin cape' – is little visited. Very few travellers come in over the Rovuma from Tanzania, or pass the other way. The province, however, has its attractions. The capital city of Pemba, itself a pleasant place, has a massive and very beautiful beach, with excellent snorkelling and deep-sea fishing. Further north you will find other, isolated villages sitting on great sweeps of white sand, fringed by swaying palms. This part of the coast is seductive, but it is very difficult to get around without your own transport, and you need to allow yourself several days to cover relatively short distances. The lack of passing traffic is compounded by the atrocious state of the roads: it can take at least five hours to cover 100km in this part of Mozambique.

Perhaps the province's greatest draw is **Ibo Island**, the ruined capital of the Querimba Archipelago, a day's journey from Pemba. Those who have visited Ilha de Moçambique will have seen what a once-splendid colonial town looks like when the occupying power has passed into history. But Ilha is a working town, whereas Ibo is in a state of elegant but terminal decay. It is one of the most astonishing relics of Portugal's African adventure: if you see nothing else in this part of Mozambique, you should get to Ibo.

PEMBA

Travellers who have spent time bouncing about on the back of the trucks and chapas that constitute the only form of public transport in the far north of Mozambique, and staying in bug-ridden local pensãos and rat-infested hotel rooms, are delighted to arrive at Pemba. By the standards of Beira and Maputo it's a quiet little place, but it has reliable electricity, good restaurants and bars, cold beers, clean hotel rooms and a wonderful beach. The huge turquoise bay with its lovely beach comes into view as you approach Pemba through the low hills to the south. As you approach, travelling companions will admiringly murmur, 'Pemba', softly emphasising the last syllable – 'Pembaaa.' As the sea gets closer it really does look like the typical paradise of thousands of tourist brochures.

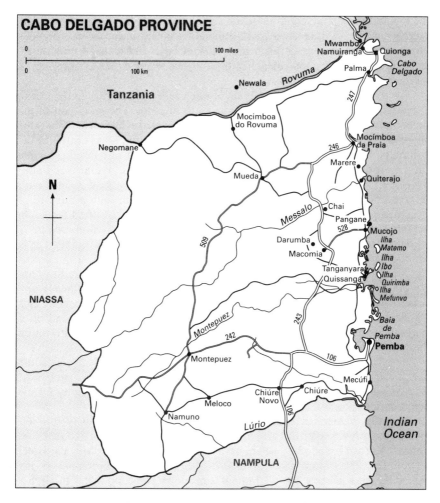

CABO DELGADO PROVINCE

Tanzania

Niassa

Nampula

Indian Ocean

Pemba, the provincial capital of Cabo Delgado, is a modern town. The Portuguese tried to set up an agricultural settlement here in 1857, when 36 settlers were granted land rights on the site of Pemba's forerunner, the city of Porto Amelia. But the surrounding land proved to be far less fertile than anticipated and the attempt quickly failed. The modern town of Porto Amelia – the name was changed to Pemba in the 1930s – was founded in 1904 when the Niassa company moved its headquarters there, and by 1928 had a population of 1,600, of which 67 were Europeans.

Today it's a backwater, but a very pleasant one for all that. A large number of aid workers from Switzerland, Finland, Denmark and the rest of Europe are based there, as well as South African and Zimbabwean road engineers, giving the town a cosmopolitan air. There are some very lively bars, most notably the outrageous Pemba Take-Away, with its blaring music, cheap beers, delicious home-made ice cream, drunken ten-year-old boys and teenage prostitutes. There are also some good cafés, like the A Tasca where expats congregate, or the Encontro in the port area.

The town occupies the outside arm of one of the biggest bays in the world, a natural, enclosed harbour, 25km from north to south. The main part of the modern town sits above the port and a picturesque reed village which hugs the shore at the tip of the peninsula. Six kilometres from the town centre, to the south, is Wembe Beach, which if nothing else will put Pemba on the international tourist map within the next five years. Wembe is being developed at a rapid rate. At the time of writing the beach road is lined with reserved plots and half-constructed residences being built with a mixture of government money, aid funds and private investment. Pemba airport is soon to get international status, and the roads are being improved month-on-month.

There is no doubt that Wembe is beautiful beach. At the moment it is practically untouched, except for a few beach chalets and a couple of restaurants. It is very much a working beach; at low tide the shallows are covered in stooping figures looking for shells, and at any time of day fishermen load and unload their boats. Their are always several cheerful kids wandering around, who will come and watch you as you camp, and offer suggestions as to how to spit fish using pine fronds. Camping is allowed on the beach and you will be able to buy crayfish, crab and other fish every evening from local fishermen. Most travellers and tourists decide to stay at the beach rather than in town (though there are a couple of good hotels). At Wembe you can either hire a beach hut or camp – the latter being by far the better option. You'll find all facilities there except for banks.

To get to Wembe beach take the road past the Pemba Take-Away, turn left at the roundabout with the globe, and right at the next major intersection. Follow the road for another 4-5km until you get to the derelict Mia Via Hotel on your left. The Complexo Nautilus is the beginning of the beach proper. It's walkable, but it takes a good 45 minutes or more; you'd do better to hitch a lift outside the Pemba Take-Away or at the roundabout.

ARRIVAL AND DEPARTURE

Air

LAM has regular direct and connecting flights between Nampula, Beira, Maputo and Johannesburg. Plan your journey carefully because all flights, especially during school holidays, get booked up quickly. Pemba-Maputo costs $300. The airport is about 3km out of town on the

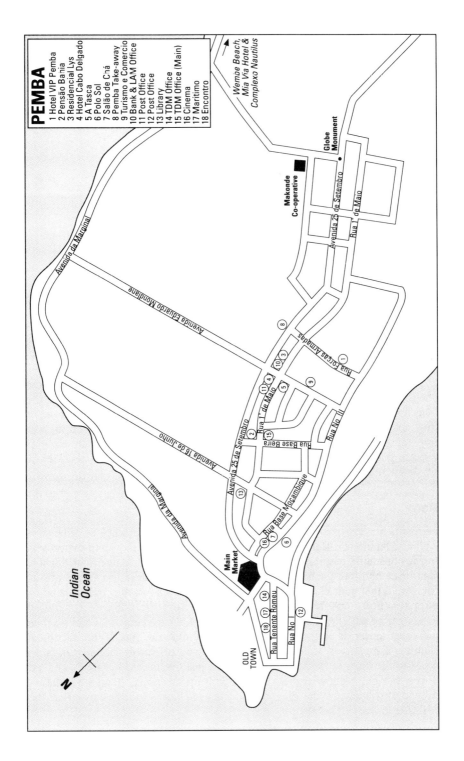

PEMBA

1 Hotel VIP Pemba
2 Pensão Bahia
3 Residencial Lys
4 Hotel Cabo Delgado
5 A Tasca
6 Polo Sol
7 Salão de Chá
8 Pemba Take-away
9 Turismo e Comercio
10 Bank & LAM Office
11 Post Office
12 Post Office
13 Library
14 TDM Office
15 TDM Office (Main)
16 Cinema
17 Maritimo
18 Encontro

Indian Ocean

Wembe Beach,
Mia Via Hotel &
Complexo Nautilus

Globe Monument

Makonde Co-operative

Avenida da Marginal

Avenida Eduardo Mondlane

Avenida 16 de Junho

Avenida da Marginal

Avenida 25 de Setembro

Rua Forças Armadas

Rua 1˚ de Maio

Rua No. III

Rua Base Beira

Rua Base Moçambique

Rua Tenente Romeu

Rua No. I

Avenida 25 de Setembro

Rua 1˚ de Maio

Main Market

OLD TOWN

N

Nampula road. There is no bus but it is easy to hitch a lift. The Nautilus on Wembe beach lays on a courtesy bus for its guests.

Private Car

The road between Nampula and Pemba is in good condition and is passable in a saloon. The journey should take between 6 and 8 hours.

Public Transport

From Nampula there is a Transnorte bus which leaves at 5am on Mondays, Wednesdays and Fridays, and takes 12 hours or more to cover the 416km to Pemba. That is by far the best bet, otherwise you are reduced to a gruelling series of chapas and trucks. Lifts aren't difficult to come by, but they take a long time when they do come and you will find yourself having to change a lot. If you are coming from Ilha de Moçambique make sure you get to the Namialo turn-off by 8am at the very latest, in order to catch the daily bus coming up from Nampula. If you miss it, you can always catch a chapa, but you will have a more comfortable journey in the bus. From the north and Tanzania there are no buses; most public transport starts at Mocimboa da Praia at 5am and take 12-18 hours to get to Pemba, over the worst roads in the country. Buses for Nampula and the south leave at 5am from outside the Pensão Bahía, and also make a long stop at the regular bus stop, 1.5km out of town and about 500m past the turn-off for Wembe beach. For the north, take any transport to Namialo and change there, but as for Ilha, get there early. If you are going to Ibo Island, get any transport going to Namialo and ask to be set down at Km 27, the turn-off for Quissanga. See *Ibo* for details.

Boat

Pemba is a major port serving ships bound for Durban and Dar es Salaam as well as Maputo and Beira. It is also a fishing town with dhow and motor-boat traffic constantly passing along the coast, and it is fast becoming a fashionable spot to anchor your yacht for two or three days during an Indian Ocean cruise. But for all that your chances of getting a lift up and down the coast depend on your ingenuity and luck. At the time of writing there are no scheduled passenger boats. There used to be one that left the harbour at 4am and went up the coast as far as Ibo, but that seems to be defunct. Ask Pieter Jacobs at Nautilus if he knows of anything, at the shipping offices in the harbour, or go down to the Paquite Quete, the reed village just outside the old town, and see if you can get a dhow captain to take you up the coast. Remember dhows depend absolutely on the prevailing winds and tides, and the voyage to Ibo will take at least 12 hours.

PEMBA

In town there are a number of hotels. *Pensão Bahía* (opposite Telecom on Rua 1 de Maio; tel 072-3435) charges $15 for a double with fan, and has a decent and reasonable restaurant attached. It is clean and neat, and very popular with travellers. Further along the same road is the *Residencial Lys* ($20-25 double room with bathroom), whose pleasant-looking wrought-iron verandah is inviting, although the author found the dining room infested with rats and the bedrooms alive with bugs. A far better bet is the *Hotel VIP Pemba* (Rua Forças Armadas; tel 072-3442, next right after Residencial Lys), which has just been upgraded and has good-sized doubles for between $25 and $35, with fans or air-conditioning and running water. The hotel has a very good restaurant with an outside terrace. The most upmarket hotel in town is the *Cabo Delgado* (Ave Eduardo Mondlane; tel 072-2558), with smart air-conditioned rooms with running water for $20-$30, and a restaurant. At the other end of the scale, but useful if you need to stay near the harbour, is the Marítimo (near the market in the old town). The rooms are small and dirty and cost $5-12.

WEMBE

If you are intending to spend a lot of time at the beach, camping could not be more highly recommended. There is nothing to stop you camping on the beach itself. Pitch your tent there and you will soon be visited by a local government official wanting $3-4 a day payment for camping on government land. You should demand a receipt which he will be happy to get you. It's not advisable to leave your tent unattended for too long, as things do go missing, but there are lots of people about during the day and it won't be difficult to get someone to watch it for you. Local fishermen will sell you their catch; pay no more than $5 per kilo for crayfish and crab, less for other fish. Firewood is quite hard to come by but you should find enough to cook with. Another camping option is the site run by the friendly and helpful Pieter Jacobs, who has the diving concession at the Nautilus. You can camp for $2-3 a day in his field at the end of the beach. It has the advantage of being guarded day and night by an affable local, but it is rather small and dirty and out of sight of the sea, and is altogether less attractive than the clean, white sand of the beach.

Also at Wembe is the *Complexo Nautilus* (tel 072-3520, or Johannesburg 011-339 7275; fax 339 7295) which has basic double-bedroomed huts for $65 each. You're unlikely to get one with a working shower. Booking is essential. There is also a restaurant (see *Eating and Drinking*, below). At the time of writing Pieter Jacobs has plans for five chalets for which he will charge around $20 for two people; for the latest information on these chalets check with him on 072-2850/3520. On the road to the beach coming from town you will see the derelict Mia Via hotel, in a splendid position on the edge of the bay. President Chissano's son has allegedly bought the place and plans to do it up.

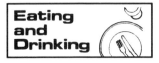

Eating and Drinking

Some of the nicest places to eat are at Wembe beach, although there are also a couple of very good eateries in town.

Pemba

The smartest restaurant in town is upstairs at the *Cabo Delgado*. It has a varied, well-cooked menu starting at around $5, but the dining room does lack atmosphere. Since its renovation the *VIP Pemba* is one of the best places to eat, with a varied and quite expensive menu. They also serve excellent coffee. At the entrance of the Cabo Delgado is a tea-room with cakes and pastries and imported chocolates. Next door to the Cabo Delgado is *A Tasca*, where you can eat outside. The menu has a selection of meat and seafood dishes starting at around $6. A Tasca is a good meeting place for expats – anyone coming into town always stops there for a coffee. Take the right turn off the roundabout just down from A Tasca and you get to the famous *Pemba Take-Away* – you'll hear the music before you arrive. It is run by a Danish-German called Pelle, who imports all his beers and sells them cheap. Not to be missed. In the old town the Portuguese-run *Restaurante Encontro* (a block away from the Pensão Maritimo) has a good reputation and is an interesting place to visit for its huge collection of Makonde carvings. On the way down to the old town, the shabby *Polo Sol* has a not-exactly romantic view of the container docks. The restaurant is run-of-the-mill but the disco on Fridays and Sundays is packed.

Other places to try are the restaurant at the *Pensão Bahía*, which does excellent chicken dishes for $7, and the *Residencial Lys*, which despite its debatable state of cleanliness has a fair reputation.

Wembe

The first place you get to at Wembe is *Nautilus*. With its shaded terrace overlooking the beach it is very popular with the better class of tourist, and it should be an exquisite spot for a lunchtime beer, or a late-night whisky watching the waves diffracting the silver moonlight as they lap the soft sand of the beach.

But the staff – despite or because of the pretentious 'native' uniform they are obliged to wear – are surly, and the food overcooked and overpriced. Moreover, the restaurant has what is known as a 'white' dog, a healthy-looking hound that nuzzles your hand if you're white, but barks and growls at the local boys who shift their boats along the beach, but know better than to come onto the terrace to sell their trinkets.

Further along the beach is the far nicer *Sol e Mar*, a friendly little place with tables on the beach, a freezerful of cold beer, and a reasonably-priced fish menu. If you are camping it may be wise to make friends with the owners, who will let you store fish in their fridge. Further on still is a massive place, the *Restaurante Boite Wimbe*, which has an enthusiastic disco at the weekends. The restaurant is popular with locals, and not too pricey.

On Wembe beach you can buy fresh bread from a couple of kiosks in the morning, and the Sol e Mar or Nautilus will sell you beer and water.

SHOPPING

The main market in Pemba is the *Mercado Municipal*, on the road leading down to the old town, past the Polo Sol. It has a wide variety of stalls selling fresh fruit and vegetables, meat and fish. There is also a market in the centre, opposite the Cabo Delgado. In the old town you will find an excellent selection of mainly Indian-run shops selling everything from bedding and furniture to electrical goods, clothing and textiles, alcohol and tools. For Makonde carvings (see the *Shopping* section of *Practical Information* for a detailed description of Makonde art) try the Encontro (see above) or the Makonde cooperative (on the way to the beach, turn left at the roundabout with a large globe in the middle and it's a few hundred metres on your left), which has a good selection of wood and ivory pieces, and you can also watch the carvers at work.

HELP AND INFORMATION

Tourist Office

There is no government tourist office, but the best place for information is *Turismo e Comercio* (Ave Eduardo Mondlane, in the square on the left going up). They speak English and arrange excursions, charter flights to the islands, fishing and diving trips.

Changing Money

Same rules apply as in the rest of Mozambique – banks will only change travellers cheques if you have a receipt. The best place to change money is the Banco Standard Totta (Ave Eduardo Mondlane, opposite the Hotel Cabo Delgado). There is another bank on the way down to the old town, opposite the Mercado Municipal.

Airline Offices

The LAM office is on Ave 25 de Setembro (tel 072-2434/5), at the bottom of Ave Eduardo Mondlane. English spoken.

Post Office and Telecommunications

The main post office is in the old town on the harbour road. There is a smaller branch around the corner from the Hotel Cabo Delgado. The main Telecom office is on Rua 1 de Maio, opposite Pensão Bahía. There is another small office on Wembe beach, halfway down opposite the Restaurante Sol e Mar.

Library

Ave 16 de Junho. The library is being re-stocked and catalogued by a Finnish aid agency, and is useful for maps, periodicals etc.

EXCURSIONS

Pemba has some of the best diving and snorkelling in the world. From the middle of the beach you can reach a coral reef at low tide after five minutes with a snorkel (at high tide it's a tougher swim); towards the far end of the beach, by the Boite Wembe, the snorkelling is supposed to be even better.

Between Pemba and the River Rovuma, which marks the Tanzanian border, there are 32 islands, all of which have something to offer the dedicated diver – the diving off Ibo is supposed to be the very best. Diving need not be prohibitively expensive – Pieter Jacobs (details above) offers trips for $11 if you have your own equipment, $35 all-inclusive. He is a qualified instructor and offers full PADI courses, up to dive master level, starting at $45. Trips around the islands can be arranged through Pieter and also through Turismo e Comercio in town (details above).

UP THE COAST FROM PEMBA

IBO ISLAND

Ibo Island is one of the most ancient European settlements in Mozambique, and certainly one of the most fascinating places you will visit in Southern Africa. The town of Ibo was a centre of mercantile activity from the 16th to the beginning of the 20th century, but nothing remains today but the crumbling ruins of once-elegant Portuguese merchants' houses, municipal buildings, two ruined forts and a church. Most of the local population live in reed huts on the outskirts of the town, leaving the mansions with their colonnaded verandahs and carefully laid-out gardens to succumb quietly to the pitilcss cmbracc of the strangler figs that climb walls, collapse roofs and undermine foundations. Ibo is a ghost town – the streets are empty, the market stalls bereft, there is neither restaurant nor pensão, and almost no electricity supply. Like all towns that have fallen from prosperity to decay, the signs of better days are everywhere. In the elegant main square with its municipal offices (of which one or two faded rooms are still used by local government officials) the low fences that surrounded the gardens are still there, and splashes of pink paintwork still adorn the broken walls of the houses.

You should make every effort to get to Ibo. It is isolated, but on public transport you can get there in a day from Pemba, and you should be able to get away again quite easily using a bit of traveller's savoir faire.

The Querimba archipelago, of which Ibo forms a part, was an important centre of Muslim trade long before the Portuguese arrived. A cloth called *maluane*, highly prized as far afield as Sofala and Zambesia, was manufactured there, and for years the Portuguese knew the archipelago as the Maluane Islands. In the 16th Century the Portuguese began to settle there, and by 1590 local *senhores*, receiving tributes from the local population, were established on all the major islands. On Querimba there was a fortified plantation house and a Dominican church that was a focus of missionary activity in the area. The ruins of plantation houses can still be seen on Quisiva and Matemo.

The islands produced millet and rice, coconuts and a variety of fruit, as well as cattle, pigs, goats and poultry, and were used as a source of food supply for Ilha de Moçambique. As well as *maluane* cloth the region produced amber and jet, ivory, turtleshell and ambergris. During the 17th and 18th centuries they increased in prosperity, even as the ivory trade declined and the centre of economic activity moved to the south and Lourenço Marques. The slave trade became a major source of wealth – the islands were dominated by two Afro-Portuguese families, the Meneses and the Moraes, who struck lucrative deals with French and Arab traffickers anxious to continue what was an illegal trade by the end of the 18th century. The maze of narrow tidal waterways that surrounds the archipelago was ideal for the running of contraband. Larger ships, especially the British gunboats the patrolled the coast after slavery was outlawed, could not penetrate the shallow channels.

In 1752 Ibo was given the status of municipality and the governor general began to build a small fort. A church and warehouses followed, and a customs house was added in 1786. In 1891 the star-shaped fort to the north of the town was built. The slave trade had brought prosperity to the islands, and to Ibo in particular, and by the early 19th Century generous streets had been laid out, gardens designed and planted, and a group of fine buildings erected round the main plaza. In 1897 Ibo was handed over to the Niassa Company, which used it as a base for exploring the interior of Mozambique.

If it was the islands' shallow waters which allowed them to continue trading slaves and to prosper, they were also responsible in part for their decline. By the end of the 19th century the Niassa company needed a deep-water port for increasingly larger modern ships, and in 1904 the headquarters were moved to Porto Amelia – Pemba – further down the coast. Ibo today has a population of around 5,000. Though it remains the administrative capital of the Querimba area it is, figuratively as well as literally, a backwater.

But being so far off the tourist track (and indeed any other track) has many advantages. The Querimba islands and their inhabitants have been unmolested for centuries: women collect oyster shells for mother-of-pearl, and the men fish for crab exactly as their most ancient forebears did. As a result the coral reefs and the mangrove swamps that make up the islands' ecosystem are still as nature intended them to be. Breeding colonies of a variety of seabirds flourish, as do turtles and dolphins in the deeper waters. A recent Mozambican-French scientific expedition to the mangrove swamps of Ibo, examining the medicinal properties of underwater animal and vegetable species, discovered new sea invertebrates and an unknown type of sponge. Much of the archipelago has still to be explored.

ARRIVAL AND DEPARTURE
Air

You can charter a plane at Pemba airport or at Turismo e Comercio in Pemba (see Pemba chapter for details). This should cost around $100 per person, though you will have to fill the plane in order to make it viable.

Private Car

The road to Quissanga from Pemba is well-covered and passable in a saloon; the track from Quissanga to Tanganyara impassable in anything but a good 4WD. In any case you should probably leave the car at Quissanga and pay someone to look after it during your stay on the island – you won't find anyone reliable at Tanganyara, which is little more than a beach.

Public Transport

Ibo is not the easiest place to get to, but the difficulty of the journey will give your visit to the island an added savour. The best way to get there is by public transport. From Pemba take any vehicle heading to Nampula and ask to be let down at the turn-off for Quissanga (pronounced 'kish-anga'), 26km out of town. If you want to be sure of getting to Ibo in one day, you should catch the 5am Transnorte bus to Nampula (which leaves from outside the Pensão Bahía). Take any transport to Quissanga, then ask directions to Tanganyára, from where boats leave for Ibo. It is a good hour's walk down a rutted track to Tanganyara; there is a short cut over the mud flats which you could get someone to show you, or you may be lucky and find a car going down there. Once at Tanganyara, look out for a dhow captain and negotiate a price for the hour-long trip. There are a couple of motor boats that ferry residents and passengers across – you'll just have to take whatever transport is available. A motorboat should cost you about $5 per person, a dhow about the same. If you are the only passenger on the dhow, expect to pay more, but don't let them charge you more than about $15. Dhows rely on the tides, so be prepared to wait a couple of hours.

Boat

This should be the easiest way to get to Ibo from Pemba, but there are few boats taking tourists up the coast at the moment. *Arrival and Departure* in the Pemba section gives details on the options. Once you are on Ibo it will be much easier to hire a motor boat or dhow to take you on up the coast. Knock on the door of the municipal offices and ask if anyone can arrange a boat for you.

ACCOMMODATION

There is no formal accommodation on Ibo. A Frenchwoman called Janine lives on the island and puts up travellers or lets them camp in her garden for a couple of dollars per tent. She is always there on Mondays for the visit of the governor, but if she's away there will be somebody at her house who will sort out a space for your tent. Ask for Casa Janine. Otherwise, there is accommodation in the big Telecom de Moçambique building near the market and the fort. If all else fails, ask around and you will find a family willing to put you up for a small fee.

EATING AND DRINKING

There is a bar of sorts just by the monument opposite the market. It seems to stock only gin, but the *senhora* will make you a chicken dinner if you give her a couple of hours' warning. As in other parts of northern Mozambique, you should ask around for someone who will prepare you a meal. If you are lucky you will find a good cook and will have an excellent piri piri or fish meal for a very reasonable price. As tourism increases this excellent and informal system will disappear. If you want to cook for yourself, take all the food you need; you will find practically nothing on Ibo. There is a market but the only stalls are run by children selling homemade honey cakes and a small amount of fruit.

The Makonde and their Art

There are two peoples who call themselves after the thicket-covered plateau (makonde) they inhabit: the Makonde of northern Mozambique and the Makonde of Tanzania. The latter live north of the River Rovuma on the Tanzanian Makonde Plateau, the latter on another Makonde Plateau, south of the Rovuma and west of Mocimboa da Praia.

The Mozambican Makonde Plateau is a natural fortress, dry but irrigated by heavy dews. The people who live there —farmers who practice crop-rotation and keep a few animals— have a reputation for fierceness: the area was not brought under Portuguese control until the 1920s, and the first Christian missionaries didn't arrive there until 1923. Many southern Makonde migrated north over the last 100 years, to escape Portuguese colonialism and forced labour, and the upheavals of the War Of Independence and the Civil War —at one stage it was estimated some 60,000 Makonde were living away from their homeland. Those that found their way to Tanzania were not enthusiastically welcomed: the Tanzanian Makonde tend to look down on their Mozambican neighbours.

But it is the Mozambican Makonde who have a sophisticated and elaborate carving tradition. Makonde sculptures, which are exhibited in the major museums and art galleries of Europe, Africa and North America, should be considered an exclusively Mozambican art form: the Tanzanian Makonde never developed beyond crude wooden carvings.

The earliest examples are the masks used in the mapiko dance (see p.39) and the figures used in initiation rituals. These were carved out of soft njala wood, and often decorated with human hair. They were kept in huts in the forest, not so much for safe keeping but to make sure women and other uninitiates did not see them. Original Makonde carvings are very rare: njala wood is soft and does not keep well. The Makonde also produced beautifully carved boxes for medicines and tobacco, basketwork and pottery, and they were known for their rich tradition of oral literature and dance.

Makonde art first came to the notice of travellers and missionaries at the end of the 19th century. It seems that as soon as foreigners began to take an interest in the intricately carved figures and masks, they also affected the way the carvers worked. It was missionaries and traders who persuaded them to use the harder wood of the Blackwood tree (known as mpingo), which was far more durable and suitable for transporting to markets all over Africa, and abroad. Carvers naturally began to produce what traders wanted to buy, and gradually Makonde art became more suited to Western tastes. Throughout the 20th century interest in African curios and artefacts gathered pace, the Makonde migrated north and south, younger carvers moved to the cities, and a whole new tradition of Makonde carving grew up.

Among the main types of carving (Binadamu, Ujamaa, and Shetani, which are described in detail on page 84) some have evolved in response to very modern pressures on the artist. A carving may portray a man in a loincloth clutching his head, weighed down by the impositions of the colonial regime; a famous piece in the Natural History Museum in Maputo shows two figures carrying a colonial officer in a litter. Producing such sculptures may have been a way of coping with the miseries of everyday life. Other carvings are rooted in more ancient traditions. Themes of fertility, domesticity, the family and the spirit world are common: gossiping women carry water pots, a teacher is surrounded by his pupils, a couple with grotesquely enlarged sexual organs face each other.

The great majority of Makonde carvings are now produced for tourists, but that is not to deny their artistic value. Carved from a single block of wood (and often, ivory) the best sculptures are intricate and beautiful. Smaller pieces can be turned in a matter of days, but a large work will take weeks or months. Carvers produce wonderfully contorted, Picasso-like figures (often inspired by irregularities in the tough wood), delicate pastoral scenes and the obscenest of grotesques. Makonde sculpture is hard to resist, and even if you are determined not to buy, no visit to Cabo Delgado is complete without a visit to at least one Makonde cooperative or workshop, where you can watch the artists at work.

EXPLORING

Ibo can be explored in half a day, but it takes at least two days to get used to the island's extraordinary atmosphere. The **forts** are worth seeing, though they are very derelict and frequently used as toilets by dogs and humans alike. Two of them date from the 18th century, the most interesting being the **star-shaped fort** to the north-west of the town centre. It is fairly well-preserved, with cannons still in place. The Portuguese used it as a prison until the 1970s and, according to some, it is haunted by the ghosts of Mozambicans who died in their cells. The third fort, by the market, was built in 1841; it's worth a visit for the view you get over the town from the top storey.

Handsome 19th century buildings, most in an advanced state of decay, line the deserted main street, at the end of which are the only houses in this part of the town still being used: the police station, the town hall and a (seemingly derelict) shop. All are generous buildings with fine sea views and attractive gardens, but they too seem to be steadily succumbing to the general air of decay. The town hall is empty of life except for a wizened housekeeper who sweeps the dust around, and the local government official, a pleasant fellow who lives and works in two echoing rooms. You will find it useful to search him out if you need to organise transport off the island.

In the square is the **Church of Our Lady of Rosaria**, built in 1752 when Ibo attained the status of municipality. Ask in the town hall or the police station if someone will open the doors for you.

QUERIMBA ISLAND AND THE REST OF THE ARCHIPELAGO

If you organise a dhow for a couple of days you could explore the other islands. On Querimba Island the ruins of fortified Portuguese plantation houses can still be seen; if you ask in the town you should be able to get someone to put you up; camping is also an option. As with Ibo, take your own food or ask if there is anyone who will cook for you. The diving and snorkelling off all the islands is reputed to be the best in the world, so take a snorkel. If you have the time and money, contact Pieter Jacobs in Pemba (see Pemba chapter for details) who runs diving trips around all the islands.

PANGANE

Pangane is a sizeable village set in a coconut grove, entirely occupying a pencil-thin peninsula that juts out into the Indian ocean. It is very popular amongst South African and Zimbabwean engineering and forestry workers. At the weekend an enclosed compound at the end of the village is full, and deep-sea fishing boats roar out into the ocean. During the week goats graze the beach, and the only sound is the soft clack of palm leaves in the wind, and the thump of mallet and chisel as someone fits a new plank into his boat. There is only one concrete building, the rest being neat mud houses roofed with palm leaves. The whole place bakes in the sun and sways in the constant wind (the western, inner side of the peninsula is more sheltered than the east). There are no cars and little electricity.

Pangane has an unrivalled reputation for its deep-sea fishing and diving, and is certainly worth a visit if you have time to spare and want a bit of calm. The beaches are beautiful and utterly deserted.

ARRIVAL AND DEPARTURE
Private Car

The roads south of Macomia and from there to Mucojo are in fair condition; there is a sandy track from Mucojo to Pangane that is only passable in a 4WD. North of Macomia the roads are the worst in Mozambique, to be attempted only in 4WD.

Public transport

Almost all traffic in the area passes through Macomia. From there get any transport to Mucojo, then walk north along the beach for an hour until you get to Pangane on your left. Very little traffic passes through Macomia – on a Sunday you will be lucky to get one or two vehicles a day.

Boat

You should be able to pick up dhow transport at Pemba and Ibo to go as far as Mocimboa da Praia, stopping off at Pangane. See relevant chapters for details.

ACCOMMODATION

Casa Suki (the only two-storey building in Pangane) is the town's store, hotel and restaurant. It has a pleasant apartment with toilet and kitchen which will sleep four to six. During the week you will be able to stay there for a reasonable price; at the weekend it is usually fully booked. Camping should not be a problem – ask at Casa Suki where you can pitch a tent.

INLAND: NORTH FROM PEMBA

MACOMIA

Anyone travelling in the region will be obliged to make several stops at Macomia, a dusty junction town with a thriving market and a bar – *Casa Chung* – which does a fine goat stew. There is also a basic, clean pensão, the *Kwetu Kumo*, if you need to spend the night. Follow the west road out of town and it is 500m on your left.

CHAI

On the main road, halfway between Macomia and Mocimboa da Praia, the town of Chai is fixed in the minds of Mozambicans as the place that began the war of independence. In 1964 the newly-formed Frelimo was divided as to the best means of opposing the colonial government, but as the Portuguese had already declared a state of emergency in response to outbursts of guerilla violence and banditry, Frelimo decided to launch its own campaign. On 25 September 1964 they duly attacked the Portuguese base at Chai, at the same time issuing a proclamation and a call to arms. The nationwide uprising that they hoped this would inspire never came about, and in the south the Portuguese crippled the movement by arresting all its key players. But over the next couple of years Frelimo managed to take control of most of the far north.

Chai is simply another dusty town on a main road, and except for a dramatic mural commemorating the liberation struggle, there is little to make you linger. Mozambicans from the south hurry through, nervous of the fierce reputation of the Makonde people, but they will always point Chai out to the foreigner as the birthplace of the liberation of their country.

MUEDA

Mueda is the unofficial capital of the Mozambican side of the Makonde plateau, a small, insignificant town, whose name resonates in Mozambican revolutionary history as the scene of one of the defining episodes of the struggle for independence. In June 1960 the Portuguese administrator at Mueda ordered his troops to fire on a peaceful demonstration of peasant farmers. Six hundred were killed in the massacre, and Mueda became Mozambique's Sharpeville. Mueda accelerated the burgeoning resistance movement (see *History*), and politicised the Makonde people, who proved Frelimo's greatest asset in its early years. This part of Mozambique had never been fully subdued by the colonial power; during the 1960s it provided Frelimo with a valuable power base and became a fruitful source of recruits.

Today there's not much in Mueda to inspire the tourist. There is a **monument** to the massacre and a couple of places to stay: notably the *pensão* on the main street, which is clean and friendly, with rooms for $8-10, no running water. It is a useful jumping-off point if you are interested in exploring the villages of the Makonde plateau – an interesting trip out of Mueda is to the small village of **Nandimba**, 10km north on the main road out of town. Remember this is the heartland of the Makonde people (who are called 'fierce' and 'terrible' by their softer, southern countrymen) and you may be welcomed with suspicion if you go hiking into the interior. Tourists very seldom penetrate these parts – there is no public transport and very few vehicles. It is advisable to get a guide in Mueda (ask in the pensão) or Nampula (ask at the Clube Tenis), not because you will be in any danger, but because you will get lost without one. The villages around Mueda are also good places to find absolutely original Makonde carvings (see *Shopping* p. 84).

The journey to Mueda from Pemba takes 10-12 hours from going via Macomia. In Macomia you should wait at the crossroads for any transport going north. It is also well-served by transport going east from Mocimboa da Praia (around 8 hours).

MOCIMBOA DA PRAIA

A depressing, shabby, frontier town inhabited by squint-eyed conmen and cross-border chancers, Mocimboa da Praia is unavoidable if you are headed for Tanzania. There is very little there to divert you, apart from the seedy disco *Casa Ramichalilah* (where you may be able to hire a cabin for $4 a night), and a tiny bar next door to the *Pensão Leeta*, which has rooms for $8, though the bathrooms are squalid and you're likely to be kept awake by rats. Down the road from Leeta, towards the town centre, is the *Pensão Mahometana Magid*, whose dining room serves passable meals, and where rooms cost $7-10.

There is a decent **fish market** on the sea front, and in the town centre is Mozambique's most northerly **post office**. In front of the market you should be able to hire a dhow or a boat to take you up or down the coast.

The road to Mocimboa from Macomia is one of the worst in Mozambique – more a series of fissured and jagged gullies than a highway. On public transport (which is plentiful) you should allow at least 6 hours to cover the 120km. South of Macomia the roads are good and will present no problems. When leaving Mocimboa you should be in front of the Mahometana Magid by 4.30am at the latest if you are going south or to Mueda. To get to Palma, the stop is in front of the Pensão Leeta.

PALMA

Palma is a pleasant little town overlooking an attractive palm-fringed bay. From Mocimboa the journey takes about four hours over a good road. There's little choice of places to stay – the *Hotel Palma* on the sea front is squalid but cheap. If you are stuck you should be able to camp if you ask around for a suitable place. Basic food and provisions are available in the town, up on the hill. If you're on your way to Tanzania this is a good enough starting point before the trip up to the Rovuma, but you'd probably find Mocimboa more convenient, and better served by public transport.

INDEX

Vacation Work publish:

	Paperback	Hardback
The Directory of Summer Jobs Abroad	£8.99	£14.95
The Directory of Summer Jobs in Britain	£8.99	£14.95
Supplement to Summer Jobs in Britain and Abroad *published in May*	£6.00	–
Work Your Way Around the World	£12.95	–
The Good Cook's Guide to Working Abroad	£11.95	–
Taking a Gap Year	£10.99	–
Working in Tourism – The UK, Europe & Beyond	£11.95	–
Kibbutz Volunteer	£8.99	–
Working on Cruise Ships	£9.99	–
Teaching English Abroad	£11.95	–
The Au Pair & Nanny's Guide to Working Abroad	£10.99	–
Working in Ski Resorts – Europe & North America	£10.99	–
Working with Animals – The UK, Europe & Worldwide	£11.95	–
Accounting Jobs Worldwide	£11.95	–
Working with the Environment	£10.99	–
Health Professionals Abroad	£10.99	–
The Directory of Jobs & Careers Abroad	£11.95	£16.99
The International Directory of Voluntary Work	£10.99	£15.99
The Directory of Work & Study in Developing Countries	£9.99	£14.99
Live & Work in Japan	£10.99	£15.95
Live & Work in Russia & Eastern Europe	£10.99	£15.95
Live & Work in France	£10.99	£15.95
Live & Work in Australia & New Zealand	£10.99	£15.95
Live & Work in the USA & Canada	£10.99	£15.95
Live & Work in Germany	£10.99	£15.95
Live & Work in Belgium, The Netherlands & Luxembourg	£10.99	£15.95
Live & Work in Spain & Portugal	£10.99	£15.95
Live & Work in Italy	£10.99	£15.95
Live & Work in Scandinavia	£10.99	£14.95
Travellers Survival Kit: Sri Lanka	£10.99	–
Travellers Survival Kit: Mozambique	£10.99	–
Travellers Survival Kit: Cuba	£10.99	–
Travellers Survival Kit: Lebanon	£10.99	–
Travellers Survival Kit: South Africa	£10.99	–
Travellers Survival Kit: India	£10.99	–
Travellers Survival Kit: Russia & the Republics	£9.95	–
Travellers Survival Kit: Western Europe	£8.95	–
Travellers Survival Kit: Eastern Europe	£9.95	–
Travellers Survival Kit: South America	£15.95	–
Travellers Survival Kit: Central America	£8.95	–
Travellers Survival Kit: USA & Canada	£10.99	–
Travellers Survival Kit: Australia & New Zealand	£10.99	–

Distributors of:

Summer Jobs USA	£12.95	–
Internships (On-the-Job Training Opportunities in the USA)	£16.95	–
Sports Scholarships in the USA	£16.95	–
Scholarships for Study in the USA & Canada	£14.95	–
Colleges & Universities in the USA	£15.95	–
Green Volunteers	£10.99	–

Vacation Work Publications, 9 Park End Street, Oxford OX1 1HJ
Tel 01865–241978   Fax 01865–790885

Visit us online for more information on our unrivalled range of titles for work, travel and adventure, readers' feedback and regular updates:
Web site http://www.vacationwork.co.uk